Rhetoric and Demagoguery

Rhetoric and Demagoguery

Patricia Roberts-Miller

Southern Illinois University Press
Carbondale

Southern Illinois University Press
www.siupress.com

22 21 20 19   4 3 2 1

Cover design by Mary Rohrer

Library of Congress Cataloging-in-Publication Data
Names: Roberts-Miller, Patricia, 1959- author.
Title: Rhetoric and demagoguery / Patricia Roberts-Miller.
Description: Carbondale : Southern Illinois University Press, [2019] | Includes bibliographical
references and index.
Identifiers: LCCN 2018021584 | ISBN 9780809337125 (paperback : alk. paper) |
ISBN 9780809337132 (e-book)
Subjects: LCSH: Rhetoric—Political aspects. | Communication in politics.
Classification: LCC P301.5.P67 R65 2019 | DDC 808/.0427—dc23 LC record available at
https://lccn.loc.gov/2018021584

Printed on recycled paper. ♻

Contents

Acknowledgments

This is the only book project in which I've been engaged that was closely connected to a course I taught on a regular basis, and so, first, I should thank John Ruszkiewicz for trusting me with the class. I am ineffably indebted to the many students who made it through that class during the various semesters, a course that began with Nazis and ended with neo-Nazis, and traveled through fascism, totalitarianism, authoritarianism, genocide, and various other cheerful topics. The students were excellent, pushing me and my thinking, and, I hope, came away more skeptical and thoughtful about public deliberation. Many of those students afterward became friends, and have continued to argue about demagoguery with me in social media—sending interesting articles, odd links, their own writing on the subject—and have generally shown that teaching is an extraordinarily rewarding profession. I wish I could name them all, but it would take pages and pages.

I'm also grateful to friends and colleagues who have indulged my fascination with the dark side of rhetoric, arguing about it with me—in person and virtually—sometimes reading drafts and sometimes commenting on blathery posts, suggesting readings, and giving me encouragement through two fairly discouraging research projects in a row. While there are too many to name, there are a few whom I have to mention: James Atkinson, Janet Atwill, Randy Cauthen, Janet Claus, Diane Davis, Alex Fischer, Gretchen Goldsmith, Joshua Gunn, Jackie Henkel, John Jones, Seth Kahn, Bill Keith, Janet Dixon Keller, Bonnie Kyburz, Donald Lazere, Drew Loewe, Owen Maercks, Dave Mauch, Cody Melcher, John Murphy, Roxanne Mountford, Kel Munger, David Newheiser, Luke Oett, Malea Powell, Danielle Terrier Reagan, Jenny Rice, Jim Ridolfo, Donnie Johnson Sackey, George Schorn, Ryan Skinnell, Martha Stockton, Paul Wallich, and Susan Wells. Casey Boyle, Rasha Diab, Justin Hodgson, Snehal Shingavi, Clay Spinuzzi, Jeffrey Walker, and Aaron Zacks have engaged in long and thoughtful conversations while I lingered in their doorways.

Various colleagues have helped me with manuscript preparation along the way, especially Megan Eatman, who prepared the list of works cited and retrieved two lost chapters; David Devine, who revised the works cited; Joshua Lee and Kirsten Holliday, who helped with article versions; and David Daniel who found sources. Davida Charney's insightful criticisms of my previous book helped with this one considerably. I'm also deeply indebted to fellow members of various writing groups over the last few years, who generously read many versions: Todd Battistelli, Douglas Coulson, Eric Dieter, Megan Eatman, Marjorie Foley, Kendall Gerdes, Megan Gianfagna, Rhiannon Goad, Hannah Harrison, Justin Hatch, Tekla Hawkins, Rodney Herring, Vicky Hill, Nathan Kreuter, Mark Longaker, Stephanie Odom, Rachel Schneider, Jeremy Smyczek, Connie Steel, Jazmine Wells. The excellent research librarians and subject specialists at the University of Texas Perry-Castaneda Library have found sources, answered odd questions, and have been tireless in tracking down information.

I am grateful to Carolyn Miller and the *Rhetoric Society Quarterly* for publishing an early version of part of the second chapter under the title "Dissent as 'Aid and Comfort to the Enemy': The Rhetorical Power of Naive Realism and Ingroup Identity," and to Martin Medhurst, who published as a forum an early version of my thinking on this topic ("Democracy, Demagoguery, and Critical Rhetoric"). J. Michael Hogan and Dave Tell responded with "Demagoguery and Democratic Deliberation: The Search for Rules of Discursive Engagement" (*Rhetoric and Public Affairs*, vol. 9, no. 3, Fall 2006, pp. 479–87), James Darsey with "Patricia Roberts-Miller, Demagoguery, and the Troublesome Case of Eugene Debs," and Steven Goldzwig with "Demagoguery, Democratic Dissent, and 'Re-Visioning Democracy'" (*Rhetoric and Public Affairs*, vol. 9, no. 3, Fall 2006, pp. 471–78). Their criticisms helped me rethink most aspects of the project, and understand ways I was being unclear. Tolerant audiences at various talks have encouraged, criticized, and usefully challenged this work. I'm thankful that Carnegie-Mellon University, University of Denver, University of Illinois, San Diego State University, Texas A&M, University of Tennessee, Michigan State University, and Furman University invited me to present parts of it. Rhetoric Society of America and College Composition and Communication conferences have been invaluable sites for discussion and criticism.

More difficult to express is the intellectual debt I owe to so many scholars whose work has helped me tremendously, including some I have never met. Tetsuden Kashima, Elliot Aronson, Herbert Simons, and Greg Robinson graciously exchanged email with me. Others, whose work informed this book, but whose scholarship I never cite, include Shirley Wilson Logan's work on nineteenth-century African American women rhetors, Michael Ignatieff's work on war and nationalism, Daniel Kahneman's work (which should be much more influential in rhetoric than it is), and Alistair Horne's haunting book *The Savage War of Peace*. Wayne Booth, Fred Antzcak (from whom I took a sophomore-level rhetorical theory course), Martha Nussbaum (whom I have never met, but whose reading of classical texts changed my thinking), and Robert Ivie (whom I met only briefly) have also been significant influences.

The faculty of the Department of Rhetoric and Writing has encouraged me, tolerated me, and listened to me, and the staff, especially Jamie Duke, Tracye Keen, Holly Schwadron, Stephanie Stickney, and Anna Crain have been supportive, patient, and endlessly helpful. For the last three years, I have also been supported and tolerated by the staff of the University Writing Center—Alice Batt, Ben Kitchen, Vicente Lozano, Natalie San Luis, Michele Solberg—and an extraordinary group of graduate students. I have a supportive dean's office, not something everyone can say, for which I am also grateful.

Another version of this argument has been published as *Democracy and Demagoguery* by The Experiment, and it shares the same proposed definition of demagoguery. The staff and editors there made suggestions that not only made that version better, but this one.

I and Southern Illinois University Press are deeply appreciative of the President's Office of the University of Texas at Austin and its tremendously important subvention grants program for contributing to the publication costs of this book and so many others.

The dogs have rather enjoyed the project, as it has meant a lot of long walks with my nattering away at them; the cats found this project just as boring as anything else I've done. My loving husband and indulgent son have found the nattering less entertaining and harder to ignore politely, and now know more about white supremacists, homophobes, eugenicists, and the epistemology/ontology distinction than they ever desired. But their intelligent questions and suggestions have been more helpful than they could imagine.

Rhetoric and Demagoguery

Introduction:
Demagogues and Demagoguery

War threatens all civil rights; and although we have fought wars
before, and our personal freedoms have survived, there have been
periods of gross abuse, when hysteria and hate and fear ran high,
and when minorities were unlawfully and cruelly abused.
—December 1941 "Statement by Attorney General Francis Biddle
concerning the Employment of Aliens in Private Industry" entered into
evidence by Richard Neustadt in the *National Defense Migration Hearings*

Once again, we're talking about demagogues, and we're arguing about whether
specific political figures are *really* demagogues—we are arguing about identity. Of course when we have this argument the identity of Hitler looms large, as
we are concerned that current political figures will do to our country what Hitler
did to his. And so at the back of the argument about demagogues is a narrative
about Hitler. We are wrong about the argument, and we are wrong about the
narrative—it may even be that we are wrong about the argument *because* we are
wrong about the narrative.

We want to believe that Hitler turned a civilized country into mass murder-
ers, but, as Ian Kershaw says, "Hitler alone, however important his role, is not
enough to explain the extraordinary lurch of a society, relatively non-violent
before 1914, into ever more radical brutality and such a frenzy of destruction"
(*Hitler, the Germans, and the Final Solution* 347). Hitler didn't cause the culture
of demagoguery in Weimar Germany, but he benefited from it. Demagoguery is
conventionally thought of as a separate category from normal political discourse,
and as something a certain kind of person does. It is popularly associated with
vehemence, nastiness, populism, and bad motives.[1] It should instead be thought
of as a way of participating in public discourse and decision making—a way that

1

can become the norm in a culture that is profoundly identity-driven. In a culture of demagoguery all political issues are reduced to the question of in-group (good) and out-group (bad). There are other characteristics that I will argue define demagoguery, but here I want to emphasize that how demagogic a culture is shouldn't be determined by identities (what sorts of people are participating in public deliberation) but by where on various axes a culture rests. Demagoguery is a continuum, and neither an identity nor a discrete category.

There are three axes that matter for thinking about how worried we should be about demagoguery at any given moment: how demagogic a discourse is; how consistently a specific out-group is scapegoated; and how powerful the media and/or rhetors are that are engaging in that kind of demagoguery. An individual text can be more or less demagogic. The more that a culture has highly demagogic texts (that is, the extent to which the normal way of participating in public discourse is highly demagogic), the more demagogic that culture is. The more demagogic a culture is, the less likely it is that political elites will be able to deliberate to find reasonable policy solutions that are inclusive and fair. The more that demagoguery is about one group the more likely it is that there will be violence, exclusion, disenfranchisement, imprisonment, expulsion, or extermination. The impact, and therefore harm, of any particular demagoguery is largely determined by its place in a culture of demagoguery, and so its harm can change when the culture changes. Samuel Morse's demagoguery about Catholics was actively harmful in the 1830s, when anti-Catholic violence was not uncommon and Catholic voting rights were actively debated—now it strikes my students as just kind of weird.

On the axis of how common (or normal) demagogic discourse is, Weimar Germany would rate high, especially since demagoguery wasn't limited to Nazis (see Evans, *The Coming of the Third Reich*). Communists, nationalists of various stripes, and rhetors across the political spectrum regularly relied on highly demagogic rhetoric. Not all the demagoguery was directed at the same out-group, but a tremendous amount demonized Jews, Sintis, Romas, and Poles, so Weimar was high on that axis (see especially Gregor, *How to Read Hitler*). And the demagoguery of those groups was promoted by powerful media, including the official and semi-official Catholic and Lutheran organizations (see especially Spicer, *Antisemitism, Christian Ambivalence, and the Holocaust*). Thus, it was high on all three axes. In the same era, Great Britain had its own demagogues, including Oswald Mosley, but his demagoguery wasn't as high on the demagoguery axis as Hitler's, he wasn't as powerful, British political culture wasn't *as* demagogic, and there wasn't as much consistency as to the objects of the demagoguery. So, it was lower on all three axes. The United States had a considerable amount of demagoguery (more than the UK, but less than Germany), and a lot of powerful political figures and media outlets engaged in it, but the objects of the demagoguery varied from one region to another.[2] None of these cultures was free of demagoguery, but neither were they all equally demagogic, nor did they all have the same levels of damage from demagoguery.

If we think about demagoguery as having three axes, then we can think more clearly about the probable harm of demagoguery. A single isolated piece of demagoguery on the part of a marginalized rhetor about a group rarely demonized (a demagogic comment on YouTube about bass players) is unlikely to do much harm. Demagoguery on the part of a major political figure (the president of the United States, for instance) that demonizes a group often presented as dangerous and violent (Latino immigrants, for instance), in a public sphere dominated by demagoguery is likely to be very harmful. Acknowledging the various axes helps us avoid an all-or-nothing way of thinking about it—for instance, whether it is always or never harmful. Later I'll discuss PETA demagoguery about snake owners—irritating but not particularly consequential, and therefore not especially harmful. YouTube comments are another field for odd and sometimes just entertaining demagoguery. There is a substantial amount of demagoguery about sports teams, especially college rivals, but again without much (or any) harm. I once spent an hour or so listening to a faculty member at another institution engage in demagoguery about university deans; much of it was funny (I didn't realize there was a genre of dean jokes), and it didn't result in persecution of college deans. It didn't even make me dislike my dean (whom I happen to like quite a bit). Enclave-based venting can be cathartic, perhaps, and some scholars have argued that demagoguery can be actively good (see Goldzwig, Darsey).

Even demagoguery that I will argue was harmful wouldn't have been had it been unusual. Had Earl Warren (discussed later) been the only person in the spring of 1942 engaged in demagoguery about "the Japanese" there would never have been mass imprisonment. Theodore Bilbo probably didn't persuade anyone to support violent protection of white supremacy who didn't already do so, but the harm of his rhetoric came from confirming those beliefs. Homophobic rhetoric enables violence because it is ubiquitous. In other words, an incident of demagoguery matters to the degree that it is part of a larger discourse, the relative power of the agent and object of the discourse, and how explicit the call for elimination is.[3]

In 1908, the issue of the Hetch Hetchy Valley was brought to the Sierra Club for a vote. San Francisco was trying to dam and flood the valley for a water and power supply, something that would be a model of Progressive use of natural resources (the "conservationist" position). San Francisco was opposed by preservationists like John Muir, who argued that national parks should be preserved in a wilderness state as much as possible, and by the Spring Valley Water Company, which had been profiting from San Francisco's limited supply for years. Muir revised an earlier piece he had published about the Hetch Hetchy, updating it to reflect his current concern about the proposed damming. In doing so, he made the piece demagogic.

Muir reduced the multiple sides to two, putting himself on the side of Jesus and John the Baptist and the conservationists on the side of Satan and the merchants in the Temple of Jerusalem. He engaged in motivism, highly fallacious argumentation, and he predicted apocalyptic consequences. Muir won the vote in the Sierra Club, but lost the larger argument, and the valley was dammed and flooded. He didn't instigate violence against conservationists, no one was inspired by his demagoguery to restrict the rights of his opposition, and dam advocates were not expelled from the Sierra Club. This is demagoguery to which I am highly sympathetic (I still think it an outrage that the valley was dammed and flooded), and shows that good people engage in demagoguery, and it isn't always harmful.

Demagoguery always exists to some degree because it appeals to what may be natural in human nature—in-group favoritism (and all that entails in terms of motivism, projection, scapegoating, false equivalencies), our preference for naïve realism and the attendant aversion to complexity and ambiguity, framing problems in terms of identity, the pleasure of seeing ourselves as victorious underdogs against a stronger and obviously evil opposition, and the joy of feeling totally and thoroughly right.

In a culture of profit-driven media, demagoguery is, in the short term, a savvy rhetorical strategy. A program that offers a nuanced and complicated exposition of a vexed issue is likely to be attractive to fewer viewers or listeners than one that promises to make its audience feel certain, confident, and confirmed. Once demagoguery is the norm, then people dependent on rhetoric for success are more likely to engage it, and thereby increase its power by making it seem that demagoguery is our only way of disagreeing. But I'm not comfortable with metaphors of it as a cancer that will grow, or an infection that will kill us unless stopped. Metaphors of disease imply policies of purification, excision, or elimination—that is, demagogic ones.

Rather than see demagoguery as a disease, it might be better to think of it as something like sitting on a couch watching TV. It's pleasurable, and doing it every once in a while won't cause much harm. But doing it a lot can be harmful, partially in that we then get worse at moving around, and doing nothing else can be deadly. The solution isn't to ban TV or burn all the couches, but to make sure we're getting enough of other kinds of activities. This project came about because I think we're spending all our time on the couch.

Train Wrecks in Public Deliberation

For some time, I have been interested in train wrecks in public deliberation—times when communities took a lot of time and a lot of talk to come to decisions that they later regretted. Part of my fascination is with trying to determine what role rhetoric had in these train wrecks. These aren't cases in which people made mistakes because of inadequate information. These are instances in which communities had all the information they needed and came to a decision in the face of disconfirming evidence, to which they recommitted even after receiving more evidence that they were making a mistake. I saw in all these cases a similar approach to public discourse—an evasion or even rejection of policy argumentation (defined below) in favor of highly polarized arguments about identity. Scholars and teachers of argumentation should intervene when any community of which we are a member seems to be dominated by that approach, which could be called demagoguery. And so I want to try to identify the specific characteristics of that demagoguery.[4]

In fairly different situations (the Athenian decision to invade Sicily and the US commitment to slavery, for example) communities have seemed strikingly determined to avoid pragmatic deliberations about the long-term costs and consequences of the various policies available to them. It wasn't uncommon for some rhetors (such as the Athenian rhetor Cleon, to be discussed later) to insist explicitly that any such deliberation was treacherous, villainous, unmanly, or even actively demonic.

Avoiding demagoguery, however, doesn't require angels of argumentation unemotionally laying out fallacy-free arguments interspersed with expressions of respect and honor for all interlocutors. We don't need to aspire to perfect public deliberation, just deliberation that is good enough. And good-enough public deliberation can involve people who are angry, vehement, snarky, hurtful, frightened, whose arguments are wobbly and whose views of other interlocutors and their arguments are uncharitable and even hostile. Rhetors can be realists, relativists, fallibilists—there isn't an epistemology entrance requirement. The low bar for good-enough argumentation is that, on the whole, the community values and rewards the fair representation of one another's respective arguments (and it's perfectly possible to be fair and unkind at the same time), internal consistency, openness to persuasion, redeeming claims (that is, providing additional evidence if challenged), policy argumentation, and honesty. Not every rhetor has to follow those rules at every moment—they are community values.

And the standard for policy argumentation can be fairly low as well—simply that the community interrogate the stock issues. First, rhetors arguing for a change in policy need to argue that there is a need (a problem or ill). They need to show that the problem is significant, and that it will not go away on its own. They need to create a plausible *narrative of causality*—what causes this problem. And they need to show that whatever conditions caused it still exist, so the ill is *inherent* to our situation. The second part of the argument is the plan. Rhetors need to put forward a plan and argue that the plan is feasible, will solve the problem, and will not have unintended consequences. In short, policy argumentation has these stases:

NEED
    ILL
    NARRATIVE OF CAUSALITY
    INHERENCY
PLAN
    SOLVENCY
    FEASIBILITY
    UNINTENDED CONSEQUENCES

So, for instance, a majority of crimes are committed by young males, and crime is a significant problem. Since this pattern of crime has continued for some time, it isn't going to go away—it's an inherent ill. One solution would be to jail all young men until they are past the age when they are likely to commit crime. It would solve the problem (the stasis of "solvency"), but it is not feasible, and the unintended consequences would be disastrous.

In the train wrecks that fascinate me, there was a genuine need, but it often wasn't the one that rhetors were emphasizing. For instance, there were a lot of possible ills that antebellum rhetors identified in regard to slavery, such as its inhumanity, injustice, and cruelty. There were pragmatic questions raised at the time, even in southern publications, such as the long-term pragmatic possibilities (given the economic reliance on expansion), the incompatibility of slavery and industrialization, the exhaustion of soil. But proslavery rhetors identified the ill as abolitionists' criticizing slaveholders and advocating slave revolt (they did the former, but the latter accusation was sheer scapegoating). Proslavery rhetors made the slavery debate an issue of slaveholder honor. There were multiple policy options available to the communities, but the dominant proslavery rhetoric reduced all possibilities to one (silence abolitionists), or sometimes a false dilemma between "this plan" and "do nothing" (which was often described as "sitting here" or "sitting there"). Cleon characterized his opposition's argument as doing nothing about the anti-Athenian revolt; pro-invasion rhetors characterized criticism of the Bush administration plan as not caring about terrorism (with a surprising amount of "sitting there" comments). In a culture of demagoguery, arguments about policy are replaced by arguments about identity. Criticism of the plan is met with the accusation that the critic has the wrong identity (is weak, treacherous, or simply a member of an out-group) or has the wrong feelings (doesn't care).

Among social groups, the "in-group" is not necessarily powerful (it might even be powerless), but it is a group important to our sense of identity. In-groups are constructed largely by opposition. The in-group is good because it isn't the out-group (and the out-group is bad because it isn't the in-group). We believe that in-group members are more likely to be honest, even objective, whereas out-group members are dishonest at worst and biased at best.

Reliance on notions about in-groups and out-groups is an instance of what social psychologists call "System 1" thinking—essentially, intuition, prior belief, previous judgment (for an engaging summary of the research, see especially Kahneman, *Thinking Fast and Slow*). One scholar calls it "in-front-of-your-nose" thinking, just looking at what seems obvious (Tetlock and Gardner, *Superforecasting*). "System 2" thinking is self-critical, self-reflective, and thinking about thinking (often called metacognition). This isn't emotion versus reason, or rational versus irrational; this is cognition versus metacognition. That's an important point, since the notion that there is a binary between emotion and reason (which is what is often meant by irrational and rational) contributes to the effectiveness of demagoguery, in that it inhibits our ability to recognize when *we* are persuaded by demagoguery. After all, we believe we are persuaded by sweet reason, and they are irrational "idjits."

In-group/out-group thinking plays into the identification of demagogues, in that we are quick to identify effective out-group rhetors as demagogues, and slow to do so with in-group rhetors. And, paradoxically, the entire project of trying to identify demagogues is too often grounded in the notion that particular figures are nearly magical, and they control the prejudiced, emotional, feminized masses with a word wand. Once the problem is formulated that way, the solution is some version of disempowering, disenfranchising, expelling, or exterminating the demagogue. And that's demagoguery. Much scholarship on demagoguery has begun with that premise—the problem is the demagogue—and then scholars have looked at all the figures they consider demagogues to see what those figures have in common. The problem with that method is that what those figures all have in common is that the scholar or commenter hates them. We end up with a list of out-group political figures.

Instead of looking for individual rhetors to blame and expel, we should look at the role rhetoric has played in helping communities climb up what Michael Mann has described as the path to extermination (*Dark Side*). Such times don't show a single figure with a word wand; there is a culture in which a particular way of participating in public discourse is common. There is often (but not always) an individual who is able to ride the wave of eliminationist rhetoric into power. But that person didn't create the wave, and there isn't even always a single individual (in the case of proslavery rhetoric, for instance). There isn't any more populism or emotionalism than is normal in politics, and, perhaps most troubling, the rhetors with the most powerful demagoguery weren't necessarily just looking out for themselves—they probably meant well. Thus, focusing on emotionalism, populism, and motivism isn't going to help us figure out when we are walking down a road toward violence.

Any project that is entirely about how badly *they* argue is going to be a self-congratulating exercise in saying the out-group is the out-group. Trying to identify the characteristics that help people climb up the latter of extermination shouldn't be in service of purifying our communities of demagogues—*we* are demagogues—but in service of reflecting on what is persuading us. That's the goal of this book. The rest of this introduction will move quickly through common ways of talking about demagogues before making my proposal (a definition, a set of criteria, and a discussion of correlating qualities). And the rest of the chapter and book pursues various studies intended to show the complexity and attraction of demagoguery—not so that we can purify our culture of demagogues or demagoguery, but so that we might have less of both.

Conventional Notions of Demagoguery

In 1941, US attorney general Francis Biddle spoke against the demands for various alarmist and alarming policies, especially toward Japanese Americans. It's a long quote, but powerful enough that someone entered it into the record in John Tolan's 1942 hearings regarding what would become the mass imprisonment of people with Japanese ancestry. Biddle said,

> War threatens all civil rights; and although we have fought wars before, and our personal freedoms have survived, there have been periods of gross abuse, when hysteria and hate and fear ran high, and when minorities were unlawfully and cruelly abused. Every man who cares about freedom, about a government by law—and all freedom is based on fair administration of the law—must fight for it for the other man with whom he disagrees, for the right of the minority, for the chance for the underprivileged with the same passion of insistence as he claims for his own rights. (December 1941 "Statement by Attorney General Francis Biddle Concerning the Employment of Aliens in Private Industry"

entered into evidence by Richard Neustadt in the *National Defense Migration Hearings*, 11044)

Biddle's argument appeals to the American topos of fairness, and his reminding people of that value in the midst of post-Pearl Harbor anxiety is inspirational and reasonable. Rights are only rights (and not privileges) if they are extended to out-groups as well as to the in-group. Unhappily, within a few months, Biddle would issue orders very much at odds with the stance he takes above, and the United States would slouch toward race-based mass imprisonment. This book is about how such reasonable arguments as Biddle's concerning in-group/out-group fairness get ignored or, as in the case of Biddle, evaporate. It is a book about the unhappily common phenomenon of how people get persuaded to try to solve our problems by scapegoating some out-group, i.e., demagoguery.

But raising the term "demagoguery" is problematic. Scholarship on demagogues went out of fashion in rhetoric in the seventies, largely because that scholarship consistently appealed to premises that were rationalist, elitist, and antidemocratic. The conventional criticism of such scholarship was four-part:

1. The criticism looked rhetorical, but it was really political—"demagogue" was simply a term for an effective rhetor in service of a political agenda that the scholar didn't like.
2. By condemning demagogues for emotionalism, scholars were assuming that the ideal public sphere consisted of technocratic discourse, an assumption that necessarily implies arguments about means and not ends, and that cannot manage significant impassioned disagreement (hence, already oppressed and marginalized groups would be discursively excluded).
3. Since the scholarship emphasized only populist demagogues, the scholarship was inherently elitist, as though elites are never suckered.
4. Scholarship condemning demagogues is demophobic; the (false) assumption is often that demagoguery is the consequence of "too much democracy," once again implying that elites don't make mistakes.

Much existing scholarship (and popular writing) on demagogues is not particularly helpful for doing much other than saying, "I don't like that rhetor," but that doesn't mean that the project is hopeless.

It's conventional in rhetoric to distinguish between a preferred and a denigrated method of participating in public discourse, such as philosophy versus sophistry, listening rhetoric versus agonism, communicative action versus strategic action, deliberative rhetoric versus compliance-gaining rhetoric. While scholars have gone to great lengths to define the preferred term in each of those binaries (philosophy, listening rhetoric, communicative action, deliberative rhetoric), there hasn't been much scholarship oriented toward differentiating versions of the denigrated term. The implication of this absence is that all forms of, say, compliance-gaining rhetoric are equally bad. And that doesn't make sense, since it suggests there is no difference between how FDR and Theodore Bilbo argued for New Deal policies.

In *Dark Side of Democracy*, Michael Mann argues that sometimes a community, for one of a variety of reasons, decides that its problems are created by the presence of some group in its midst, and that that group *must* be disenfranchised, expelled, or exterminated; the issue is not subject to the normal political processes of inclusive deliberation, bargaining, or compromise.[5] The world of complicated, contingent disagreement about the feasibility, solvency, and unintended consequences of various policy options is blocked off by a cultural obsession with arguing about just how bad the out-group is, what rhetors have the most in-group loyalty, and how extreme the repression and exclusion of the out-group should be. If the out-group resists, that resistance is reframed as aggression, and then the repression is escalated on the spurious grounds that it is actually self-defense (see O'Shaughnessy's elegant discussion of how Nazi propaganda framed WWII as self-defense). The out-group's resistance is narrated as something that "forces" the aggressors to be more violent (*Dark Side*, see especially 503). The conflict then escalates through a series of increasingly radical and violent solutions, which, at each step, are rationalized as reasonable or necessary because dominant media insist there are no other options. In Giorgio Agamben's terms, the community is persuaded it is in a "state of exception." In such a state, the supposed respect for law is paradoxically demonstrated through its suspension (what Agamben calls "not-law"):

> The normative aspect of law can thus be obliterated and contradicted with impunity by a governmental violence that—while ignoring international law externally and producing a permanent state of exception internally—nevertheless still claims to be applying the law. (87)

We decide we have to destroy the law in order to save it.

There are often rhetors who end up epitomizing that eliminationist rhetoric —Cleon, Adolf Hitler, Joseph McCarthy—whom we call "demagogues." And, many scholars have focused on those individuals, but there can be odd consequences of that focus. Take, for instance, Kenneth Burke's brilliant analysis of Hitler's *Mein Kampf,* and the odd logical problem it falls into by trying to explain Nazism through Hitler's individual psychology. According to Burke, Hitler became obsessed with the Jews because he lost arguments to them in Vienna, but if that's what made him anti-Semitic, why did his anti-Semitic rhetoric work with so many of his listeners and readers? Did every member of his audience go to Vienna and lose an argument to a Jew? Of course not. Whatever Hitler's personal motivations were—he was anxious about his heredity, he was outargued by Jews—they don't explain why he was effective with people who didn't have those anxieties or experiences. Kershaw puts it more forcefully.

> Concentrating on Hitler's personal worldview, no matter how fanatically he was inspired and motivated by it, cannot readily serve to explain why a society, which hardly shared the Arcanum of Hitler's "philosophy," gave him such growing support from 1929 on—in proportions that rose with astonishing rapidity. Nor can it explain why, from 1933 on, the non-Nationalist Socialist élites were prepared to play more and more into his hands in the process of "cumulative radicalization." (*Hitler, the Germans, and the Final Solution* 57)

That isn't to say that Hitler didn't have those motivations, but that the motivations of the rhetor don't explain the success of the rhetoric.

Scholarship on demagogues too often focuses on the motives of the demagogue—demagogues, unlike statesmen (thank Plutarch for that fallacious distinction), look out for themselves.[6] They want power, but statesmen (and I use the gendered term deliberately) want what's best for the country or community. But distinguishing good politicians from demagogues on the basis of motive is deeply flawed. We do sometimes have evidence of motive—diaries, moments we think someone was speaking confidentially, testimony of intimates, consistency across time—but we more often rely on highly speculative inferences, and those inferences are largely determined by the extent to which we already trust someone. Thus, making assertions about motives almost always lands one in the realm of circular and nonfalsifiable beliefs about in-group members having good motives and out-group members having bad ones for precisely the same actions. Loyalty to group is admirable in group members, but blind obedience in out-group members; we are clever, they are scheming; we are responsible with money, they are grasping.[7]

To the extent that we do know the motives of many people who end up on the list of demagogues, we know they thought they were doing the right thing. That's a somewhat horrifying realization. As will be discussed later, Theodore Bilbo almost certainly believed that forced repatriation was a good, and he was sincere in advocating segregation. (Had he been motivated purely by ambition, he would have softened his racism on the national stage.) As is demonstrated by Hitler's prioritizing the extermination of Jews, Romas, Sintis, and other groups over the war, Hitler wasn't engaging in genocide for political gain, but because he sincerely believed in it (for more on this, see especially Yaron Pasher's *Holocaust versus Wehrmacht*). Kershaw argues that not only was Hitler sincere in his belief that Judaism must be exterminated, it was "firmly planted in his thinking" by 1924 (*The Germans* 52). Timothy Snyder emphasizes that Hitler really did see history in apocalyptic and racist terms, and did believe his plan regarding the Soviet Union "would allow the right master race to starve the right subhumans for the right reasons" (21). That notion was widely shared; Antony Beevor says that soldiers in Hitler's Sixth Army who were dying outside of Stalingrad "buoyed themselves up with the idea that future generations would see them as the defenders of Europe from Asiatic bolshevism" (349). It might be more comforting to imagine that people defending segregation or genocide know that they're among the bad guys, but they generally think they're the good guys, and they sincerely mean well.

Trying to identify demagogues is not helpful for trying to improve public deliberation because in the train wrecks, there is demagoguery, but there isn't necessarily *a* demagogue. Proslavery forces didn't have a single rhetor who led everyone along—the antiabolitionist alarmism, scapegoating, and general demagoguery wasn't emanating from one rhetor, but was almost ubiquitous. It was in newspapers (even of opposing parties), in congressional speeches on all sorts of topics (including the question of the Sunday mails), in novels, poetry, and plays; it was used by major figures and minor figures. Prosegregation rhetoric was similarly demagogic, ubiquitous, and headless—there wasn't *a* figure from whom it emanated. There wasn't an individual who led the United States in his wake; there were a lot of figures who decided to ride a wave.

For instance, in the buildup to the Iraq invasion, a situation with no urgency, inclusive deliberation was characterized as unmanly dithering, cowardice, anti-American, and proterrorist. It was not George Bush alone who was making that argument; had he been the only one, his administration would never have succeeded. Had proslavery demonizing of deliberation been limited to James Henry Hammond, his self-destructive proposal of the "gag" rule would have died without discussion. We invaded Iraq, imposed the gag rule, engaged in massive race-based imprisonment, and enacted various other policies because these policies were supported, often demagogically, by many rhetors who were appealing to widely shared premises about public discourse.

There was demagoguery on the part of opponents to the invasion, but not as much, and it wasn't coming from media or rhetors as powerful or ubiquitous. And demagoguery was (and is) not something in which "both sides" engaged equally, in regard to slavery, the Mytilenean Debate, the Sicilian Expedition, the

Holocaust, the Iraq invasion, or the various other train wrecks. "Both sides are just as bad" fails as an accurate description of a political disagreement, since there are rarely two sides. This is a tremendously important point, and one ignored by the compulsion to equate "fairness" with "condemning both sides equally." In regard to slavery, for instance, there were at least six different positions, ranging from immediate emancipation and full citizenship to slavery as a "positive good." In between were such positions as the proslavery "necessary evil" argument, racist antislavery, antiracist antislavery, proslavery procolonization, antislavery procolonization, antislavery antiexpansionist, and others (for more on this, see Roberts-Miller, *Fanatical Schemes* 6–7). The debate over the Iraq invasion included people who supported invasion but not at that moment, or with that number of troops, or only with international support, or not until Afghanistan was more secure (see chapter 2 in this book). There were people opposed to any invasion and in favor of lifting sanctions, people opposed to invasion who wanted the sanctions to remain, people opposed to invasion because they thought it would help Israel (such as David Duke), people opposed to invasion because they thought it would hurt Israel, and so on. Noam Chomsky, James Fallows, and David Duke were all opposed to the Iraq invasion, but on very different grounds. It certainly doesn't make sense to call any of them synecdochic of the anti-invasion side generally. Similarly, Christopher Hitchens, Ann Coulter, and Colin Powell are not usefully grouped.

Even if, for the sake of argument, one takes that rich and complicated array of positions and reduces it to two sides, the notion that "both sides are equally guilty" is an abandonment of judgment. While it might be fair to say that Chomsky and Hitchens engaged in similar rhetorical strategies regarding the war—demonization of the enemy and motivism—that wouldn't be an accurate claim to make about James Fallows and Anne Coulter, or Colin Powell and David Duke. Coulter (proinvasion) and David Duke (anti-invasion) both engaged in demagoguery, but neither Fallows nor Powell did.[8]

We do have a tendency to worry the bone of whether rhetors are good people, and whether they mean well, as though answering that question would enable us to characterize their rhetoric definitively. But, if we're talking about political deliberation, and not whether people are going to hell, then the question of their goodness becomes less interesting. Earl Warren, Madison Grant, and Theodore Bilbo all relied on demagoguery, but I'm not claiming that they were thoroughly evil people. Earl Warren is a personal hero for his courage in *Brown v. Board of Education;* Madison Grant was instrumental in the conservation of species and beautiful natural spaces; people I love and respect supported the invasion of Iraq; even Theodore Bilbo had his defenders (such as Chester Morgan), as a supporter of various policies that directly benefited poor whites. And their opponents were not necessarily good people. Not everyone who opposed Bilbo, for instance, did so because they objected to racism or segregation. Some opponents of eugenics were more motivated by misogynist opposition to birth control than antiracism. The Japanese American Citizens League agitated against mass imprisonment, but has been criticized by other opponents of internment for colluding too much with military authorities. There were not "two sides" to any of these issues, let alone a binary of good versus bad people.

Our tendency to focus on the feelings of the supposed demagogues is probably the consequence of a flawed model of public discourse. There is a tendency to assume that hostility and effective public deliberation are mutually exclusive. It's assumed that, at its worst, hostility leads to exterminationist or exclusionary policies, and even at its best clouds our judgment, inhibits reasoning, and interferes with good decision making. The logical consequence of this assumption is that we shouldn't feel hostility toward other groups, and we should ban expressions of hostility from the public sphere. There is a corollary inference—that people who express their view without obvious marks of hostility are rational, and are making a rational argument; see, for instance, positive reviews on Amazon.com of David Duke's work.

That notion gets muddled with the notion that language can be a kind of aggression, and so verbal expressions of hostility are aggression—aggression and hostility are the same thing. Therefore, if we don't want a violent public sphere, we shouldn't have any degree of aggressive *or* hostile language. And there is a strong tendency to assume that aggressive or hostile language is a mark of demagoguery. As with many muddled concepts, this notion isn't entirely wrong, but the ways in which it is wrong are importantly damaging—this assumption that hostility is demagoguery contributes to our tendency to overidentify demagoguery in the out-group and underidentify it in the in-group. Much of this book concerns demagoguery that avoided looking hostile or aggressive and yet which was in service of violence toward out-groups; looking for discursive hostility and aggression is a red herring. What makes Warren's argument demagoguery is his argument, not his affect.

If we assume that the problem with demagoguery is that it is an expression of hostile feelings, then the solution appears to be calling for prohibiting expressions of hostility in the public sphere. There are three major flaws in the argument for banning hostility and aggression. One is the notion that hostility and aggression are the same. Feelings of hostility don't necessarily lead to acts of aggression, and it's historically clear that nonviolent political campaigns have often been motivated by considerable hostility toward practices, arguments, policies, institutions, and sometimes even individuals (as in the case of the anti-Marcos movement in the Philippines; see Chenoweth and Stephan). Quaker abolitionists were clearly hostile to the practice of slavery and to regulations that protected it such as the gag rule and censorship of the mail, but they continued to advocate nonviolence. Equating hostility and aggression collapses the distinction between very different kinds of acts, since expressions of hostility toward a group on the part of powerful rhetors might well constitute aggression, whereas the same expression on the part of someone relatively powerless about a powerful group might not.

The second flaw is the assumption that hostility is necessarily damaging to decision making. Hostility isn't necessarily an impediment to good deliberation. Hostility toward bad arguments, toward racism, toward genocide, and toward various other kinds of hostility can help us make better decisions (including the decision to engage in aggression, a decision that is, unfortunately, sometimes a good one). People who are oppressed will feel hostility toward the institutions, and even groups, that oppress them. Perhaps, were they saints, they could feel hostility only toward institutions and practices and never groups, but sainthood may not be a viable precondition for participation in public discourse. And, since people in power are likely not to feel much (or any) hostility toward the institutions that keep them in power, banning hostility (or expressions of hostility) makes sainthood a requirement only for the oppressed. That favoring of the powerful is the third way that banning all expressions of hostility (or characterizing them all as demagogic) is flawed.

Focusing on expressions of hostility tends to favor the powerful insofar as we are very attuned to noticing threats to ourselves and our groups, and less so to other groups. We are especially bad at noticing marks of hostility directed at groups by whom we feel threatened. We will take offense at arguments that presume *we* have bad motives or are stereotyped on the basis of our group's worst members, but we aren't as likely to notice the same moves toward out-groups because they won't immediately strike us as unreasonable. And setting the bar at open hostility means we will not notice microaggressions against out-group members. For instance, it is irritating (and perhaps even entertaining) if you happen to be extremely good at math to have someone patronizingly explain a simple math concept to you; if that happens to you over and over because your gender, ethnicity, or sexuality don't fit common stereotypes about who is (and is not) "good at math," it's a hostile world. The nth person who has engaged in that kind of patronizing is likely to get snapped at, and feel victimized because she or he was the object of hostility (failing to see the microaggression).

We should have a public sphere in which people get angry and snarky, because people should care about politics. It would, on the whole, be more productive to keep hostility directed at arguments, ideas, policies, and practices rather than identities, but that isn't always possible. I admire Earl Warren, but I get angry every time I read his testimony, and I don't think that my anger distorted my understanding of his argument or my perception of Japanese internment. It might have clarified both.

Having said how we shouldn't think about demagoguery, I should explain my proposed solution. My proposal has three parts: a definition, a set of criteria, and a description of how and why demagoguery works. I'm proposing a definition that comes, not from looking at political figures I dislike, but from times that cultures talked themselves into disastrously bad decisions even they later regretted. This is a proposal, intended to contribute to a conversation about the advantages and disadvantages of various definitions.

Defining Demagoguery

A useful definition of demagoguery looks something like this:

> *Demagoguery is a polarizing discourse that promises stability, certainty, and escape from the responsibilities of rhetoric through framing public policy in terms of the degree to which and means by which (not whether) the out-group should be punished and scapegoated for the current problems of the in-group. Public debate largely concerns three stases: group identity (who is in the in-group, what signifies out-group membership, and how loyal rhetors are to the in-group); need (usually framed in terms of how evil the out-group is); level of punishment to enact against the out-group (restriction of rights to extermination).*

There are certain characteristics discourse must have to be demagoguery: in-group/out-group(s); scapegoating of an out-group; emphasis on identity (which is group membership); motivism; the insistence that the in-group is victimized; and a call for purifying the community of the out-group(s). Other characteristics demagoguery consistently has, or that consistently correlate with the definition above, are summarized below and will be given close analysis throughout the chapters.

Scapegoating is a prominent feature of demagoguery, exhibited when an in-group holds an out-group completely responsible for something the out-group didn't do at all, or for which it is only partially responsible. The behavior or occurrence might be something for which the in-group is responsible, or partially responsible, or for which neither the in-group nor the out-group is responsible, such as the scapegoating of a group for a natural phenomenon (e.g., Jews and the plague). Scapegoating is directly related to the promise of simple solutions, since punishing (or expelling or exterminating) the guilty group is all we need to do.

Demagoguery always depends on binaries—though they can be somewhat complicated. There might be multiple identities within the out-group, for instance, but there is still an absolute distinction between "in-group" and "other." But, more than that, demagoguery relies on various binaries that are assumed to be logically connected to one another, through *binary paired terms*. A concept described by Chaim Perelman and Lucie Olbrechts-Tyteca (who call them philosophical paired terms), paired terms are sets of disjunctive binaries that are taken to be necessarily chained to one another. In regard to Cleon, for instance, there is a binary between punishing and rewarding (all possible policies in regard to Mytilene fall into one of those two categories). There is also a binary between submitting and dominating, and another between being just and unjust. So, punishing is to rewarding as dominating is to submitting as being just is to being unjust.[9]

punish		dominating		being just
——	::	——	::	——
reward		submitting		being unjust

To fail to punish is rewarding, which is the same as submitting, which is necessarily unjust.

As Perelman and Olbrechts-Tyteca note, binary paired terms are common, and specific sets are connected to particular texts, ideologies, or cultural moments. For instance, demagoguery about the civil rights movement worked by insisting that there was a set of paired terms connecting segregation to Christianity. Since integration is the opposite of segregation, and communism is the opposite of Christianity, then integration was necessarily communist.

segregation		Christianity		us
——	::	——	::	——
integration		communist		them

The central pair is in-group/out-group ("you are either with us or against us") or "us" and "them." That pair implies other clearly connected pairs, such as "loyal/disloyal," but, also, others that are more obliquely connected, such as "objective" (us) and "biased" (them). That particular pair is behind the tendency in demagoguery to dismiss disconfirming evidence purely on the grounds that it *is* disconfirming. It is, therefore, disloyal, and therefore out-group, and therefore biased, and it need not be refuted. Thus, in demagoguery, the accusation of bias is made through assertions about group membership, and such assertions release the rhetor from the responsibility of actually engaging the *argument*.

These terms aren't presented (or, perhaps, even perceived) as ideological or cultural; they represent categories that claim to be *grounded in the ontic logos*. "Ontic logos" is Charles Taylor's term for the concept that some things are spoken into the world itself—the concepts we have are not socially constructed, but part of the universe itself (*Sources of the Self*, see especially 187). Just as God's will is spoken in Scripture, so the world, as God's "other book," speaks in a stable and timeless way. "Woven into the fabric of the cosmos" is another metaphor that is sometimes used to mean, again, that certain kinds of distinctions are ontologically grounded and inescapable. So, for instance, pro-imprisonment rhetors in the hearings regarding Japanese "internment" (discussed in chapter 2) asserted an *essential* and ontological distinction between "the Japanese" and "Americans," ignoring that many of the people who would be imprisoned were American citizens. Madison Grant (chapter 3) tries to make "Nordic" an ontological category, as racist discourse generally does with "race."

Perhaps because demagoguery relies on binaries, it also relies on (and reinforces) the assumption that either things (ideas, perceptions, values, illnesses, identities, personalities) are entirely subjective (that is, defined by idiosyncratic belief, transient, and essentially unreal) or entirely objective (that is, eternal, ontologically grounded, and existing entirely outside individual perception). Thus, demagoguery has tremendous difficulty with socially constructed "facts" (such as race, money, gender norms, cultural practices). Such concepts are assumed to be either subjective (so that a person can claim not to see race) or grounded in the very fabric of the cosmos (and therefore beliefs to which we *must* submit). The odd consequence of this ontological grounding of cultural constructs is that a fairly recent practice gets projected back through time, as happens when opponents of equal rights in regard to marriage assert that monogamous companionate marriage was the Hebrew practice. To give simply one example, not discussed elsewhere in this book, Mark Hitchcock's *The End of Money* is a recent book exemplifying the anxiety that many people feel at the reduction in (and possible end of) the use of cash; Hitchcock connects the shift from cash to electronic transfers of money as, not the end of *cash*, but the end of *money*, presumably because, in his life (and the life of his intended audience) cash was money for their entire lifetimes. That has so much been the case that it is easy to forget that cash is itself a signifier, neither more nor less real than electronic transfers. For Hitchcock, the end of cash—the shift from cash to credit cards—is a sign of the apocalypse, whereas, somehow, the shift from gold to cash was not, because it happened before his lifetime. The premises of our life become the premises of life.

Demagoguery appeals to the hope that people with good judgment (usually, but not always, male) can perceive those timeless and ontological categories because they have direct perception of the world; this model of knowledge is *naïve realism*. Naïve realism is the dominant lay epistemology—it posits that one's perception of the world is based on "realistic, unbiased interpretations" (Van Boven, "Naive Realism" 602–3). It is implicitly a narrative about what happens we think—we have sense perception, *then* cognition that might corrupt that sense perception. Naïve realism privileges simple explanations (since they are most likely to correspond to direct perception), and increases the tendency toward confirmation bias (since people tend to perceive more easily and quickly any information that confirms their current beliefs). Naïve realism is oddly blinding, in that our belief that our beliefs are unmediated representations of the world means we are less likely to notice errors, and more unwilling to admit them.[10]

Naïve realism is connected to the assumption that since we are misled by things that get in the way of our own perception (biases, prejudices, emotions), the only process of verification that we need is to reflect on whether we are allowing biases, prejudices, or emotions to get in the way of our beliefs. We can know whether we know by asking ourselves if we *really* know. For naïve realists, diversity of opinion is not a good, let alone necessary, quality in public discourse, because the truth is available to any person of good judgment. Diversity is a sign that people (usually "those people") are letting their judgment be clouded by their prejudices, or are secretly agreeing with us but pretending to disagree out of nefarious motives.

In general, demagoguery appeals to naïve realism, but not always. Over the last thirty years, I have spent a lot of time creeping around dark corners of the digitally connected world arguing with jerks (I'm sure people who've argued with me would say they've also argued with a jerk). And I have often found myself in a fascinating exchange. Initially, it starts with someone repeating in-group talking points as facts that everyone knows; they're appealing to naïve realism. This—in and of itself—is interesting. They're in an argument, so they know that not "everyone" knows the facts; the very first move is a false assertion. When presented with other data, the response is often a reassertion of the FACTS (by the second exchange, the word is in caps), an attack on my person ("libtard" if I'm disputing right-wing talking points, "tool of Big Pharma" if I'm disputing antivaccination arguments, and so on). I often find that showing that my interlocutor's own arguments contradict each other goes nowhere. They cannot understand that there is a problem with holding the out-group to different standards than one holds the in-group, or the basic concept of a major premise. If I present data from sources that are in-group for my interlocutor, and show him that his "facts" are disputed by an in-group authority, things get very strange. A person who has been arguing from the perspective of a naïve realist might suddenly assert that "everyone has biases and prejudices and everyone just sees things from their own point of view."

In other words, in my experience, the most common response to a person being presented with in-group–endorsed evidence that his or her "facts" are false is to jump from naïve realism to incommensurability (and a kind of sloppy moral relativism).[11] Vice President Cheney made a similar move in a 2008 interview when he said—after having insisted prior to the invasion that Iraq had weapons of mass destruction—that intelligence is "not a science, it's an art form in many respects and you don't always get it right" (ABC News, December 15, 2008).

What strikes me as strange about internet conversations is that they often start with a person condemning the out-group for being prejudiced and subjective. What does one make of all the accusations of prejudice and talking points, directed at the other on the part of someone who might, if pushed, defend her positions as arbitrary and irrational? One possibility is that it is another instance of one of the consistent qualities of demagoguery: *projection*. Demagoguery relies on condemning the out-group for what the in-group is doing, something that enables scapegoating. This projection has several forms.

- Sometimes a rhetor engaged in demagoguery admits that the in-group is violating (or has violated) in-group ethical codes, but tries to justify that violation on the grounds that the out-group is violating those same codes (generally an instance of the fallacy tu quoque). It can be what Gordon Allport called *"mote/beam" projection* if the accuser is trying to equate two things that are distinctly different, as when single instances of violence are framed as "just as bad" as mass violence, minor in-group inconveniences are equated to denial of rights, or criticism is framed as "just as bad" as hate speech (i.e., calling someone racist is "just as bad" as saying something racist).[12]
- *Cunning projection.* Condemning the out-group for the same thing the in-group does effectively distracts onlookers, insofar as it invites them to have one of two responses: conclude "both sides are equally" bad or take the time and energy to try to determine the relative responsibility of various participants (and that's work).

Projection is effective because, especially if condemnation of out-group behavior is performed with a very likeable persona, then onlookers are likely to conclude that the rhetor would never engage in the behavior she or he is condemning. This maneuver is effective with people who believe that you can know what someone believes by listening to what values he claims to have—that is, that there is no difference between what a person says and what a person believes.[13] Thus, a person who continually condemns corruption couldn't possibly be corrupt. Someone who rails against homosexuality couldn't possibly be homosexual. The actions or proposed policies of such people need no examination other than a consideration of what they (claim to) believe. If people say they love the "little guy," then their policies *must* help the little guy. Assertions of commitment to the middle class can then be used to defend policies that significantly hurt the middle class.

Sometimes projection goes further than claiming "everyone is doing it," into claiming that one is the "true victim" of the situation, such that the in-group's violation of the law, ethics, etc., is not a violation of the law, but self-defense necessitated by the out-group's actual or threatened actions (Agamben's not-law). The in-group is being *victimized* by the situation. Sometimes the "victimization" is simply the loss of a privilege, as when Christians claim that teachers and administrators no longer being allowed to proselytize in public schools is a war on faith (even when not claiming that Satanists, Muslims, or even other kinds of Christian teachers should be allowed to proselytize). If the in-group has historically been oppressing the out-group in some way, then the "victimization" is that they are no longer allowed to engage in that oppression, as in the case of segregationists claiming that integration was victimization, or employers calling it oppression if they are no longer allowed to discriminate on the basis of gender. Not uncommonly, the violent attempt to protect privilege is renamed a kind of restrained control, and repression is reframed as compassion. This "control," "compassion," and "victimization" are all instances of *strategic misnaming*, in which something is simply called the opposite, as Burke points out Hitler did by characterizing his attitude toward Jews as "love."

Demagoguery sometimes justified repression and violence by positing or implicitly appealing to an *apocalyptic metanarrative*. Since the in-group is, supposedly, facing extermination, to advocate negotiation, deliberation, thinking carefully about the situation, or even debating the best policy is arranging deck chairs on the Titanic. There are three intriguing correlates of this apocalyptic metanarrative. First, it is, of course, an end-of-times battle between good (in-group) and evil (out-group): we are good, we are the chosen (by God, Nature, History), which suggests and enables a language of determinism. Yet, if we do not act, we will be exterminated, so our fate is not actually determined by God. We are, and are not, predestined to triumph—a flickering determinism.

Second, this narrative of our being in a supernaturally determined battle between good and evil has no place for thoughtful policy argumentation. Policy argumentation has two parts: deliberation about the need (Is there a problem? How serious is it? Will it go away on its own? What is the cause?) and the plan (What plans should we consider? How do they compare to one another in terms of feasibility, solvency, and unintended consequences?). If a supernatural force

(God, Nature, History) is on our side in a battle between good and evil, then there is no point in careful and thoughtful inclusive deliberation concerning the causes of our problem. Instead, we should pray. Similarly, in end times, it is irrelevant that the plan might not be feasible, might have costs higher than the benefits, or might not be logically related to the need we've identified. The feasibility of a proposed plan, for instance, doesn't really matter; any plan will work, as long as we stay right with God/Nature/History. It may even be that committing to an unlikely plan, with very little chance of success, after little or no deliberation, is the best approach to take: our refusal to worry about feasibility shows that we have extraordinary faith in the in-group's relation to God/history/nature, and it is faith, not feasibility, that is most likely to invite divine assistance. In this narrative, heroes are irrational and impractical. Thus, this apocalyptic metanarrative prevents pragmatic and inclusive deliberation.

Third, this posture of standing strong in the midst of the end of the world can be fairly complicated: demagoguery has to square the circle of inspiring fear while not looking fearful (since fearfulness is being paired with thinking and deliberating). As will be shown with the segregationist William Workman, rhetors engaged in hyperbolic fear-mongering often present themselves as controlled and courageous. We should be terrified *and* brave.

Desperate times require desperate measures, and those desperate measures are usually some kind of punitive policies that will control out-group behavior, prevent in-group/out-group contact, or purify the in-group. Demagoguery seems to correlate closely with what George Lakoff has called the "*strict father model*."[14] Lakoff's argument is that many people imagine the relationship of governor and governed as one of two models of the family. The strict father model posits that the main value fathers should teach children is obedience to known norms, and that obedience (framed as "self-control") is best achieved through punishing bad behavior. If the bad behavior continues, the punishment needs to increase. Lakoff's point is that this view of the government and public policy is reflected in *metaphors* associated with good behavior (control, strength, rigidity, rectitude, hierarchy, being at the center, going up) and bad (lack of control, chaos, disorder, laxness, equality, being at the fringe, going down). In addition to the ones Lakoff argues are associated with the strict father model, demagoguery associates metaphors of insects, rodents, infection (and disease generally), contamination, hybridity (things that cross categories, such as effeminate men),[15] impaired masculinity, deliberation or thinking, and demonic possession with the out-group. It associates metaphors of purity, masculinity (especially tumescence), order, action, decisiveness, and control with the in-group. It associates dithering, wavering, impaired masculinity, and weakness with people considering protecting or defending the out-group in any way, or any criticism of the in-group.[16]

Thus, demagoguery tends to be *authoritarian*. Authoritarianism as a world-view (rather than political system) has three main aspects:

> First, authoritarian submission is one's willingness to comply with es-tablished authorities placing very narrow limits on people's rights to criticize authorities. Second, authoritarians advocate sanction against those whom they deem detrimental to established authorities. Authoritarian aggression is enhanced by the belief that established authority at least tacitly approves it or that it will help preserve established authority. Thus, the theory of authoritarianism is closely related to the theory of social dominance. Finally, authoritarians tend to commit to the traditional social norms that are endorsed by society and its established authorities. Targets of authoritarian aggressiveness are often directed toward unconventional people or those defined as social deviants, such as homosexuals. (Lim 45–47)

Demagoguery can be used to argue for nontraditional social norms. As will be discussed later, Cleon was arguing for a new way of dealing with rebellions in allied city-states, but he claimed his policy was traditional. Slavery, as practiced in the southern United States, relied on new practices and new justifications, yet it was defended as a timeless phenomenon. The Iraq invasion was a radical departure in American foreign policy, the first preemptive war, yet it was defended as "conservative," what "real Americans" had always wanted, and a mere continuation of the Persian Gulf War. The Flint War Council statement was an explicitly new program, but framed as the submission to what was always already there, and its rejection (by the Prairie Fire Organizing Committee, the group that put together a new Weatherman manifesto) was similarly framed as a submission to a pre-existing shared truth. These new practices can be renamed "traditional" if one takes that term, not as a historically falsifiable claim, but a personal claim (that these actions fit what the individual feels has always been the case). All of these examples are authoritarian insofar as they demand submission to in-group authorities.

Demagoguery not uncommonly claims to be anti-authoritarian, and accuses others of being mindless slaves to authoritarian thinking. The submission to the authority of the in-group is not uncommonly represented as a kind of liberation from false authorities. The Weathermen demagoguery of *Prairie Fire* is a fairly obvious example of that move, but one can also see it in odd places like a more or less randomly selected piece of anti-Bernie Sanders demagoguery ("Fuck Bernie Fucking Sanders") which, among other things, accuses "a disturbing number of well-meaning progressives" of having "fallen for the Jedi mind trick," and being "duped," "brain-washed bots," engaging in "groveling lickspittle" and ass-kissing, and having "the kind of mindless religious zeal that flies planes into buildings" (Rendel).[17]

Coupled with naïve realism, the assumption that taxonomies are ontologically grounded means that demagoguery presents (and enacts) public deliberation as a place in which people with accurate perception point out the "real truth" to others who, if they are also capable of unmediated perception, will instantly see it. Public discourse is imagined as primarily a realm in which one expresses opinions and demonstrates in-group membership. The best evidence that one's claims are true is some kind of demonstration of personal certainty, so *assurances of certainty count as evidence of accuracy.* Because willingness to go to extremes demonstrates certainty, irrationality becomes an odd kind of evidence.

As I will argue throughout the book, that sense of identity as proof doesn't mean that demagoguery is free of claims about facts, statistics, and data, but that the data functions to illustrate the point, not logically demonstrate it. This distinction between illustrating and logically demonstrating is often confusing when I try to explain it, since demagoguery so habitually invokes language of logic and demonstration, but it's a relatively straightforward one: if a claim is *supported* by particular evidence, then the loss of that evidence means the claim collapses. The claim must be supported by other evidence, refined, or abandoned. That isn't what happens in demagoguery. In fact, quite often, people will claim that it doesn't matter if the evidence is true, because the evidence *should* or *could* be true. As will be discussed later, for instance, an approving reviewer of Grant's *Passing of the Great Race* admits that Grant's evidence is wrong, but still praises the book for being true.

Demagoguery often deduces from what "must" be true, even in cases when there is adequate empirical evidence to come to reasonable conclusions. For instance, in proslavery demagoguery, proslavery rhetors often insisted that race war *would* happen were there emancipation, although race war had never happened in any area where there had been emancipation. Demagoguery about gay marriage describes apocalyptic outcomes that haven't happened in any of the many places in which it is legal. Premises are thereby protected from falsification. The very things that might throw them into question (conditions in which they are shown to be falsified) are rejected precisely on the grounds that they would falsify the premises. The dominant form of reasoning is *deductive reasoning* from premises that *must* be true.

This notion that certain beliefs necessarily follow from the premises the in-group holds dear, coupled with naïve realism, generally leads to a denial of interpretation as a process in which someone has engaged: "You aren't arguing with me; you're arguing with the Bible/God/Nature/the Constitution/Science." While the stereotype about demagoguery is the racist thumping a Bible that he claims to understand in an unmediated way, the Bible is not the only text one can claim as an unmediated basis for demagoguery. Grant claimed to be reading Nature. Much prosegregation demagoguery claimed to have "the Constitution" as its basis, and much of it was claimed to be unequivocally grounded in "Science." It's quite possible that any foundational text can serve as the foundation for demagoguery.

Because demagoguery (and much political discourse generally) presumes that political debate should focus entirely on the question of the identity of rhetors (rather than their policies), it relies heavily on *motivism*. Deirdre McCloskey elegantly summarizes Wayne Booth's definition of motivism: "the notion that an argument is wrong if it can be shown to arise from a hidden motive" (192). And it is "shown" to arise from that motive simply by asserting that the motive exists. Motivism is the dismissal of an argument purely on the grounds that the person making the argument has bad motives. Motivism is a problem in that it depoliticizes policy deliberation by replacing argumentation about policies with nonfalsifiable assertions about motives.

Motivism isn't always wrong, and not all arguments about inferences are motivism. Raising questions about logical premises is not motivism, for instance, even though it relies on inference; claims about the honesty, good faith, consistency of an interlocutor aren't motivism insofar as they are arguments that can be defended and disputed by appealing to other things an interlocutor has said. Those claims are all falsifiable. And even considering motives might be necessary for determining how (and whether) to proceed in an exchange, in the sense of trying to determine whether an interlocutor is motivated by a desire to solve the problem, gain compliance, bargain, deliberate, lie, and so on. If an interlocutor isn't engaged in good faith argumentation, then we aren't cutting short an argument—it never was one. Considering one's own motives seems to me a necessary part of a rational discussion, and therefore should be *part* of a community's deliberation. After all, the deliberation over mass imprisonment of Japanese Americans would have been more rational had the motives of all parties been up for discussion (including those people who wanted the land). Motivism, as I'll use it in this book, is the move that says a person's policy argument can be dismissed *without any engagement* because she or he is a member of a group, and that group is made up of people with bad motives. The argument qualifies as motivism when attacks on identity and motives are the *only* support given for dismissing the opposition argument. Speculating about motives *and* refuting an argument are not motivism.

Finally, demagoguery is *not rational argumentation*, although it often purports to be. Like many theorists of argumentation, I want to argue for using "rationality" in a relatively straightforward way:

1. I don't think the answer is to establish a lot of rules that have to apply across all arguments, but whatever rules are in play should apply equally to all participants. If proof-texting from a foundational text is presented by one interlocutor as a rational argument, then she has to accept that it's a rational kind of argument for the opponent to make;
2. The argument is internally consistent. The major premises of various arguments don't contradict each other. Definitions are consistent (not necessarily identical), claims cohere;
3. Rhetors take responsibility for what they say and imply, including fairly representing the positions of other interlocutors, and those responsibilities apply equally across interlocutors; and
4. The issue is up for argument—that is, the people involved are making claims that they are willing to reconsider.

Demagoguery violates all four of those rules—it's internally inconsistent, holds the out-group and in-group to different standards, rejects rhetorical responsibility, and puts forward claims as inviolable (even if they contradict one another). Not every discussion has to fit those rules. There are some topics that are not open to disproof, and that therefore cannot be discussed this way. And those sorts of nonrational discussions can be beneficial, productive, enlightening, and fun. But they're not rational; they're doing other kinds of work. Those nonrational discussions can contribute to public deliberation, but they are not sufficient.

The conventional focus on demagogues (rather than demagoguery) is still a question of what identities are allowed in the public sphere, who is and is not a good person; it still dodges the argument about policy. To argue that demagogues are a cancer on the body politic, or a dangerous bacterium, is still to rely on the basic model of demagoguery that causes so much trouble: that we should purify the public of people who are essentially bad. I don't think *they* are the problem; I'm not sure they are a *they*. We all engage in demagoguery, and we are all attracted to it, and the point is to recognize when we do so and what are the risks attached to it.

Central to many scholarly and popular discussions of demagoguery is the person of the demagogue as a rhetorical sorcerer, consciously manipulating the ignorant (and generally feminized) masses. Kenneth Burke says of Adolf Hitler's rhetorical skill, that he was "a man who swung a great deal of people into his wake" ("Rhetoric" 191). William Shirer, in his memoir of his time as a journalist in Germany in the thirties, refers repeatedly to the force of Hitler's rhetoric in terms that make Hitler the dominant master. Listening to a "vulgar and nonsensical" two-hour speech on art, Shirer "was again fascinated by [Hitler's] oratory, and how by his use of it he was able to impose his outlandish ideas on his audience" (131). Shirer calls Hitler's oratory "overwhelming" (127), and says he "appeared able to swing his German hearers into any mood he wished" (128). It was, Shirer says, "his eloquence, his astonishing ability to move a German audience by speech, that more than anything else had swept him from oblivion to power as dictator and seemed likely to keep him there" (127).

Biographers of other notorious demagogues—Theodore Bilbo, Joseph McCarthy, Charles Coughlin—similarly emphasize the political power such figures gained as a consequence of their rhetorical skill. Michael Signer puts it particularly forcefully:

> When [demagogues] emerge, it is because the people, rather than using
> their freedom, their wits, and their self-restraint to select leaders who
> would ensure liberty for the ages, willingly hand over their power to
> a leader who enslaves them. Democracy self-destructs, and the most
> hopeful and optimistic of dreams—a system based on pure freedom, and
> on possibility itself—becomes the most monstrous of nightmares. (26)

Signer's narrative makes the demagogue the dominating puppet master, and the masses are the powerless and submissive servant. The relationship that scholars like Signer give us is fairly clear:

$$\frac{\text{Demagogue}}{\text{Masses}} :: \frac{\text{Dominance}}{\text{Submission}}$$

Yet, that might be wrong.

A few years ago, while guest teaching my undergraduate course on demagoguery, a friend and colleague pointed out this ambiguous passage in *Gorgias* (467b). Socrates and Polus have been disputing whether learning rhetoric is a valuable pursuit, and the disagreement has turned to the value of rhetorical power itself. Polus has argued that rhetoric can make one as powerful as a tyrant (which Lamb translates as "despot"), in that powerful speakers, like tyrants, can put to death or expel from the city anyone they want. Socrates replies that orators and tyrants have the least power of any:

> For I say, Polus, that the orators and the despots alike have the least
> power in their cities, as I stated just now; since they do nothing that
> they wish to do, practically speaking, though they do whatever they
> think to be best. (466d-e)

Josiah Ober interprets the passage (and dialogue generally) as arguing that "public speech caters indiscriminately to the desires of the many (thereby corrupting them) while simultaneously serving to corrupt the speaker and to enslave him to the multitude" (*Dissent* 190). In contrast to the relationship mapped above, then, Socrates presents something like this:

Masses		Dominance
Demagogue	::	Submission

The demagogue must submit not only to his (or her, although the dialogue assumes only male demagogues) uncontrolled passions, but to the desires of the masses.

It has come to seem to me that both models are correct. The demagogue presents herself as dominating, but in a way that the ideal audience ("masses") shares in the domination, through "agency by proxy." And Socrates's point is insightful: the demagogue is powerful only insofar as she submits to the constraints set by the current beliefs of the ideal audience, and how much those beliefs can be moved.

Demagoguery invites people to imagine themselves members of a particular group by telling them that is who they already are (interpellation).[18] When it's effective, demagoguery persuades people to see beliefs, policies, and so on as "naturally" deriving from who they "essentially" are (good). The opposition's arguments derive from who they essentially are (bad), and therefore need not be taken seriously. When it works, there is sometimes the puzzling consequence that people often end up believing false histories of their own group identities (such as that evangelicals have always been opposed to abortion, Christians have always read Genesis literally, "races" were pure until recently, Democrats have always been supportive of civil rights, and conservatives have always been opposed to increasing national debt). If the audience accepts the invitation to see themselves as part of the rhetor's in-group, then they can deduce that any policies advocated by the rhetor are *essentially* and *inevitably* good, and policy argumentation is unnecessary. All that matters is loyalty.

Demagoguery doesn't give the rhetor unlimited power, though: demagoguery invites the audience to inhabit an identity that cannot be too far from how we see ourselves in the moment. Despite the tendency to describe rhetors like Hitler, who are notorious for their demagoguery, as "imposing" (to use Shirer's term) or "enslaving" (to use Signer's metaphor), a single speaker, especially in a single text, is limited as to how far he or she can move that audience. Mann says in regard to the narrative that genocides are the consequences of wicked leaders who make good people go astray: "That would be to credit leaders with truly magical powers of manipulation" (*Dark Side* 8). And scholars of individual demagogues invariably note the extent to which they were already not saying anything new.[19]

For instance, Madison Grant and his 1916 *Passing of the Great Race* are often given credit for some of the horrors of the twentieth century—eugenics, anti-immigration laws, lynchings, forced sterilization, segregation, and even the Holocaust. Grant's book was one of only two books by non-Germans recommended by the Nazi Party, and "Nazi racial thinkers often pointed to Madison Grant and his disciples as the inspiration for their work" (Spiro 357). Karl Brandt's defense counsel Robert Servatius introduced several pages from the book into evidence during the Nuremberg trials (presumably to argue that Brandt's actions were endorsed by American authorities, *Medical Case-USA v. Karl Brandt* 10179). Alain Leroy Locke listed Grant's book among the "influential racist works" against which *The New Negro* was a "note of protest" ("Introduction" xv). Jonathan Spiro argues that Grant's book had a "direct influence" on biologists, geneticists, zoologists, psychologists, university presidents, and geologists (168). Theodore Bilbo's *Take Your Choice* (arguing for sending African Americans "back" to Africa) cites and paraphrases Grant, as did his speeches against antilynching laws. David Duke, the white nationalist, cites Grant's book as influential (173, 575), and current white nationalists "prize" Grant especially for his role in the 1924 immigration restrictions (Swain and Nieli 66).

Historians who study Grant sometimes argue that it was not his theory that was so influential (since it was not especially new), but how he presented it—that is, his rhetoric. Michael Mezzano explains the paradox that people like Grant and Stoddard were taken as authorities despite their lack of formal training "because they explained these difficult subjects in easily understandable terms" (83). As Daniel Kevles says in regard to the use of intelligence tests in eugenics rhetoric:

> The majority of mental testers and their audience, their views shaped in considerable part by the racial or class prejudices that pervaded eugenics, found the biological theory of intelligence, advanced in the seemingly neutral language of science, persuasive. (84)

But the claim that Grant's rhetoric was effective is complicated—what *effect* did it have? It is also common to say that Grant, and authors like him, did not change anyone's mind, but simply naturalized and legitimated existing racism. Kenan Malik describes racialist science generally as functioning "to validate the idea of a hierarchy generated outside of society and governed by natural rather than social laws" (88), and K. L. Garver and B. Garver describe rhetoric like Grant's as functioning primarily "to justify prejudicial viewpoints."[20] Scholars say that Grant did and didn't change anyone's mind. That's interesting.

The role of demagoguery in public deliberation *is* interesting, especially the question of what impact it has, and this book argues that we should pay more attention to it. The first chapter considers an instance when minds were changed—the debate over the Iraq invasion (during which time a large portion of US voters did become persuaded regarding the invasion). My argument in that chapter is severalfold. First, the demagoguery surrounding the invasion was not coming from *a* rhetor, but constituted discourse. The demagoguery might have been the consequence of (among other things) the decision on the part of the Bush administration to engage in nothing but compliance-gaining rhetoric instead of political deliberation, but the record suggests that the administration did not, ever, deliberate. And the disastrous outcome of the invasion shows the importance of policy argumentation. Had there been deliberation, even the GOP would have benefited. The Bush administration didn't just successfully demonize Saddam Hussein, but effectively demonized democratic deliberation, especially policy argumentation. The case for war was a case about identities, which presented the American public with the false choice of being a hero in an action movie or the effeminate intellectual who ineffectually tries to think things through. Americans were invited to eschew deliberating in favor of believing. And we took that invitation.

The second chapter examines three instances of demagoguery, emphasizing in each the way that the rhetors argue against deliberation itself, insisting that the correct course of action is the correct act of submission. Cleon, a rhetor from the fourth century B.C.E., tried to persuade his audience not to listen to plans for anything less than brutal destruction of Mytilene. Using a set of philosophical paired terms (what Laclau calls an "equivalential chain"), Cleon enumerated two categories of people: manly realists who act quickly and want punishment, and dithering fools prone to weak-willed pity. Cleon's argument is openly emotional, and openly a call to act on emotion (specifically anger and not pity), but demagoguery can also present itself as a rational and unemotional, even "middle" position, as shown by the second case in chapter 2. William Workman's *The Case for the South*—an argument for segregation that, like Cleon's, relies heavily on cunning projection, a rhetoric of realism, contradictory premises, and dividing things into a set of binary and paired terms—is an internally inconsistent argument, but one that consistently presents the in-group as manly, controlled, and acting rationally and decisively to prevent the catastrophe of integration. The argument is irrational, but the posture is rational.

Cleon and Workman were probably acting in ways they sincerely believed benefited their community, although taking the postures they did also helped them politically. Demagoguery, however, is not necessarily (or even most commonly) engaged in by people on their own behalf; demagoguery can be in service of handing decision making over to some other entity. The third case in this chapter concerns the United States Supreme Court's demagoguery defending what has come to be called "Japanese internment" in the case *Hirabayashi v. United States*. In this case, too, there is an argument against deliberation and for submission to "the facts" (which were fabrications) and to the military.

Chapter 3 uses the testimony during the hearings of John Tolan's House Select Committee Investigating National Defense Migration regarding the "evacuation" of various groups from "military zones" (especially the testimony of then-California attorney general Earl Warren) to argue for a more complicated understanding of the role of emotions in demagoguery than is assumed in the common conception that "demagoguery is distinguished by its emotionalism." While some people who testified were openly racist, quite a few, especially Warren, adopted a posture of manly submission to facts and rational and unemotional assessment of the situation. Their demagoguery was in the service of an irrational, incoherent, and even fascistic way of managing their own fears. Their discourse lacked many of the surface features of emotionalism (such as boosters), and Warren's, in particular, relied on linguistic features associated with caution (such as hedging). Opponents of mass imprisonment sometimes (but not always) used boosters and other marks of emotionality, but in service of more internally consistent and rational arguments. Thus, it's pointless to try to distinguish one kind of argument as more or less rational on the basis of surface features. Nor was one set of arguments worse (or less rational) because it was more emotional. The problem with Warren's testimony—and the arguments made by other pro-imprisonment rhetors—was not that he felt fear and suspicion and a lack of control, but that such emotions were bracketed out of deliberation.

Chapter 4 similarly discusses demagoguery engaged in by (and for) the elite, and a kind that presents itself as scientific. While Warren was a member of the political elite, his argument and evidence, albeit not logically connected, were easy to follow. Madison Grant's 1916 *Passing of the Great Race,* on the contrary, is almost impossible to follow. The general argument was a remix of Arthur Gobineau's and William Ripley's racist taxonomies, as was noted at the time. Grant's book is interesting for a variety of reasons. It is an example of the kind of text that, at the level of argument, does nothing new, and, yet, it is cited as moving and powerful. Since the book is almost unintelligible, and what is intelligible was taken from other authors, the puzzle is why so many readers (including current white supremacists) familiar with previous versions of Grant's racial hierarchy would insist that his argument was *new.* The book is demagoguery, having the same characteristics of paired terms, appeals to contradictory premises, the posture of submitting to facts, cunning projection, and so on. In this chapter, I argue that the book did not change readers' minds, but it might have made them feel that their racist beliefs could be defended scientifically. Most importantly, the book models an epistemological stance on the part of the in-group. In-group members, the book claims, are *essentially* entitled to dominate others; members of the in-group can see that. Adopting the posture of the book through having read it is to demonstrate one's membership in Grant's entitled elite. It is race as reason.

Chapter 5 examines several instances of demagoguery—two of which are closer to common conceptions of it, in the work of E. S. Cox and Theodore Bilbo. All the instances discussed in this chapter involve puzzling attempts to invoke the authority of "science" to support positions that are non- and even antiscientific. Although eugenics fairly consistently supported racist notions about racial hierarchies until discredited by Nazism, other sciences were less clearly supportive from earlier in the twentieth century. Cultural anthropology and linguistics early in the century explicitly rejected racist policies, and physical anthropology increasingly shifted to rejection. As segregation lost its scientific support, segregationists formed their own organizations and journals, and continued to claim expert endorsement of their position, even while (contradictorily) whingeing about being academically marginalized. Similarly, while homosexuality was pathologized by psychology for some time, in the 1970s, it was officially determined not a mental illness. Groups committed to the now-outdated characterization of homosexuality as a mental illness formed their own journals, conferences, and impressive-sounding names. It is puzzling that homophobes and segregationists claim that their positions originated in science. It's easy enough to point out that rhetors such as Cox, Bilbo, and various homophobic groups rely on *bad* science, but why rely on science at all? Why invoke as an authority something the audience doesn't find particularly authoritative, and particularly in order to invoke bad versions of it badly? This chapter argues that these cases exemplify epistemological populism, which posits that disagreement is the consequence of bad people more or less deliberately deceiving themselves. All truth is obvious truth, and group identities are obviously written into nature itself. I argue that the image of "science" to which these rhetors appeal is an older and Romantic version of the "knower" who can see what is obvious to all good people. Good science, then, tells good people what they already know to be true.

1

Invasion of Iraq and
Evasion of Policy Deliberation

> It is a requirement of a real democracy that significant elements of
> critical discussion should be involved in serious political debating.
> A speaker in a political discussion should be willing to change his[/
> her] position if offered convincing arguments by the other side.
> —Walton, *Place of Emotion*

In August of 2002, around the same time that various prominent Republicans
(including Brent Scowcroft) were expressing doubts about the Bush administration plan for war, Ann Coulter wrote,

> Democrats claim to support invading Iraq—just not yet! . . . But first—
> there are many worthless objections to be raised. Sore loser Al Gore has
> said that before invading Iraq we need to establish peace in the Mideast,
> create a perfect Jeffersonian democracy in Afghanistan, and get the Amer-
> ican-hating French and Germans on board. Also invent cold fusion and
> put a man on Mars. Then will the time be ripe for a pre-emptive attack!

The argument relies on a fairly clear enthymeme: the Democratic stance on the
war can be dismissed because Gore's argument can be dismissed. Of course,
the grounds on which Gore's argument can be dismissed aren't entirely clear;
this passage (and the article generally) works through association, rather than
logical implication. It isn't clear whether the "sore loser" epithet is intended
to indicate that Gore is an unreliable rhetor (because he has a bad character)
or to imply that his argument is purely the consequence of his having lost the
election (that is, motivism). It also isn't clear whether the last part of the passage
is making a slippery-slope argument (once we try to meet the conditions Gore

has set, he will set more), a reductio ad absurdum (since we are doing one set of things, why not do these), a straw man (since Gore had said nothing of the kind), or perhaps all three.

The article would simply alienate someone who thought Gore's criteria were reasonable, who realized that not all critics of invasion were Democrats, or who was even familiar with the AP article she quotes (but doesn't cite). To the extent that this article would have "impact," it would polarize the situation just slightly more by alienating anyone who didn't already agree with the surprisingly complicated associations Coulter is assuming and reinforcing (all criticism of the Bush plan is opposition to the invasion, all opponents of invasion are Democrats, all Democrats are typified in Gore, Gore is a sore loser, Gore's criticisms are ridiculous). In general, the argument is that objections to the Bush case for invasion are worthless and not worth listening to. But, that's an odd point, even if common, for a professional pundit to make. After all, Coulter's living comes from writing and speaking about politics, and she is, presumably, writing and speaking to people who choose to read about politics, listen to radio shows about politics, and watch television shows about politics. Yet, one of her recurrent themes (and perhaps the main theme throughout her writing) is that democratic deliberation is worthless. So, as with Cleon's speech, this is a lot of talk about how political talk is a waste of time. And there is a considerable audience for such rhetoric—people for whom participating in politics means reading and listening to arguments that policy argumentation is unnecessary and dangerous. That's an interesting paradox.

There is another interesting aspect of this piece. This dismissal through association works through a series of synecdoches, so that Gore stands for Democrats, who stand for opposition to the invasion. The argument presumes a factionalized binary, with perfect proinvasion unity on the side of one political faction, and any opposition to any aspect of the Bush plan on the other. And yet this article came out while there was still a kerfuffle going on about Scowcroft, Baker, Kissinger, and other conservatives who had expressed concern and criticism about various aspects of the Bush administration plan for invasion. Coulter's demagoguery reduces the complicated and nuanced arguments about the Bush *plan* to a binary of identity that maps factional lines perfectly.

My desire to write this book began with the debacle that passed for public debate over the proposed invasion of Iraq. That people disagreed with me about what we should do didn't bother me—that's a fact of having an opinion. But it did bother me, and still bothers me, that there was so little *debate*. Instead, the argument quickly shifted to the motives of the "other" side, and whether there even should be an argument. Unhappily, the Bush administration and its "water carriers" (as Rush Limbaugh once characterized various parts of the media) succeeded in persuading Americans not only that we should invade Iraq, but that we shouldn't deliberate about it. According to Amy Gershkoff and Shana Kushner, polls through the pre-invasion period indicated that "more than 40 percent felt that those opposed to the war should not be allowed to speak out or hold protest marches or rallies" (529). Americans came to the conclusion that the invasion was a mistake, and many have come to blame the Bush Administration, or Bush personally, but we haven't admitted that the process whereby *we* came to a decision was a mistake.

Identity as Policy

Coulter's attempt to use political party as a shorthand for political agenda may or may not have been in bad faith. It's hard to imagine she was unaware of the Republicans who argued against a unilateral war, or the Democrats who argued for it, especially since the article from which she quoted made exactly that point (assuming I have correctly inferred the source—she doesn't give one). The AP article to which Coulter refers is almost certainly Will Lester's "Democratic Hopefuls on Iraq" as that has the quote she gives. Not only does the article point to division within Democrats, but also among Republicans: "Democratic voters have mixed feelings about war with Iraq, polls suggest, and some Republican leaders are showing even more doubts than the Democrats." Coulter's argument, then, was based on a false assertion of perfect polarization, and is supported by a quote from an article that falsifies Coulter's claim. Coulter's argument is an identity argument, a kind of argument with troubling consequences for political deliberation. If policy is purely a consequence of identity, then there is never any reason to debate policy.

Traditional rhetorical theory identifies two parts to policy debate: need and plan. The "need" portion of a debate concerns such stases as whether there is a serious "ill," what causes it, and whether the problem will go away on its own. The "plan" portion should allow the investigation of what various options are, how they compare to one another in terms of solvency (do they actually solve the problem identified in the "need" portion of the debate), feasibility, and unintended consequences. The Bush case for war persistently and consistently evaded any debate of its plan. Robert Ivie refers to it as the way that "American insecurity [was] amplified beyond the limits of critical thinking and thus placed outside the reach of pragmatic political critique" ("Fighting Terror" 222). Instead of policy debate, we had performances and assertions of identity.

The explicit public case was, as Chaim Kaufmann summarizes it, entirely about the person of Saddam Hussein:

(1) he was an almost uniquely undeterrable aggressor who would seek any opportunity to kill Americans virtually regardless of risk to himself or his country; (2) he was cooperating with al-Qa'ida and had even assisted in the September 11, 2001, terrorist attacks against the United States; (3) he was close to acquiring nuclear weapons, and (4) he possessed chemical and biological weapons that could be used to devastating effect against American civilians at home or U.S. Troops in the Middle East. ("Threat Inflation")

It is striking that the administration entirely failed to make the "plan" portion of their case. In fact, it may even be that there was no plan: "As numerous analyses have compellingly documented, the United States invaded Iraq without an effective plan to secure the peace" (Diamond, *Squandered* 282). John Murphy discusses Bush's September 20, 2001, speech, pointing out that it was not a policy speech, but a performance of identity: "He did not preview policies for the union's betterment nor did he suggest expediency arguments. Rather, he was representative of the people; he stood as a part for their whole" (613). Murphy says that later in the speech Bush approached policy issues, in that he "announced" what he would do, but even then "no arguments were presented as to their practicality" (616). As Murphy argues, this aversion to policy deliberation was how Bush consistently presented his own thinking:

> This was not a mind that regarded the slow and messy processes of democratic deliberation, diplomacy, and compromise as useful tasks. In his private view, as in his public address, character made policy and there was no need to lawyer the thing to death. (617)

To make the issues not just character and identity issues would open them up to argument. As Ronald Krebs and Jennifer Lobasz point out, "Claims advanced by national leaders" are "more contestable in principle when wrapped in pragmatic rhetoric than when offered in a rhetoric of identity" (425). Or, in Murphy's words, "Extraordinary public pressure is brought to bear on those who oppose the president because opposition based on practicality and expediency makes no sense in a world governed by theistic essence" (627).

Denise Bostdorff says that Bush

> relied on the rhetoric of covenant renewal, which allowed him to place blame for September 11 on evil, external enemies and to cast the U.S. and its citizens as a blameless, exceptional community that had been attacked because of its goodness. (298–99)

Krebs and Lobasz called this rhetorical strategy "national identity discourse" and argue that it "overshadowed all others" in the weeks following September 11 (423). In fact, it persisted throughout the selling of the invasion. In September of 2002, Robert Kaiser wrote an editorial for the *Washington Post* in which he argued that Bush's explanation for the September 11 attacks ("they hate our freedoms") was part of ignoring the list of grievances made by bin Laden and others, which attributed their hatred to fairly specific practices and policies:

> By ignoring the items on this list and denouncing an enemy that hates us for what we are, not for what we say and do—or what they think we do—President Bush has created an all-purpose bad guy whose existence allows him to sidestep any examination of American policy. ("The Long and Short of It" September 8, 2002)

This reduction of political action to expressions of identity not only excludes the debate of policies *qua* policies, including their feasibility, solvency, and unintended consequences, but complicates any dissent at all. Krebs and Lobasz say, "It appeared to compel opponents to do the unthinkable—support the War on Terror or make common cause with evil" (428).

Characterizing going to war as our only choice was not only frequently connected to the binary of "this action or no action at all," but connected to stereotypes about Muslim identity and beliefs. In December of 2001, Reuel Marc Gerecht, a Middle East specialist in the CIA, propounded an argument in the *Wall Street Journal* that (as the title of the article says) "crushing al Qaeda is only a start." The premise of his argument is that,

> If we really intend to extinguish the hope that has fueled the rise of al Qaeda and the violent anti-Americanism throughout the Middle East, we have no choice but to re-instill in our foes and friends the fear and respect that attaches to any great power.

Michael Kramer's response to Scowcroft, horrifyingly called "The Case for Bagging Saddam" (explicitly making him an animal one shoots for bragging rights), approvingly quotes two unnamed officials who argue that the Iraq invasion was a deliberate attempt to intimidate, not just terrorists, but "the Islamic world," and that a practice of intimidation is grounded in "Islamic psychology." Taking into account "Islamic psychology," Kramer acknowledges profound anti-Americanism in the world, but doesn't consider that such anti-Americanism might be the consequence of anything the United States actually does—to our foreign policies. Resistance to the United States is, Kramer says, "rooted in a perception of American weakness" and is "immune to diplomacy." Approvingly quoting a Bush adviser, Kramer says that reversing the perception of weakness is the importance of a war against Iraq.

> "That's the perception we have to reverse," said a Bush adviser. "It is for that reason, not just to keep Saddam from using his weapons of mass destruction, that a war against Iraq makes sense. If we don't appear all-powerful, and as willing to use our power, we're doomed."

The quote from the unnamed advisor is an interesting instance of projection: it is itself an irrational and hyperbolic perception, that infuses a particular action with almost chiliastic meaning; and yet, supposedly, it is because of *their* excessive interpretation that we *must* go to war.

Gerecht also evokes the myth of Muslims' perceiving deliberation and diplomacy as weakness: "America actually loses face in Muslim eyes by not enforcing an unabashedly pro-Western, pro-Israeli agenda." Our goal should be to inspire awe. Kramer, in a piece that evokes several myths about the "Arab" psychology, calls for a "war against mythology"—a clear instance of cunning projection. The profoundly irrational character of Muslims not only forces us to go to war against them, but in a way that is profoundly irrational and entirely about awe. The pro-invasion rhetoric scapegoated the vague entity of "the Muslim world" twice over: Saddam Hussein was scapegoated for 9/11, and for our having no possible response other than invasion.

This stereotype of the irrational Muslim was easily contradicted not only by the actual behavior of actual leaders in the "Muslim world," but also by how those actions had been characterized previously by Bush administration figures. While there are ways in which the presentation of Saddam Hussein as irrational evil personified remained a constant in political discourse through the 1990s (as Krebs and Lobasz argue, "The Sound of Silence," see especially 124–6), there was considerable evidence that he was quite rational, as was often unintentionally admitted. Condoleezza Rice argued in a 2000 *Foreign Affairs* article that Saddam Hussein was susceptible to deterrence. In a passage discussing the Clinton administration handling of North Korea and Iraq, she said,

> These regimes are living on borrowed time, so there need be no sense of panic about them. Rather, the first line of defense should be a clear and classical statement of deterrence—if they do acquire WMD, their weapons will be unusable because any attempt to use them will bring national obliteration. ("Campaign 2000")

Chaim Kaufmann says, "Hussein's behavior since the first Gulf War showed him to have been successfully deterred at almost every turn." He was "not a crazed aggressor prone to wild chances, but a ruler profoundly concerned with retaining power and aware that his greatest danger was that the United States might exert itself to remove him" ("Threat inflation" 101).

What one has to notice about the two unnamed officials in Kramer's article (and much discourse at the time) is that it was textbook homogenizing of the Other, treating the extraordinary range of Muslim identities, behaviors, psychologies, and worldviews as fixed and transparently knowable—a fundamental attribution error those officials would have been unlikely to make about, for instance, "Christians." As Andrew Flibbert says, "A black-and-white understanding of international politics blurred the distinction between US adversaries like Iraq and al-Qaeda, diminishing their marked political and ideological antagonism" (86). This Manichaeanism meant that there was no need to think very carefully, and certainly not in worst-case scenario terms, about what would happen after the invasion: "The war and its aftermath were expected to be relatively easy, because Manichaean thinking implied that Iraq after Saddam's demise would shift naturally from negative to positive political valence" (90).

And shifting to positive valence would involve submitting to US policy agenda, becoming a placid client-state. Kramer quotes "a State Department official" as saying,

> Winning the war against terrorism will only happen "if we dent the Islamists' view of their 'manifest destiny.' . . . Because they see their cause as inevitable, they accept and even welcome any sacrifice that advances their goal of driving the West out of the entire Islamic world."

The goal is not to dent their sense of manifest destiny because there is something wrong with the notion of manifest destiny per se, but because there is something wrong with *Islamists* believing in *their* manifest destiny. After all, the Bush administration frequently invoked a narrative of manifest destiny to justify our actions. J. K. Cramer and E. C. Duggan persuasively argue that the foreign policy goal, especially of Cheney and Rumsfeld, was "nothing less than full, unquestioned US primacy" (230). One of the four crucial beliefs that Andrew Flibbert identifies as contributing to the commitment to invasion is "benevolent hegemony," which he describes as the United States using its power to ensure "not only a safer United States, but also a more peaceful world . . . to change the world for the better" (83). Our actions would be good—must be good—"since US intentions were believed to be irreproachable" (83). Because we are good people, our actions are necessarily good.[1]

Like Athens's client-states (discussed in the next chapter), other members of this hegemony would defer to us, in what would be, magically, a good economic deal for us, an extension of a superpower's hegemony, *and* an act of kindness and liberation. Paradoxically, this exceptionally good identity as a liberator not only means that other states should submit to us, but that rules don't apply to us. Our superior ethical identity enables us to live by different (even lower) ethical standards. Advocates of American exceptionalism, in Flibbert's words, believe that the United States "was entitled to a degree of deference from other states by virtue of its exceptional nature, and it was exempt from the conventional rules of international interaction in light of the leadership role it played" (83). In other words, the rhetoric that sold the war (we are good people and they are bad people) wasn't just a sales pitch—it signified the philosophy of identity behind the foreign policy being sold. The Bush administration wasn't just selling a policy, they were selling a way to think about the role of the United States in the world, *and* a way to think and argue about politics in general. It was demagoguery all the way down.

And all the way across. Part of what made me despair about our situation (and what made it seem so similar to antebellum America) was that the demagoguery wasn't restricted to political elites—it was how people argued in letters to the editor, comment threads on blogs, on the bus, over Thanksgiving dinner. Demagoguery was clearly becoming, not a cunning strategy adopted for Machiavellian purposes, but the dominant model of public discourse. Elsewhere I take the more or less random example of a 2007 interview with Gene Simmons and its reception on a popular news aggregator to argue that it is commonplace for political arguments to be little more than performances of loyalty to group identity (Roberts-Miller, "Dissent Is 'Aid and Comfort to the Enemy'"). My argument is that reducing political discussions to expressions of condemnation of the out-group and praise of the in-group makes policy questions feel simpler and less uncertain.

While some people are generally uncomfortable with uncertainty (especially people who are what Ariel Kruglanski calls prone to epistemic closure), most (perhaps all) people find it somewhat unsettling, and research suggests that we're likely to respond to uncertainty of any kind by reminding ourselves of in-group membership, by reasserting in-group entitativity. The most threatening kind of uncertainty, according to Kees van den Bos and Annemarie Loserman, is the kind that raises the possibility of failure. Such a situation, they argue, triggers "hot-cognitive responses because it is a warning sign that our current or past efforts may not pay off in the future" ("Radical Worldview" 76). I'd suggest it's precisely that kind of uncertainty that Simmons's performance of perfect certainty reduces. By taking the posture of an in-group member who is not at all troubled by recent events, he demonstrates his own loyalty to the in-group, while reinforcing the definition of that in-group as people of clear and perfect judgment.

After all, by 2007, advocates of the Iraq invasion were facing not just uncertainty, but a distinct possibility of failure: both politically and epistemologically. Reality had disconfirmed many (if not all) of pro-invasion rhetors' claims about Iraq and the invasion—regarding weapons of mass destruction, the possibility of a quagmire, the cost of the invasion, its consequences for US security—and that future efforts might not pay off. That policy failure was a failure of judgment—that they had been wrong about what the situation was (and would be) suggests that their judgment had been wrong, raising the prospect that in-group membership does not guarantee flawless policy. For people for whom uncertainty is a fact of life, for whom mistakes are likely (whom Philip Tetlock [borrowing the formulation of Isaiah Berlin] calls "foxes" as opposed to "hedgehogs" *Expert*), such a prospect is not particularly frightening.

But, for people for whom in-group membership means unmediated and unbiased judgment, some kind of direct contact between perception and reality, the prospect of in-group disagreement is destabilizing. Pro-invasion rhetors might have been wrong, not just about the war, but about their own sense of themselves as people who were grounded in reality. Such uncertainty about in-group identity was heightened by the presence of disagreement within the in-group about what should be done. That is, in 2007, with the invasion going badly, people who believe themselves to have perfect vision were faced with cognitive dissonance ("I am always right" and "My judgment about Iraq might have been wrong"). Acknowledging that not all conservatives agree(d) about the invasion would make that dissonance even worse. Admitting heterogeneity within the in-group means admitting that "good people" disagree, and, therefore, the situation is uncertain; a group with heterogeneity, especially in regard to opinions, fails to provide a clear prototype (or closure). A heterogeneous group highlights uncertainty; hence, if one is uncomfortable with uncertainty, one will reject any information about dissent within the in-group, through such strategies as the "no true Scotsman" move, denying that people *really* disagree, policing group membership (calling dissenters a "RINO"), or relying on abstract language and concepts that are harder to disconfirm (Kruglanski and Orehek 14).

Under such circumstances, rhetoric that says "you and I are right, and we were right all along, and will continue to be right" would be tremendously pleasing. In short, part of the "effectiveness" of the interview with Gene Simmons, and one reason some people liked it, was probably that he persuasively identified himself as a member of their in-group, and he implicitly and explicitly defined that in-group in ways that they found satisfying—as a homogeneous group that accurately and easily perceives the right and wrong of the situation. This in-group was constructed in opposition to a vague out-group (Sean Penn, critics of the war, "the" media,

Hollywood "idiots") that pleased people who saw themselves as part of that in-group and opposed to that out-group. Simmons promised his audience that there is a stable taxonomy of political persuasion and identity, this taxonomy is ontologically grounded, and it is easy to perceive. That is, the "argument" in the Simmons interview, like the argument in much political punditry, is not about the specifics of policies (which, as in the Simmons case, are often muddled, muckled, and internally contradictory) but about the stance of being a member of a group that operates with perfect certainty, direct perception, and a direct connection to reality.[2]

In-group/out-group confirmation is closely related to naïve realism. The conclusion of various researchers is that thinking in terms of in-groups and out-groups provides a tremendous amount of epistemic security.[3] People with a high need for "cognitive closure"—defined as "the need to pursue, possess, and rely on information that is unambiguous, clear, and unlikely to change" (Federico and Deason, "Uncertainty" 201)—tend to be drawn to authoritarianism, and, in fact, the two can be mutually reinforcing. Mark Hetherington and Jonathan Weiler say authoritarians have "(1) a greater need for order and, conversely, less tolerance for confusion or ambiguity, and (2) a propensity to rely on established authorities to provide that order" (34). More likely to support physical punishment in parenting (3; in fact, there is a strong crossover between authoritarianism and George Lakoff's "strict father model"), prone to black and white thinking (3), they tend to "make stronger than average distinctions between in-groups—the groups they identify with—and out-groups—groups that they perceive challenge them" (4). While prone to submit to authorities, it is only to authorities who themselves present the world in clear-cut terms (34)—that is, one of the ways that a rhetor marks him/herself as an authority to authoritarians is in using authoritarian rhetoric. Hetherington and Weiler say authoritarians are "more likely to feel threatened by, and dislike, out-groups; more likely to desire muscular responses to conflict; less politically well informed; and less likely to change their way of thinking when new information might challenge their deeply held beliefs" (37). To be blunt, an authoritarian has more at stake in a disagreement than a nonauthoritarian. Similarly, someone who perceives group (or individual) goodness at issue in every contest enters every argument with much higher stakes.

That is, if I believe that what is really at stake in an argument about whether to invade Iraq is whether "liberals" or "conservatives" are essentially better people, then admitting lack of clarity on a single point, let alone error, has all sorts of attendant admissions: that I'm not sure who is better, that I am not sure what is true, that people like me can be wrong. Nonauthoritarians faced with disconfirming and compelling evidence may feel stupid, chagrined, and may even look stupid to anyone watching the disagreement, but are left with confirmation of the basic worldview that the world is an uncertain place. That they have made an error confirms the notion that people make errors. Authoritarians must admit either that they are not members of the epistemologically elect (that is, the in-group), or that the in-group is not epistemologically elect. It shakes their world.

Authoritarianism is simultaneously a hermeneutic, a model of group identity, an ontology, and an epistemology. For instance, authoritarians reject "context-specific interpretations" of texts.

> Whether one is talking about the Bible or the Constitution, for instance, one can identify an outlook that would reject multiple, layered interpretations in favor of an outlook motivated by the belief that too much slack and uncertainty in rule application could yield disorder, chaos, and social breakdown. (Hetherington and Weiler 35)

For many people—not just authoritarians—the world is a text, and written into that text is group identity. If authoritarians admit to misreading group identity, they have misread a foundational text. To admit uncertainty is one more step down the road to chaos. Uncertainty is terrifying.

Something like the Iraq War is a terrible challenge to naïve realism, authoritarianism, and faith in the epistemologically elect. The Bush administration presented an unambiguous narrative of good triumphing quickly and easily over evil. It was obvious, they argued, that Saddam Hussein was a bad man. It is obvious that people who fight evil are good. It is obvious that good triumphs. And, finally, *that* was the Bush administration case for war. That is, the Bush administration case for war was, in many ways, not political deliberation, but the plot of an action movie. As Robert Ivie summarizes Bush's pro-invasion rhetoric, it was a world "filled with heroes and villains, divided by good and evil, and given purpose by God's will, which was to be fulfilled by people of faith and character opposed to evil" (*Dissent* 63).[4] Krebs and Lobasz summarize how the 9/11 attacks were immediately cast by the Bush administration as an issue of "the goodness and virtue with America" versus "the 'evil'" of her terrorist adversaries. "At the core of these contending accounts lay a common narrative element: 'we' were attacked because of 'who we are,' not because of 'what we have done'" ("Sound of Silence" 122).

The Iraq "debate" played out like a blockbuster action movie, in which a common and blunt-speaking male is up against dithering bureaucrats who want to run things through channels, discuss things, negotiate with evil, or otherwise get in the way of the obviously correct course of action: blowing things up.[5] A complicated situation, with a variety of legitimate opinions and options was reduced to—as Bush famously said—you are either with us or against us. (Since Christ says this in Matthew 12:30, Bush made going along with his political policy a demonstration of piety.) For many supporters of the war, this bifurcation was an attractive (perhaps even persuasive) way to think about the issue: some people (good people) recognized the threat and therefore supported Bush in all of his polices, and others (bad people), whose judgment and masculinity were impaired, were engaged in unmanly quibbling and cowardice.

The tendency toward bifurcating policy options served the Bush administration well, as it effectively silenced the anti-Saddam Hussein–antiwar position. To acknowledge that position, and the goodwill and intelligence of people who held it, would be to acknowledge the inadequacy of naïve realism: it would mean that there was not perfect agreement among good people, and that the true course of action was not obvious. The Bush administration, and the various media figures who "carry the water" for them (in Rush Limbaugh's phrase), may have been cunning in presenting a bifurcated view of the options. Silencing the anti-Saddam Hussein–antiwar position may have been a deliberate strategy on their part, but I think it is more likely (and, perhaps, more troubling) to consider that it was perfectly sincere.

How, then, can the dissent of other in-group members be explained? It can be denied, as in arguments like Coulter's that equated opposition to the Bush plan with being a Democrat; it can also be dismissed through psychologizing. One of the more disturbing examples of this process was the response to Brent Scowcroft's *Wall Street Journal* editorial, "Don't Attack Saddam." In that August 2002 piece, Scowcroft, national security adviser under George H. W. Bush and Gerald Ford, refuted the Bush case, arguing largely on the grounds of unintended consequences: "An attack on Iraq at this time would seriously jeopardize, if not destroy, the global counter-terrorist campaign we have undertaken." It would do so, he argued, because most actors in the Middle East are primarily concerned about the Israel-Palestine conflict, and,

> If we were seen to be turning our backs on that bitter conflict—which the region, rightly or wrongly, perceives to be clearly within our power to resolve—in order to go after Iraq, there would be an explosion of outrage against us. We would be seen as ignoring a key interest of the Muslim world in order to satisfy what is seen to be a narrow American interest.

The media response to that argument was deeply discouraging for the prospect of democratic deliberation. The low points were the various responses that dismissed Scowcroft's arguments by relying on the "strategy schema," as some kind of neurotic contest between George W. Bush and his father rather than a policy argument. Maureen Dowd, for instance, in a syndicated article variously titled "Family Feud" (*Pittsburgh Post-Gazette*), "In Need of Some Bush Family Therapy" (*Tulsa World*), and "Bush Jr. Gets a Spanking" (*New York Times*), framed Scowcroft's article as "Poppy" (as she calls the elder Bush) using Scowcroft as a pawn in the conflict with "Junior," concluding, "Who needs a war plan? We need family therapy."[6]

My criticism of Dowd's article is not that she takes swipes at either George W. Bush or George H. W. Bush, nor that she speculates about psychological motives or strategies either president might have had, but that those things are *all* she does; she summarizes Scowcroft's actual argument in one sentence, and never engages it. The point of her article is that we don't need a plan, and that doubt about the unilateral invasion was not the consequence of some family drama. But history shows that we did need a plan. It was a reasonable assessment of the problems inherent in an unprecedented invasion of another country on the basis of scant factual support for its necessity, wisdom, or feasibility. Family therapy would not have resolved the issues of feasibility, solvency, and unintended consequences inherent in the plan of the Bush administration. We needed to argue about the plan.

Selling the War

It is (and was at the time) clear that the Bush administration decided at some point to use the public sphere to sell the war. That isn't particularly unusual; the practice of trying to control public discourse in order to be as favorable as possible to an administration agenda is implied in the very notion of the "marketplace of ideas" (for more on this, see Roberts-Miller, *Deliberate Conflict* 98–122). Elsewhere, in regard to the notion that many people perceive public discourse as war, I've argued that it matters what kind of war (*Fanatical* 198–200). Similarly, it isn't just a question of perceiving the public sphere as a marketplace, but of what kind of marketplace. And one model of the marketplace is that consumers benefit the most from a variety of sellers, with the role of the government being to ensure standards of fairness, honesty, and quality. In this model, competition fuels improvement and efficiency, and so everyone benefits from an inclusive marketplace with a variety of competitors. That was the kind of marketplace that Oliver Wendell Holmes probably had in mind when he used the metaphor in defending free speech, but it isn't the dominant model now. We now have a model that puts the power in the sales and not competition. Conservative and neoconservative policymakers seem increasingly drawn to the efficient monopoly model, in which the goal is for a single firm to dominate the market entirely. By crushing, pushing out, or acquiring all other competitors, the single provider can reduce inefficiencies. Singularly impervious to falsification, this model operates on a zero-sum, in which oppositional relations are necessarily negatives, and pluralism is a flaw. *That* is the "marketplace" we had for the debate about Iraq.[7]

The Bush administration did not value ideological pluralism or deliberation, either in the general public or even internally. Rather, it marketed the war to the general public.

> Much of the information and many of the assessments used by the Bush administration in its pre-war public relations campaign were inflated, distorted, or selectively disclosed to the public. The administration did not simply rely on rhetorical devices—such as invoking rhetorical images of mushroom clouds and the like—it selectively used its executive advantages on intelligence collection and analysis to frame a particular version of the threat in order to influence public opinion. (Western, "The War over Iraq" 169).

That is, the Bush administration treated the war as a product to be sold, and American citizens as consumers to be wooed into buying the product.[8]

This evasion of deliberation and disagreement wasn't just an approach they took to public discourse; it's how decision making operated within the administration. As Jane Cramer and Edward Duggan say, "What is most notable about the records of the decision-making process is the absence of any debate about whether to invade Iraq within the Bush administration" ("Primacy" 212). John Prados and Christopher Ames say, "President George W. Bush and Prime Minister Tony Blair, the record suggests, made their real decision privately and restricted knowledge to a very few individuals" ("Was There Even a Decision?"). From December 2001, Prados and Ames argue, actions on the part of the administration were not to resolve the conflict with Iraq, nor to consider whether to invade, but to gain compliance to an invasion: "Such diplomacy as took place was designed to recruit allies for an invasion or to coerce the Saddam government into admitting international teams of weapons inspectors—not to disarm Iraq but to justify invasion." Prados and Ames quote Richard Armitage and George Tenet on the absence of debate within the administration. Even more persuasively, among major figures who have written about the buildup to war—George W. Bush, Rumsfeld, and Cheney—not one describes debate within the administration, nor describes himself as having considered worst-case scenarios. When Bush worried about his decision, he didn't talk to people with differing points of view or look carefully at potentially disconfirming evidence—he prayed.[9]

And he succeeded at getting public support for an unprecedented move in American foreign policy. I said earlier that there were two arguments at play in the public discourse over the Iraq invasion: one about whether to invade, and the other about how to argue politics. The Bush administration won, and lost, both arguments. The outcome of the relative success at displacing policy argument with a rhetoric of identity shows the importance of policy argument, and that displacing policy argument with identity claims so successfully is not in the long-term best interest of anyone. The irony is that everyone—including the GOP—would have been better off had the plan been more thoroughly debated. Had there been skepticism and pushback from the public, at the very least, the Bush administration would have had to prepare a more thorough set of fallback plans. The issue of financing the war would have been confronted. Perhaps the invasion would have been delayed until Afghanistan was in better order. A thorough debate might not have prevented the war, but it would, *at worst,* have led to a better-planned war. Michael O'Hanlon says,

> The problem was simply this: The war plan was seriously flawed and incomplete. Invading another country with the intention of destroying its existing government yet without a serious strategy for providing security thereafter defies logic and falls short of proper professional military standards of competence. It was in fact unconscionable. (36).

Larry Diamond says,

> Instead of preparing for the worst, Pentagon planners assumed that Iraqis would joyously welcome U.S. and international troops as liberators. With Saddam's military and security apparatus destroyed, the thinking went, Washington could capitalize on the goodwill by handing the country over to Iraqi expatriates such as Ahmed Chalabi, who would quickly create a new democratic state. Not only would fewer U.S. troops be needed at first, but within a year, the troop levels could drop to a few thousands. ("What Went Wrong" 36)

We didn't get that best-case scenario. Andrew Bacevich says, "Instead of a quick victory followed by an early departure—Desert Storm without the loose ends—U.S. forces got a recurrence of Mogadishu, on a much larger scale" (*New American Militarism* 64). Had the administration been coerced into better defenses of its plan, it might have come up with plans for worse cases. The consequence has not been good for the United States: "American shortsightedness played a large role in creating this war. American hubris has complicated it unnecessarily, emboldening the enemy, alienating old allies, and bringing U.S. forces close to exhaustion" (*New American Militarism* 203).[10] Fallows says, "I have sat through arguments among soldiers and scholars about whether the invasion of Iraq should be considered the worst strategic error in American history—or only the worst since Vietnam" (*Blind* 114).

Others argue that the idea of invading Iraq to install liberal democracy was not flawed, but the Bush administration's handling of the invasion and occupation was. O'Hanlon says,

> The post-invasion phase of the Iraq mission has been the least well-planned American military mission since Somalia in 1993, if not Lebanon in 1983, and its consequences for the nation have been far worse than any set of military mistakes since Vietnam. ("Iraq without a Plan" 33)

A "senior figure at one of America's military-sponsored think tanks" told Fallows, "I voted for these guys. But I think they are incompetent, and I have had a very close perspective on what is happening" (115).

United States military casualties were around four thousand; estimates of the number of Iraqi casualties range from a hundred thousand (*Iraq War Logs*) to over six hundred thousand (Burham). In addition, the war probably cost the United States $3 trillion (Stiglitz); at the very least it was $1 trillion (far higher than Bush administration estimates), and possibly as high as $23 trillion.[11] Richard Haass summarizes the costs of the war.

> In American lives (more than four thousand), American casualties (more than twenty thousand), and dollars ($1 trillion plus or minus depending upon the accounting . . .). There is the human cost in Iraq, a cost that includes not only the tens of thousands that lost lives but the four to five million Iraqis who fled from their villages and homes and ended up as refugees in neighboring countries or as displaced persons within their own country. The war in Iraq certainly stimulated terrorism there in the short run; what we do not know is what the long-term consequences of the war will be when it comes to thousands of young men who have been radicalized and trained in Iraq's streets. (265)

The war was disastrous for American foreign policy. Fallows summarizes the outcome of our handling of Iraq: "But about the conduct and effect of the war in Iraq one view prevails: it has increased the threats America faces, and has reduced the military, financial, and diplomatic tool with which we can respond" (*Blind* 115). Diamond says, "As a result of a long chain of U.S. miscalculations, the coalition occupation has left Iraq in far worse shape than it need have and has diminished the long-term prospects of democracy there" ("What Went Wrong" 34).

Diamond attributes much of the postwar problems to the small number of troops, noting that Bush did so "despite the warnings of the U.S. Army and outside experts on postconflict resolution that—whatever the needs of the war itself—securing the peace would require a force two to three times that size" (*Squandered*

281). Another extremely important omission, indicating a sincere commitment to wishful thinking, was that, "As has been documented in a number of excellent investigative reports, the United States invaded Iraq without a coherent, viable plan to win the peace" (*Squandered* 27). Diamond reports that a participant in the discussions of what would happen after the war described the situation.

> "There was never any discussion of *how* the Pentagon would implement their plan, or anybody else's. There was never any dialogue on it. Each group had its own plan, but nothing ever got done or decided because of the infighting. Each plan had its good aspects, but the president needed to get behind one plan and say, 'This is going to be it.' He never did." (*Squandered* 29)

It was not in the best interest of the administration for the occupation to go as badly as it did, so one has to infer they thought it wouldn't. That is, their unwillingness to listen carefully to dissent and their tendency toward wishful thinking may be connected, and may indicate an approach to decision making.

Daniel Kahneman and Jonathan Renshon have argued that the standard collection of cognitive biases heavily studied by Kahneman and others (and an important part of what Kahneman calls System 1 thinking) contributes to a propensity to settle conflicts through violence rather than discourse. Kahneman and Renshaw mention seven such biases: positive illusions, the fundamental attribution error (FAE), the illusion of transparency, endowment effect/loss aversion, risk seeking in losses, pseudocertainty, and reactive devaluation (3). The first, positive illusions, is essentially what one might infer concerning the Bush administration; people are likely to have "unrealistically positive views of one's abilities and character, the illusion of control, and unrealistic optimism" (4). Given that everyone has these tendencies, to say that the Bush administration might have been prone to them is not any kind of attack on their character or competence, but it does raise a question about policy and process—whether there was anything in place to try to counter these natural tendencies, and the answer appears to be no.

Descriptions of the Bush administration decision-making processes suggest two recurrent (and connected) characteristics: a tendency for the administration to arrive at goals and objectives through thinking about them (and perhaps some discussion among like-minded individuals); and a tendency for optimism about their abilities and likely outcomes. The biases would be enhanced by this process, since decision making would either be done without discussion, or discussion with someone who had opposite biases. The three that are particularly important for miscalculations in regard to Iraq, and that recur throughout descriptions of the decision-making processes are: positive illusions, FAE, illusion of transparency.[12] Loosely, positive illusions involve rating confirming evidence (signs that success is likely) higher than disconfirming evidence, such as interpreting the Afghanistan enterprise as completed, deciding there was no need to plan for a large amount of resistance, or to have a clear plan for occupation, or to think about how to fund the occupation, and so on. FAE, "perhaps the single most studied bias in social cognition" (Khaneman and Renson 6), is the tendency that people have to assume that the motives of others are easily inferred from observable behaviors—that I can simply look at people and know their motives. Coupled with in-group/out-group thinking, this bias also means that I tend to assume that the out-group's motives are not only bad, but *obviously* bad.

The case against Saddam Hussein exemplifies this bias. He was, I'm perfectly willing to grant, a bad person, although not necessarily an irrational one—that is, he appears to have been fairly cunning in his decisions, and, as mentioned earlier, his actions can be interpreted as showing a person capable of deterrence and rational self-preservation. But, if one assumes that he is completely irrational, then the actions that show rational choices are reframed as random and insignificant; his horrific treatment of political opponents, instead of being seen as a sociopathic (but appallingly rational) way to reduce dissent, is reframed as indicating a completely irrational person who will stop at nothing.

The illusion of transparency is, in a way, the flip side of FAE: that the goodness of one's own motives are obvious to everyone, so obvious that they don't really need to be made explicit. There remains powerful disagreement about the political goals of the Bush administration in the Iraq invasion, but there are several points of agreement among scholars: that the Bush administration hoped to put in a pro-US and pro-Israel stable government, favorable to US business interests (especially in regard to oil), and establish a politically and economically reliable client state. All of this would be achieved with minimal occupation, the assumption being that the citizens of Iraq would go along with it fairly enthusiastically, that they would, in short, see US goals as good goals, and believe that the US had nothing but good intentions for them.

In other words, the characteristic of Bush administration rhetoric often called "Manichaeist" was not just a set of rhetorical tropes useful for persuasion; I'm saying it was their model of determining policy. It is worth thinking about the conditions under which the Bush administration plan (or, more accurately, lack of plan) would have worked:

- if Saddam Hussein presented a purely (and not very popular) military resistance that collapsed quickly;

- if the majority of Iraqis welcomed American political and economic interests (relatively secular, hostile to anti-American terrorism, supportive of US Middle East policy);
- if we quickly and efficiently put into place a stable government without the destabilizing shift to extremism or collapse into warlordism that is typical of transition;
- if we quickly and efficiently built and rebuilt a stable economy, especially in regard to oil; and
- if all the vagaries of historical events—"one thing happening after another"—did so in ways that were beneficial to the United States.

In other words, the Bush administration would have had to have been destined by supernatural forces to be protected from risk. They had to be on the side of God. Flibbert argues that there were four "reinforcing ideas" that made the gamble seem less risky (74, quoted previously), seem dependent on the three biases mentioned above, and seem perfectly sensible in a world in which group identity is the single most determinant factor. If Americans are good, then American hegemony is good; if Americans are good, then those opposed to us are bad; if Americans are good, then our kind of regime is good and leads to good policies; if Americans are good, then our military can solve problems.

And, finally, the Iraq invasion, and especially the failure of the pre-invasion public discourse to focus on the stock issues that turned out to be the fatal flaws in the plan (feasibility, solvency, and unintended consequences) shows that public discourse that focuses on whether the people making the decision are good people who mean well is not an effective deliberative shortcut. Many of the people advocating invasion were (and are) good people, or as good as those arguing against it (many of whom were probably not especially good people). I think they all meant well, and there is no reason to believe that they thought it would turn out as badly as it did. And, not only was it not a case of good versus bad people, but it wasn't even clearly an instance of clearly delineated groups neatly bifurcated on the issue. The problem is not that the American public misidentified which "side" had the good people on it—it was never one side versus another, let alone one group of homogeneously good people versus homogeneously bad people. The problem was the Bush administration's plan, and that the plan was never debated, in the administration or among the public. We can blame Bush for what happened within the administration, but the failure of the American public to insist on debate is on us.

Punishment/Reward and
Binary Paired Terms

I have tried to show in Hitler's writings the two trends that we have
already described as fundamental to the authoritarian character:
the craving for power over men and the longing for submission
to an overwhelmingly strong outside power.

—Fromm, *Escape from Freedom*

Pro-invasion demagoguery operated on three levels. It wasn't just a way to
gain compliance, but a set of assumptions about how publics should make
decisions, and a set of assumptions about how to generate policy. Demagoguery
can be a rhetorical strategy, a theory of public deliberation, and a method of
policy determination. And that isn't new. Although we are in an era when it is
commonly understood that the problem of demagoguery is new (we are *now* post-
truth), it's important to ground the discussion of demagoguery in terms of a very
old and famous democracy. In his *History of the Peloponnesian War*, a narration
of Athens's and Sparta's deliberations and military actions during a long war,
Thucydides describes the debate between Cleon and Diodotus over the fate of
the city-state of Mytilene, and Cleon remains a classic example of demagoguery.

Some number of Mytilenean citizens had used the opportunity of Athens's
war with Sparta to break from the Athenian empire. The anti-Athenian revolt
was crushed, and the Athenian general Paches sent back to Athens the people
he considered responsible for the attempted revolt. The Athenians were feeling
particularly vindictive, and decided to hold the entire populace guilty, condemning the women and children to slavery and all the men to death. The next day
after this decision, Thucydides tells us, the people regretted their rash decision,
"and they began to reflect that the design which they had formed was cruel and

monstrous" (3.36). At the assembly to reconsider their decision, Cleon, the person who had successfully argued for the exterminationist policy, again spoke in favor of the total destruction of Mytilene. Thucydides, when introducing Cleon to the reader, describes him as one who "was not only the most violent of the citizens, but at that time had by far the greatest influence with the people [*demos*]" (3.36).

Some scholars have tried to redeem Cleon, arguing that he was an able military leader (for his attack on Sphakteria) who was intentionally set up for failure in order to remove him as a political force. These scholars have argued that Cleon was less powerful than Thucydides presents him, and "performed a vital service by opening space for public deliberation and for reasoned consideration of alternative modes of thought and conduct" (Whedbee, 82, paraphrasing Grote 6:271). While Grote and Whedbee have argued that Thucydides objected to Cleon's politics and rhetoric because Cleon had brought a lawsuit against Thucydides, that might be precisely reversing cause and effect. Since lawsuits were often used to settle political scores, it's equally likely that Cleon brought the lawsuit because he and Thucydides disagreed politically.

Whatever Thucydides's criticism, and regardless of whether his Cleon is an accurate representation of the historical figure, this attempt to recast Cleon as *opening* space is precisely wrong; Thucydides's condemnation of Cleon is based on how much Cleon *closes* deliberation. I will argue that, while Cleon's stance in his debate with Diodotus exemplifies demagoguery, it is not because of his appeal to emotion, his political aspirations, or his supposed populism. He doesn't appeal to emotions any more than rhetors clearly admired by Thucydides (such as Pericles). If he wanted power for himself, that simply makes him a politician, and his relationship to his audience is not straightforward pandering. Rhetorically, Cleon's goal in his Mytilinean speech is relatively clear: to persuade the audience to stick with their previous decision; that is, enact an extremely punitive policy on all inhabitants of Mytilene. Cleon's strategy is to set up a series of paired terms that, on the whole, present a bifurcated worldview of good and bad, with punishment related to good, and reward related to bad, so that disagreement with him is rewarding rebellion. It's a very consistent view, in many ways, insofar as it consistently values certainty over uncertainty and perfectly fits Lakoff's "strict father model," but it's hardly prodemocratic or a new form of reasoning.

That Cleon's rhetoric is emotional, populist, or even rhetorical, is not especially interesting; much political discourse is emotional and populist, and not all of it is demagoguery. Cleon is troubling because he shifts the argument from what is the best policy in regard to the Mytilineans to whether anyone can disagree with him. The speech isn't just an argument for genocide, but an attack on any democratic process that requires people to disagree *with* one another. Central to

Cleon's argument, like his political theory, is submission—his listeners to him, other city-states to Athens. His speech, like much demagoguery, is demophobic in that democratic deliberation is presented as a disease of democracy that needs to be cut out and cut off. It is troubling that the speech denies its own rhetoricality, thereby—to the extent that it is successful—putting its own arguments outside of the realm of the debate. This is not just an argument for killing citizens of resisting city-states, but for killing dissent in Athens.

Killing Dissent

One view of the demagogue is that he panders to his audience; as Reinhard Luthin says, he promises "everything to everybody" (3). The positive and negative taxonomies that Socrates sets out in *Gorgias* set pleasurable acts against painful ones—pastry-cooking versus medicine—implying that what is wrong with people like Callicles is that they try to please their audiences, rather than bleed, cup, or otherwise chastise listeners. Socrates criticizes Callicles for his unwillingness to contradict the masses. As Ober summarizes the argument: "Callicles' burning desire for the approval of the demos puts him under its control and forecloses the option of asserting his own genuine opinions in public debate" (198). Callicles follows what the masses say; again, quoting Ober, "So, if when you are addressing the Assembly, you say something that is contradicted by the Athenian demos, you change your position (metaballomenos) and you say just what the Assembly wishes" (*Dissent* 198). Pericles, as opposed to Cleon, was thought to be so good because he had "the capacity to contradict and speak angrily" to his listeners (Ober, *Dissent*, 93).

Cleon, like many rhetors engaged in demagoguery, doesn't flatter his audience; he chastises them. His speech begins, "On many other occasions in the past I have realized that a democracy is incompetent to govern others," and he goes on to condemn and criticize his audience repeatedly. Even his praise for the "common" (*phaulotoi*) people is hardly flattery—calling them ignorant (*amapherteroi*), deferential, and too stupid to realize they are engaged in an oppressive tyranny. Victoria Wohl says, "If Cleon is merely flattering his audience in this speech (as is often charged), *phauloteroi* is an odd word to have used" (118). Arlene Saxonhouse puts it more strongly: "In no way does he flatter his audience" (153). Were Plato's binary accurate—good rhetors chastise their audiences, and bad rhetors flatter them—Cleon must be counted as a good rhetor.[1] Given that he is advocating genocide, that is a conclusion I would rather not draw.[2]

Cleon is engaged in what scholars of rhetoric call "parrhesia," the posture of speaking fearlessly, espousing hard truths, and brutal honesty. It's a posture, in that (as in Cleon's case) his actual argument is neither particularly fearless nor honest. It hardly takes courage to advocate a policy that triumphed the previous day. Cleon is advocating a popular policy—and the policy itself is better characterized as fearful rather than courageous. Cleon's whole argument is that client states are in a state of near rebellion, and our only hope is what amounts to state-sponsored terrorism. Cleon's policy comes from fear of what client states might do.

In addition, Cleon's apparent truth-telling invites his audience to stop being the kind of person he chastises. Cleon engages in interpellation, in which he invites his audience to become a certain kind of person, a kind he does flatter; thus, he chastises who his audience is, but praises whom they would become if they followed him. Interpellation is not always demagoguery; Pericles, in his Funeral Oration, had done exactly the same thing, inviting Athenians to become the Athenians he praises: fond of deliberation, tolerant of diversity, lovers of beauty *and* action, brave but not militaristic, and so on. Cleon, on the other hand, praises the Athenians he invites his audience to become: angry, vindictive, suspicious of deliberation, quick to punishment.

Cleon characterizes the out-group as both clever and stupid, too judgmental and not judgmental enough, given to overthinking and easily swayed by pity, too much under the control of rhetoric. The in-group, however, is praised for uncritical submission to rhetors and being excited by speech. His listeners should think critically about the arguments of other speakers, but not about his arguments; those they should simply feel. People should submit without thinking to Cleon, not because submission without thinking is good, but because submission *to him* without thinking is good. Cleon's audience should submit to his (and not his opponent's) speech, and other city-states should submit to Athens, and other city-states are wrong to act as though Athens should submit to them.[3] This is politics of submission to the *appropriate* authority, a relationship grounded in fear.

The question as to the ideal relationship between a dominant and subordinate city state is raised throughout Thucydides's history, and Cleon is not the only one to characterize Athens's relations as inherently oppressive.[4] And Cleon tries to characterize Athens's treatment of Mytilene as kind—too kind, in fact.

> Our mistake has been to distinguish the Mytilenians as we have done: had they been long ago treated like the rest, they never would have so far forgotten themselves, human nature being as surely made arrogant by consideration, as it is awed by firmness. (3.39.5)

Athens was mistaken in its failure to subjugate Mytilene: the failure to punish was itself a kind of kindness that bred arrogance. A city-state not in subjection, through fear, is one that might at any moment rebel. There are, then, two possible roles for other states: submission or war. To fail to enforce the submission through fear is to reward and encourage rebellion and resistance. The world that Cleon presents is a world of domination and submission, in which one must punish those who resist subjugation. Sincere resistance to domination is the same thing as attempting to dominate.[5]

Cleon does not claim they otherwise treated the city-state especially well; the "different treatment" (*diapherontos*) they received was simply not punitive. He claims both that Mytilene should have known that they would be punished if they revolted (by looking at "the calamities of their neighbors who had already revolted from us and been subdued," 39), although they did not, and that other city-states will learn from harsh treatment of Mytilene ("if you inflict upon those who willfully revolt no greater punishment than upon those who revolt under compulsion" others will revolt on the slightest pretext, 39). Punishment functions as a persuasive text.[6]

His argument follows from seeing the options in a kind of geometric relation: justice is, in the words of Simonides (qtd. in *Republic* 1.6) "to render each his due," or to "benefit friends and harm enemies" (1.7). Everyone is either a friend (good) or an enemy (bad), and every act is either punishment or reward. Friends do things that help one, and everyone else is an enemy. Thus, one can generate a kind of ratio; punish is to enemy as reward is to friend:

$$\frac{\text{Punish}}{\text{Enemy}} :: \frac{\text{Reward}}{\text{Friend}}$$

This is the set of paired terms to which Cleon is appealing when he argues that someone who argues for not punishing the Mytileneans must be arguing that "the crimes of the Mytileneans are beneficial to us" (3.38), or that people who do not support him are "traitors to themselves" (3.40).

Cleon, like other rhetors engaged in demagoguery, perversely uses public discourse to deny the agency of public deliberation. Cleon is populist *and* demophobic; he condemns people who like speeches, and who enjoy deliberation.

> You are adepts not only at being deceived by novel proposals but also at refusing to follow approved advice, slaves as you are of each new paradox and scorners of what is familiar. Each of you wishes above all to be an orator himself, or, failing that, to vie with those dealers in paradox by seeming not to lag behind them in wit but to applaud a smart saying before it is out of the speaker's mouth. (3.38)

Cleon, the supposed populist, attacks the populace's ability to reason; it is Diodotus who, as Arlene Saxonhouse says, "asks only for an honest deliberative body. He argues for the arguments and disagreements that constitute debate. The speech of Cleon tried to bar that debate. Cleon demanded uniformity, not disagreement, submission, not freedom" (158). Cleon insists that there is no real *choice* in this matter: either punish Mytilene or give up the empire. But, of course, were there really no choice, he would not need to speak; it is precisely because there is a choice, and a strong likelihood that the assembled might make a choice different from Cleon's, that he has to speak. This assertion of "no choice" in the midst of many choices is an example of strategic misnaming, such as segregationists using the term "democracy" to mean a segregated system that disenfranchises large numbers of citizens, rhetors whose positions are entirely religious claiming they are engaged in "science," racists disavowing racism. Cleon is speaking because there is a choice.

Cleon's claims might look as though they are assertions about a reality external to his text and shared with his listeners ("assertoric"), but they are attempts to *create* the reality he is claiming already exists ("performatives"). If, by insisting that there is no choice, he persuades his audience not to consider any other choices, if, by naming all Mytilenes as obviously the enemy, he persuades his audience to treat them as enemies, he has created the reality for which he is arguing without seeming to have argued for it.

After all, if the correct course of action is indisputable, why is there any dissent? Cleon gives several different answers to that question in the course of his speech. The speakers have been paid to speak on Mytilene's behalf; they are arguing for that case because, like all sophists, they like to make paradoxical arguments; they don't care what is true, and only want to make a great rhetorical show. Audience members are persuaded by being too kind, by letting their love of rhetoric overwhelm their good sense, by losing track of the real issues, by misunderstanding the essentially coercive and brutal nature of the empire, and by not taking the issue seriously. With all of these explanations, people have no *reasons* for disagreeing with Cleon, only bad motives, and those motives are related to a kind of softness, a mistaken kindness.[7]

Cleon's accusation is that other people are persuaded by rhetoric, an accusation he makes using rhetoric—an irony on which scholars have often remarked. It is, however, typical of rhetors who identify their stance as the realistic one. As James Aune argues, "Realism is a rhetoric that must deny its own rhetoricity in order to function" (61). And Aune's description of a rhetorically "realist" passage perfectly describes Cleon's stance: "a claim to objective seeing, an obsession with security, and an assertion that opponents are caught in a web of textuality" (61). Robert Hariman, in his discussion of the "realist style" emphasizes the ways that rhetors who use the realist style insist that "whereas other writers are described in terms of their textuality, he is aligned with the natural world . . . his text is indigenous to reality itself" (*Political Style* 19).

In addition to claiming to be in touch with reality, Cleon claims to represent (even embody) tradition (*nomos*).[8] This, too, is strategic misnaming. The policy Cleon was advocating was entirely new; it represented a new level of brutality. Common practice was closer to Diodotus's—to distinguish among the innocent and guilty in a rebellion.

It is because of this embodied tradition that Cleon's claim to embody Athens is so rhetorically and politically powerful. Cleon's argument operates on multiple levels: he advocates a policy of genocide, but he also advocates, assumes, and models a specific approach to community decision making. His rhetorical relationship with his audience models the relationship he calls for between Athens and the other city-states: subjugation that is reinforced through punitive behavior, a relation of anger and coercion. If his audience submits to him, they become him. If they don't submit, they are rebellious. Similarly, the relation between city-states that Cleon offers is that they can submit to Athens, and become part of the Athenian empire, or they can put themselves in open rebellion.[9] Cleon's vision of the relationship between Athens and the other city-states (he uses the term *summachos* [translated "allies" but simply meaning "people who fight with"] without implying equality) is that of subordinate client state and master. If the city-states are good, they will submit to Athens; if the audience is good, it will submit to his will; both the other city-states and the audience can be bullied into submission, because that is the right order of things.

The relationship that Cleon promises to his reader is simultaneously dominating and submissive: the person can be, like Cleon, dominating of others in the hierarchy, but submissive to the system itself. Douglas Madsen and Peter Snow, building on Bandura's concept of "proxy control," describe the paradox in the process of bonding with a leader: "Only by yielding personal control is a sense of control retained; only by accepting the leader's 'understanding' of events is a sense of personal understanding restored" (15). Demagoguery invites the audience to participate in this domination/submission; one submits to the will of those higher in the hierarchy, but participates (through proxy control) in the in-group's domination of the out-group. Erich Fromm identifies this as "fundamental to the authoritarian character: the craving for power over men and the longing for submission to an overwhelmingly strong outside power" (261). Demagoguery offers this complicated pleasure.

This is an erotically charged relationship, both as Cleon represents it, and as Thucydides tells the story of Athens's seduction by bad lovers. Wohl summarizes Thucydides's narrative: "Cleon wins the demos over by offering it pleasures of the most venal sort and turns the citizens into whores by acting the whore himself"

(64). Cleon offers to his audience a pleasurable and honorable submission, and the pleasure of dominating others in an honorable way. Dominating, in his argument, is chained to punishment, and his argument that "the Mytileneans" deserve punishment because "they" rebelled means scapegoating the Mytileneans as a whole for what some did. Diodotus wasn't arguing for no punishment (despite how Cleon tries to characterize him) but for trying to identify the guilty. (The same argument comes up in regard to mass imprisonment of "the Japanese" in the next chapter).

Cleon grants that his policy is brutal, but for him that is its virtue—the very brutality of it. The lack of proportion between act and consequence makes the punishment an effective rhetoric. Diodotus not only disagrees that the excess will necessarily send such a message, but, at a more basic level, Cleon and Diodotus disagree about political decision making: for Cleon, it is essentially the same as forensics (determining guilt or innocence, and assigning punishment); for Diodotus, it is about deliberating (*bouleuô*) what would make the Mytileneans most useful (*chrêsimos*) for Athens.

In *The New Rhetoric*, Chaim Perelman and Lucie Olbrechts-Tyteca argue that one can infer the "system" of philosophical pairs that a writer establishes.[10] The system of pairs characteristic of Cleon's reasoning creates two groups.

In-group	*Out-group*
Sticking to decision	Reconsideration
Common people	Clever people
Deference to "convention" (nomos)	Confidence in their own judgment
Ignorance and self-restraint	Cleverness and recklessness
Good citizens	Bad citizens
Submission to him	Judging him
Enraged by Mytileneans	Kind to Mytileneans
Action	Deliberation
Substance	Style
Realistic	In "thrall" to sophists
Familiar, traditional, previously decided	New, tricky
Punishing bad people	Rewarding bad people
Anger	Pity
Manly	Unmanly[11]
Killing and/or enslaving all Mytileneans	Any other policy

On the one hand are manly good citizens who stick to their decisions, out of self-restraint, deference to convention (*nomos*), and submission to speakers like Cleon who represent realism; they prefer substantive, punitive, action, grounded in anger against people who have done them harm. On the other hand are unmanly,[12] weak, cowardly (*malakizomai*), bad citizens, who re- (even over-) think decisions because they trust their intelligence more than conventional wisdom (*nomos*), who recklessly take it on themselves to judge speakers like Cleon, and get excited by rhetoric to feel pity for bad people, consequently engaging in policies that reward those people and endanger the polis. Cleon may have sincerely believed that his policy was best for Athens—he wouldn't be the first or last person to want to make state-sponsored terrorism the basis of international relations—but that isn't what makes his rhetoric demagogic. Instead, it is that his rhetorical strategy is to polarize the situation and his community in such a way that careful investigation of the various policy options is equated with unmanly treachery, and the only *real* option appears to be violent purification.

Claiming the Middle Ground

For many, especially authoritarians, political decision making is, simultaneously, an act of self- and other-control; if you don't have self-control, you cannot be trusted to control yourself enough to come to good decisions about how others should be controlled. Therefore, people incapable (or prohibited from the practice) of domination and control are inherently emotional, and cannot be trusted with the power of political decision making. In this model, rationality is not about metacognition, but about control.

The consequence of our equating control and rationality is that we assume that "being emotional" is signified by being "out of control" and being rational is signified by being in control. Thus, we infer whether someone's judgment is good (whether they have made a "rational" decision) by whether they seem to be in control, and we infer their degree of self/other control by their stance. If we accept this set of paired terms, then, in judging the rationality of an argument we look to see:

- whether the author takes the posture of being in "control" of the material, dominating the topic by performing an apparent mastery of details and data;
- whether the author expresses certainty about the topic;
- whether there is the presence of a booster rather than attitude marker metadiscourse.

Metadiscourse consists of words or phrases that are about the discourse itself, that help identify the relationship with the reader; it is, in a way, group identification. Ken Hyland defines it as "the cover term for the self-reflective expressions used to negotiate interactional meanings in a text, assisting the writer (or speaker) to express a viewpoint and engage with readers as members of a particular community" (37). Control and emotionality are inferred from: self-mention, attitude markers, common knowledge markers, and what we might call rationality markers.

Self-mention (the use of first person) "refers to the degree of explicit author presence in the text" (Hyland 53), and the absence of such metadiscourse can contribute to a perception that the rhetor has an "objective" stance. Shifting between "hedging" (using phrases and words that indicate precision and even lack of certainty) coupled with "boosters" (when rhetors foreground their own feelings of certainty about their claims) gives the impression of a rhetor who is carefully self-reflective and therefore even more reliable. Hyland calls shifting between hedging and boosting a "strategic deployment," "where hedges and boosters work together to vary the strength of statements. By contrasting caution and assertion, this works to give a clear indication of precisely the commitment the writer grants to different parts of the argument" (101). Attitude markers are words and phrases that "indicate the writer's affective, rather than epistemic, attitude to propositions" (53). Hyland mentions verbs like "agree" or "prefer," adverbs like "unfortunately" or "hopefully," and adjectives like "appropriate, logical, remarkable" (53). If Hyland is right, that they signal affect, then readers would interpret texts with a large number of attitude markers as "emotional," and ones with very few as "calm" or "not emotional." Demagoguery can involve explicitly advocating reliance on emotions. Cleon tells his audience they should make their decision while angry and vengeful, but they don't necessarily do so. Demagoguery can claim a middle ground, a reasonable affect, and a posture of calm control, often achieved through a combination of hedging and boosting.

For instance, in 1960, William D. Workman, "a leading apologist for segregation" engaged in an argument for segregation that was, in terms of overall argument, hyperbolic and irrational, that the South was "under siege by black activists, northern politicians, and a reckless Supreme Court" (Ward 166). But, rhetorically, Workman opted not for the explicit calls for anger, vengeance, and violence that Cleon did; instead he "embodied the ethos of responsible segregation that had guided South Carolina's resistance campaign for over a decade" (166). Workman both embraces and rejects the position of a "moderate" (depending on what suits his argument in the moment), but the tone of his argument is carefully nonhyperbolic. David Chappell calls the book "the most dispassionate and well-documented segregationist book" (142). Workman's book does not rely heavily on attitude markers in his own prose (although they appear in considerable numbers in quotes from others). Workman uses "boosters," which, according to Hyland, "allow writers to close down alternatives, head off conflicting views and express their certainty in what they say" (52). They are statements of belief, and not feeling. Thus, for instance, Workman says, "There is an artificiality, a deliberate warping of the situation, in allegations that racial preference is necessarily based on racial hatred" (112). He presents this information, not as though these are feelings he has about the situation, but as though he is describing a situation about which he has cognitive certainty.

That sentence has compressed within it several fairly complicated arguments: that people allege racial preference is necessarily based on racial hatred; that racial preference is not based on racial hatred; that the people who say racial preference is based on racial hatred have deliberately warped the situation. Workman provides no evidence for the first or third claim, and relies on a somewhat weak analogy for the second (that "Harvard men can band themselves together without hating Yale men" 112, an analogy that has nothing to do with race). To support the first claim, Workman would have to quote people making it. Since he doesn't say who has made this claim, it's nonfalsifiable—it isn't possible to show that he has misrepresented an argument, since we don't know whose argument he is describing. It's possible that he was paraphrasing the argument of someone like Ruth Benedict, who had argued in her infamous 1947 pamphlet (*In Henry's Backyard*) that there is a kind of animosity to racist policies, but, if so, Workman has significantly changed her argument by adding in one word: "necessarily."[13] Similarly, showing that the unidentified people who make this claim have done so deliberately would be difficult. He might quote them advocating his position (thereby implying that they knew one thing and said another), or he might quote them saying that they were making such changes deliberately. Obviously, he doesn't. My point isn't simply that his arguments on these three claims are insufficient, but that the very insufficiency of his arguments is part of what would give him, with certain audiences, a posture of mastery and control. He is so familiar with the discourse that he can simply refer to "allegations," and he knows the minds of the people who make those allegations. What for some people is a weak argument, for another audience will look like a particularly powerful one precisely *because* it is unexplained, unqualified, unsupported, and nonfalsifiable. The very fact that we have nothing on which to rely other than Workman's perception (that people who make this claim really exist, that the claim is false, and that they are engaged in falsehood deliberately) means that the support for the claim comes from him and his authority, and his authority is derived from the certainty with which he makes the claim.

Yet, Workman doesn't present his views as his alone; he avoids self-mention, and instead relies heavily on what Dimitra Koutsantoni calls "common knowledge markers": "words and expressions that exclusively underscore authors' beliefs by presenting them as given, as knowledge shared by all members of the community" (166). Koutsantoni argues that "by emphasizing certainty in and attitude toward claims, and by presenting them as given and shared, authors control readers' inferences and demand their agreement and sharing of their views (power entailing solidarity)" (170). Instead of saying, "My racial preference is not based on racial hatred" or "I think they are lying," Workman's claims are in the world itself. To the extent that Workman is successful at persuading his readers that his views are not interpretations, but qualities in the world itself, he has made it much harder for anyone to contradict his (very problematic) claims. To argue with Workman is to argue with reality, and to separate oneself from what all good Southerners "know" is an act of in-group disloyalty.

Workman's book is demagoguery—he presents a complicated situation as polarized, scapegoats various groups as Southern,[14] reduces the issues to questions of in-group loyalty, and calls for a purification of the South. It is an irrational argument in that it is internally contradictory and highly fallacious, but it is not a particularly emotional one, and his polarizing of the situation is not incompatible with the posture of being on a middle ground. That posture may be sincere. The tendency to make distinctions in the in-group and homogenize the out-group can mean that we are far more aware of almost-in-group members whom we consider more extreme than we are of gradations in the out-group. We don't generally recognize when we are being drawn to demagoguery, and one reason is almost certainly the tendency to assume that it is obviously extreme rhetoric in service of obviously extreme policies. Barry Goldwater notwithstanding, extremism is usually an accusation we make about others, perhaps even project onto others.

Even when demagoguery is being used to advocate extreme policies, as it is in Workman's case, it can adopt a posture of reasonableness through claiming to be a middle position. When this claim of a middle position works, it does so because the audience has a truncated view of the range of policy options and stances. In addition, because we tend to perceive the out-group as more homogeneous, and to essentialize them on the basis of their most extreme members (or even on the basis of our fantasies and projections about what their most extreme members believe), we don't recognize the truncation. Like the "both sides are at fault" claim being taken as a sign of fairness, this claim of being in the middle can seem to be a quick check for reasonableness; it isn't. But it *seems* as though it should be, and therefore demagoguery that adopts that posture can go unnoticed. This false assumption that demagoguery would be discursively marked as extreme is one of the things that makes us *more* likely to fall for it.

Now that Martin Luther King Jr. has become a cultural icon, and we all want to believe that we would have been at his side and on his side, the obstructionist role of the "white moderate" has been forgotten, or even (in the case of it having come out that George W. Bush left the National Guard to support Winton "Red" Blount) deliberately obscured. Anders Walker neatly summarizes how our both-sides narrative of the civil rights movement similarly obscures that the self-identified "moderates" were actually working to resist integration.

> By pushing for a dramatic, almost fictional account of civil rights—one in which nonmanipulative black leaders led a crusade against violent racists—moderate whites in the post-civil rights era could endorse the symbolic moral victory of the movement, while erasing their own role in the larger stories of resistance to integration, and leave historians to focus almost exclusively on white extremists. (156)

Walker's argument is that this focus on extremists leads us to miss the ways that white "moderates" were able to get into place legal responses that would ensure that gains against racism were limited (see, for instance, Walker's discussion of Coleman's career 141–143). The civil rights movement ended with a whimper, not because of an extremist white backlash, but because white moderates enabled a set of restrictive legislation much like that which ended Reconstruction "that both reinforced racial stratification and complied with constitutional norms" (Walker 157). The narrative of civil rights workers against racist extremists is not just inaccurate history, but consequentially so, because we miss the ways that "moderation" assists the racist political agenda.

Part of the success of white "moderates" came from their ability to represent their position as a middle ground between extremists, which they characterized as the Citizens' Councils on one side (who advocated open defiance of *Brown v. Board*) and the NAACP on the other, yet they were not halfway between the two positions, nor was the NAACP as "extreme" in its agenda as the Citizens' Councils. "Moderates" were, in fact, quite similar to the Citizens' Councils in terms of end goals (to prevent *Brown v. Board* and any other antisegregation judicial rulings or federal policies from being enacted). They only disagreed on the best means to prevent integration from happening. White moderates advocated delay tactics, such as tying up progress in the courts, shifting from explicitly to implicitly race-based segregation (such as school assignment on the basis of morals, test scores, or "free" choice of schools; see Walker 101), a shifting of stasis from the harms of segregation to the responsibilities of African Americans to earn the respect of whites (Walker 87, 109), and resisting integration in order to "preserve peace" (Walker 95). Moderates, according to Walker, worried that open defiance, especially in light of highly publicized incidents of violence, would result in more federal (especially judiciary) intervention in southern states (see especially Walker's discussion of the "Pearsall Report" 55). They argued that southern states should look as though they were complying with *Brown v. Board* while actually preventing desegregation. That is, the case that Workman advocated was "middle," if and only if the range of political options is nothing more than KKK and white moderate.

Workman presents his position as moderate, and it wasn't; nor was his attitude toward deliberation. He is not saying that he's willing to compromise, consider multiple sides, or treat his opponents as reasonable. His "moderate" policy is the only possible one. He begins *The Case for the South* by comparing the current situation to the apocalypse.

> The South is being scourged by four pestilential forces which impose an almost intolerable burden upon Americans who cherish state sovereignty, constitutional government, and racial integrity. On the one hand are these three: the Supreme Court of the United States . . . , the National Association for the Advancement of Colored People, . . . and the Northern politicians and propagandists who pervert small truths into big lies. . . . On the other hand is the Ku Klux Klan with its unlovely cohorts who substitute muscle and meanness for the intellect which by rights must be the defense of the South. (vii)

This passage surprisingly pairs two claims that should be contradictory—apocalyptic language and a claim of the middle ground. Throughout the book, that is Workman's position—a person who has been patient in the face of near extermination, but whose powers of manly self-control still stand.

His next paragraph begins, "The man in the middle is the one whose voice needs to be heard" and he claims that is the posture he will adopt in the book. This man has "his quiet but determined resistance to tyranny from either side" (vii) and "a strong case, rooted in American soil and nurtured in Southern tradition" (viii). This "quiet" resistance suggests that the case has not previously been made or heard (an implausible claim), and his posture of resisting the "tyranny" of treating others equally reinforces the fantastical narrative that sharing rights is the same as being victimized. Sean O'Rourke summarizes how Workman (and others) tried to frame their defense of segregation. They sought to embed the themes of "good relations," minimal local discontent, and "outside agitation" into the media's coverage of civil rights protests and to wrap them in what Jennie Hill has identified as a frame of "victimage"—the notion that somehow the South was a victim of the slander, discrimination, and violence of northern integrationists and their southern stooges. (687)

Their case is American and traditional, and made by someone who has retained control; resistant, yet in the middle, "he" is both intransigent and claiming a middle ground, a peaceful and patient person, yet willing "to fight for what he believes" (17).

Workman's somewhat paradoxical self-presentation as both intransigent and reasonable runs throughout the book, with attendant contradictions. For instance, he has a chapter insisting there is no moderation on the topic (chapter 14, "The Myth of Moderation"), saying, "Philosophically, the matter of integration, like that of pregnancy, leaves no middle ground" (270), and "it is virtually impossible to arrive at a point of moderation between two such diametrically opposed sets of circumstances as segregation and integration" (270). Yet, he argues for allowing African Americans to vote (268), getting rid of legal impediments to voluntary "bi-racial activities" (287), and "simply substituting an attitude of cooperation rather than condescension" (288); that is, he advocates compromising on some aspects of segregation. He claims that segregation is separate but equal *and* admits that African Americans have received "harsh treatment" "for more than a century" (134), which he blames on abolitionists. His insistence on the "separate but equal" argument is complicated by his racist arguments about African American inferiority (see especially 165, 215–18, 289), and his abuse of "equality cultists" (239). Although he argues at the end that whites should cease to be condescending toward "Negroes," his discussion of the role of Negro servants, his irritation that African Americans now express a preference not to be called "Uncle" (63), and his limited praise of African Americans as childlike can only be characterized as condescending. He says that "complete repugnance" to race mixing is natural (212) *and* that race mixing is a snowball that cannot be stopped once started (212) *and* admits that it has been happening for quite some time: "the presence in our midst of considerable numbers of negroes of mixed blood" (218) shows that there has been a lot of "race mixing" (220).

His representation of the white Southerner (a term Workman sometimes uses interchangeably with "Southerner") as having "been remarkably placid in submitting to the unrelenting stream of abuse" (73) and who has borne the "unconscionable burden" placed upon those Southerners "who seek to preserve the social order through peaceable, although adamant, resistance to arbitrary and unreasonable changes imposed from afar" contradicts his admission that whites have taken out their rage about this abuse in violence against African Americans (135, 139) and have a propensity to rape African American women (218). His admissions about the treatment of African Americans belie an even deeper claim of his, that the South was spared turmoil and upset because it remained more racially Teutonic than the North (3, 6, once again flopping around on whether there is complete repugnance at race-mixing); his story is actually one of tyranny, arbitrary violence, and abuse of African Americans. Yet demagoguery commonly relies on this fantasy of a long tradition of stability, now threatened with disruption due to outside influences (in this case, interference from Northerners, see especially 16).[15] His claim to the middle ground is similarly troubled by his endorsing what was often called "interposition" (27–37, see also 248), the notion that the "final voice" rests with the states and not the federal government. As Walker says, this argument "made little constitutional sense in 1955" (21), let alone in 1960, by the time Workman was making it, but it was rhetorically powerful, "a formal way of dressing groundless constitutional rebellion in legal language, useful mainly as a rhetorical tool for extremists to gain uninformed votes" (21). Interposition was not a reasonable policy, as much as it was a rhetorically powerful stance for someone with political aspirations to take.

That Workman presents himself as decisive but is inconsistent on policies not only contradicts his claim of deep commitment to principle, but also suggests that the point of the book is not to advocate a specific policy agenda other than opposition to desegregation. As a set of claims about policy, or even as a set of claims, his book is irrational: he contradicts himself, appeals to contradictory premises, and makes assertions about reality that are unreal (in several senses of the word). But he is consistent in his presentation of self, and the paired terms he sets up about groups. Like Cleon, he invites his audience to adopt his supposedly calm and reality-based determination to stick to tradition, a determination that might manifest itself in violence (which is then blamed on the victims). It is, largely, an argument for framing the segregationist extremism and violence as calm commitment to principle. Like proslavery rhetors of the antebellum era, Workman presents himself and his in-group as made of up manly men who are barely resisting irrational violence, but whose self-control necessarily manifests itself in punitive action from time to time, for which they are not responsible.[16]

Workman's book relies on a binary (violence and disorder versus the stability of segregation), the rhetoric of realism (so that his position is presented as not just true, but obviously true), and a call to refuse to deliberate segregation, so that it is just a question of what kind of segregation there will be (that is, the extent to which African Americans will be punished for their own poverty, employment discrimination, victimization by violence, and so on). The chapter "Home Guard of the Nation" claims for the South (by which, at that moment, he means WASP Southerners) racial integrity unfound in the North, and, therefore, the true character of Americanness (see especially 3). His side has principles; the out-group has motives. The book continually condemns the out-group for the same behavior praised in the in-group, such as intransigence, concern for minority rights, engaging in political organizing, imposition of tyranny; that isn't merely hypocrisy, but something much more complicated. It is projection, and a kind that rhetorically enables preemptive violence. The violence and oppression of the out-group is justified because they might do what the in-group is already doing. So, what the in-group is doing is justified by what the out-group would do (that is, behave like the in-group). The in-group can thereby adopt the posture of being opposed to tyranny while engaging in it *and* holding the out-group responsible for the oppression.

The vexed logic of Workman's argument belies his claims to be reasonable, realistic, and grounded in facts. My point is not that Workman appeals to a reality and set of facts with which I disagree, but that he appeals to a "reality" and set of "facts" with which *he* disagrees. Negroes are equal and inferior, happy and enraged, childlike and rapists. Southerners are peaceful and violent, pure and mixed, moderate and extreme, tolerant and intransigent, calm and enraged. There is and is not race mixing, lynching, injustice, and so on. Workman's claim of being reasonable is not, then, a claim about how the assertions in his argument fit together: it is a claim about his tone. His argument is demagoguery, but his stance is the (barely) controlled realist willing to speak the truth, and while submitting to the facts, standing up to emotional, prejudiced forces of chaos unwittingly abetted by people who refuse to take his side.

Proxy Control and the Demagoguery of the Elite

One criticism of the deliberative model of decision making is that it is too slow and unnecessarily cumbersome; many argue that it is impossibly idealistic for most of us, who have little time to assess evidence on our own. Yet, if there is one group that ought to be able to take the time to deliberate carefully on the basis of evidence, it would be the Supreme Court of the United States. When it came to defending their decision about the constitutionality of what is generally called "Japanese internment," however, the Supreme Court engaged in demagoguery. It adopted a posture of realism and reasonableness, submission to facts, and a willingness to behave with necessary pragmatism. It also engaged in cunning projection, fallacious reasoning (such as assuming what's at stake), and a tendency to posit the rhetors' feelings in the ontic (that is, rather than say that people were frightened, it asserted that the situation was dangerous). The court's ruling was based in fear-mongering, but without the discursive markers associated with appeals to fear.

Gordon Hirabayashi, a US-born student at the University of Washington, had deliberately disobeyed the "curfew" orders and was arrested. His case came before the Supreme Court in May of 1943, and was decided in June 1943. By this time, almost exactly a year after the Battle of Midway, the notion of a Japanese attack on the mainland United States was even less plausible than it had been in 1942. It was known that sabotage had not played a part in the attack on Pearl Harbor, but there was still good reason to be concerned about the cost and even outcome of the war with Japan. Anti-Japanese war alarmism was still being stoked in the Western states (and, as has been argued, anti-Japanese racism would remain strong for many years after the war), and a decision declaring mass evacuation unconstitutional would have had complicated economic and political consequences. But, the court is not supposed to be influenced by political consequences, and, judicially, the justices had options, including refraining from endorsing the most problematic aspects of the administration's handling of Japanese Americans. Unhappily, the unanimous decision (written by Stone, with three concurring decisions by Douglas, Rutledge, and Murphy), like Cleon's speech, frames the situation as one in which the justices have no choice, argues for the substitution of judgment, demonizes deliberation, appeals to a just world hypothesis, nationalism, authoritarianism, monolithic values, naïve realism, cunning projection, weak determinism, and scapegoating. It is demagoguery.

Throughout the decision, Stone insists that the situation was extraordinary, a state of exception, and Douglas says, "Peacetime procedures do not necessarily fit wartime needs." Even Murphy (in a concurring opinion that, as Paul Finkelman says, "reads more like a dissent" 128, and was originally a dissent) says that "determinations as to the loyalty and dependability of individual" Japanese "could not be made without delay that might have had tragic consequences." This topos of urgency is repeated throughout the decision, and yet it is odd; it is even odder to say that there might have been tragic consequences had the military not acted quickly, since it is all premised on the notion that Japan was poised to invade the continental United States. That some people might have believed in 1941 that Japan would invade the West Coast is understandable; by 1943, it was known that such an attack had not happened. The sabotage topos, rickety enough in the spring of 1942, could hold no weight by 1943—there had been no sabotage in Hawaii, where there was no mass imprisonment. Yet, the decision asserted those myths as though they were true. That this invasion would be assisted by sabotage was proven by the assistance given by the "fifth column" to the German invasion of Europe and by people sympathetic to Japan in the attack on Pearl Harbor.

This is a strange argument in several ways in that it is based, twice over, on myth. Neither the German invasion of Europe nor the Japanese attack on Pearl Harbor were assisted by sabotage. Although anyone with access to a globe or world map, and even minimal understanding of military logistics, would have to be skeptical of the premise that Japan could invade the West Coast, let alone successfully and without warning. Yet, this was not simply asserted by the court, it was asserted as undoubted: "That reasonably prudent men . . . had ample ground for concluding that they must face the danger of invasion, take measures against it, and in making the choice of measures consider our internal situation, *cannot be doubted*" (emphasis added). The decision dismisses as entirely unreasonable the position that even advocates of mass imprisonment such as FDR and even General DeWitt (and who knows how many other advocates of the policy) actually had.[17]

I want to emphasize this point, as recent defenses of mass imprisonment try to ignore that the position that is being put forward as obvious—there was military necessity—was not shared by the major military experts of the time.[18] That is, it was *not* obvious to everyone looking at the situation; it was not even obvious to DeWitt. This insistence on the obvious and indisputable nature of a nonobvious and disputed position continues throughout the decision (and through current defenses of mass imprisonment). The curfew, according to the decision, "is an *obvious* protection" (emphasis added). At best, what one could say is that General DeWitt believed there to be such a need, but, given the amount of dissent on the issue, to claim a highly debated perception as an obvious one is strategic misnaming. Douglas similarly insists that "the threat of Japanese invasion of the west coast was not fanciful but real." The assertion was fanciful, of course, as was the notion that the German invasion of Europe or the Japanese attack on Pearl Harbor had been substantially aided by fifth columnists.

The situation was not urgent, but it *felt* urgent to some people, whose feelings are allowed to define reality. The Japanese, somewhat obscurely, end up responsible for the feelings of Americans like DeWitt. The decision regularly refers to threats (i.e., "a time of threatened air raids and invasion") but Japan had never made those threats, and they were not even plausibly inferred from things like the bombing (but not invasion) of Pearl Harbor. The threat was *felt* by Americans, although never made by Japan, so "the Japanese" are constituted by the feelings DeWitt and others have about them.

The court's decision states that these extraordinary circumstances require that people other than the military, including the Supreme Court justices, stop thinking for themselves and cease deliberating on these issues: "We cannot sit in judgment on the military requirements of that hour." Even the military should not have been expected to deliberate on the loyalty of individuals: "To say that the military in such cases should take the time to weed out the loyal from the others would be to assume that the nation could afford to have them take the time to do that."[19] Hence, the decision, like Cleon's speech, insists upon people substituting someone else's judgment for their own; unlike Cleon, however, the justices do not present themselves as rightful decision makers. They embody the American people as they (we) submit to the judgment of the military: "We must credit the military with as much good faith ... as we would any other public official acting pursuant to his duties." This might be called demagoguery without a demagogue, or demagoguery on behalf of another demagogue.

The decision argues that such rights (and such reason) must be viewed "in the light of the conditions" after the attack on Pearl Harbor—I want to emphasize that "the conditions" are the feelings some people (specifically DeWitt) had about the situation. Their feelings are not marked by self-reference, which would make them personal and specific and possibly wrong, but by common knowledge markers, which suggests they are descriptions of brute facts in the world.

Conducting the war "necessarily involves some infringement of individual liberty." Murphy grants that this decision "is the first time, so far as I am aware, that we have sustained a substantial restriction of the personal liberty of citizens of the United States based upon the accident of race or ancestry" (a distinctly odd assertion, given previous cases on segregation, denial of naturalization to Asians, and even *Dred Scott*). But, the "great emergency," "critical military situation," and "urgent necessity" were such that "the military authorities should not be required to conform to standards of regulatory action appropriate to normal times." In other words, universal rights and universal reason are not universal, but simply normal, for normal times; traditional solutions (that is, the way that potential espionage on the part of Italians or Germans was handled) are not appropriate because the feeling of crisis overwhelms such concerns.

Hirabayashi had not argued that the fears were groundless, but that the military should have made some effort to distinguish among people of Japanese ancestry—people like him, who had no contact with Japan, and the people used to stereotype Japanese (and thereby rationalize the treatment). That is, people of Japanese ancestry should be treated no differently from people of German or Italian ancestry. To defend this racist treatment, the decision argues that Japanese are dangerous because they have failed to assimilate: "large numbers of children of Japanese parents" go to Japanese language schools (in addition to, not instead of, American public schools); as many as ten thousand American-born Japanese children visit Japan "for all or part of their education." Even if one accepts the dubious premise that such behavior in Japanese (as opposed to strikingly similar behavior among many Germans or Italians) signifies excessive, even dangerous, attachment to Japan, that does not make jailing all Japanese Americans a sensible policy; at best, it rationalizes identifying Japanese Americans who attend Japanese language school, or who visit Japan. But, in their decisions, both the military and the Supreme Court make the same assumption that Cleon did in regard to Mytilineans—attributing homogeneity to the out-group (as individualism is a quality of the in-group). The military's response was that they all look (or behave) alike, and the court's response was that the military had to do the thinking for both of them.

Further, Americans of Japanese descent were scapegoated for their own potential unhappiness. The decision argues that Japanese have never really assimilated.

> There has been relatively little social intercourse between them and the white population. The restrictions, both practical and legal, affecting the privileges and opportunities afforded to persons of Japanese extraction residing in the United States, have been sources of irritation and may well have tended to increase their isolation, and in many instances their attachments to Japan and its institutions.

This is a variation on the "wolf by the ears" argument so important in defenses of slavery: because we have treated this group badly, they are angry with us. Their anger makes them so dangerous that we must treat them worse. This is, simultaneously, an appeal to the just-world hypothesis (the United States is just, so our history of treatment of Japanese immigrants must be just) and projection. We must punish them for the consequences of our racist treatment of them while maintaining the fundamental justice of the system that so discriminates.[20] Unwillingness to let Japanese become Americans becomes projected onto Japanese Americans in the form of being opposed to (albeit also prevented from) assimilation, something for which they can then be punished. Japanese are responsible for our admittedly repressive policies, and they are dangerous for resenting our admittedly repressive policies. Bizarrely, Japanese resentment becomes the post hoc justification for the policies that caused the resentment: sort of a Mobius strip of causality.

Just as Americans are not really responsible for the mass imprisonment of Japanese, so the Supreme Court justices are not responsible for their decision. A group that is supposed to be committed to deliberation, they endorse a decision that frees them from the responsibility of deliberating. They (we) are forced into it. Japanese Americans, says Douglas, "constituted a menace to the national defense and safety, which *demanded*" mass imprisonment (emphasis added). The imprisonment,

Stone says, was *"necessary* to meet the threat of sabotage" (emphasis added), and the "menace" constituted by the existence of some unknown (and unknowable) number of "disloyal" people *"demanded* that prompt and adequate measures be taken" (emphasis added). Granted, the decision says, the military might instead have taken the route suggested by appellant—"impose the curfew on all citizens within the military area, or on none"—but, it says, that forces the military into polarized policy: "It is a choice between inflicting obviously needless hardship on the many, or sitting passive and unresisting in the presence of the threat."

This polarizing of the situation is typical of demagoguery, and typically incoherent. Mass imprisonment itself was "obviously needless hardship on the many" if (as the Supreme Court should have) one sees the interned Japanese Americans as actually counting as part of "the" many. No one, not even the military who lied about the threat, pretended that the majority of those interned were spies or saboteurs. But, "obviously needless hardship" against members of the out-group doesn't really count, because, as members of the out-group, they are never entirely innocent. And, like Cleon, Stone uses this false dilemma to accuse the opposition of passivity. Either we are active ("inflicting") or passive ("sitting"). He, and his fellow justices, applaud the decision of the military to act, rather than be the passive "sitters" the (Japanese American) opposition wants them to be. Because the opposition wanted the military to think, to consider individuals and specific evidence, then, oddly enough, the Supreme Court ends up denigrating thinking and deliberating as passive behavior.

To put this argument into paired terms:

Inflict on Japanese	Protect US	Defer to military judgment	Action	Support internment
Sit	Endanger US	Question military judgment	Consider issues of constitutionality	Deliberate

This was a common binary used to argue for mass evacuation and/or imprisonment. As one of the American Legion resolutions states:

> This is no time for namby-pamby pussyfooting, fear of hurting the feelings of our enemies. . . . It is not the time for consideration of minute constitutional rights of those enemies[; rather,] . . . it is time for vigorous, wholehearted, and concerted action (11389).

The Supreme Court decision does not use the term "namby-pamby," but it does rely on the opposition of action versus concern about constitutionality. That the decision would seem to accept the racist premise that Japanese deserve to be treated differently is troubling; more troubling, though, is that the US Supreme Court would make an argument that associates deliberating, including about constitutionality, with dangerous inaction. There is something very disturbing about the Supreme Court arguing, even through association, that deliberation, thinking, and a system of checks and balances is un-American, but that is what this decision does. Deliberating is treasonous because it asks that we think and talk and look at a policy issue from the perspective of the people whom that policy might hurt—that is, it means identifying with the people who have been identified as the enemy.

There were deliberations in regard to the decision, of course, and there is speculation that there was instrumental bargaining—that the FDR administration made promises (or even gestures) of ending imprisonment in exchange for a favorable decision. If the decision-making process was instrumental and bargaining, then the decision itself was purely performative, albeit pretending to be deliberative. That it may not have been deliberation, however, does not explain why it dismisses deliberation. As does Cleon, *Hirabayashi v. United States* models, assumes, and advocates the abandonment of deliberation. That we were at war does not, in fact, matter. Deliberation is never a luxury in a democracy—it *is* democracy.

3

Scapegoating and
Rationality Markers

No matter how great our resources, no matter how strong our man-power, this country of ours can never withstand the pressure of internal conflict arising out of this policy of hunting down saboteurs and spies by race, nationality, or creed. During a period of hysteria there are always those who think they can save their own skins by joining in the persecution of another minority group. When it comes their turn to be kicked around it is too late to reconsider.
—Louis Goldblatt, *House Select Committee Investigating*
National Defense Migration Hearings

As Robert Ivie has pointed out, even in a democracy, public discourse is often conceived of "as a rational process best reserved for experts and privileged political leaders, a process easily degraded by the common people under the irrational influence of a demagogue" (*Democracy* 5). Because the masses are imagined to have "unruly impulses" (*Democracy* 6), unlike the elite, the dangers of demagoguery are assumed to be peculiar to conditions of mass participation. As Ivie argues, this model is "elitist, culturally biased, and generally tone deaf to the challenges of pluralism and diversity" (*Democracy* 5), but it's also very present, even where one wouldn't expect it. It is, fundamentally, a narrative: that the masses, unlike the political and cultural elite, are less self-controlled, more emotional, more prone to panicked reactions, and therefore more susceptible to demagoguery. The narrative is wrong on two counts. First, as is clear in many of the examples in this book, elites participate in demagoguery in various ways, as producers and consumers. While Cleon was a leader of the less elite, and Workman was reinforcing a popular political agenda, both Workman and the Supreme

Court were members of the elite speaking to other members of the elite. Earl Warren (discussed in this chapter) was very much a member of the elite, also making a popular argument, but Madison Grant (discussed in the next chapter) was an elite writing purely to other elites. Second, the problem is not that demagoguery distorts decision making by causing people to be more "emotional" (whatever that would mean); the problem is that it reduces all issues to questions of in-group loyalty and purity, thereby ensuring we don't deliberate policy. That reduction can be done with a "reasonable" tone and with a rhetoric of realism, as happened in Warren's testimony.

It seems common sense to say that mass- and race-based imprisonment would depend on dehumanization, and we can think we know what dehumanization is like.

> By means of a dehumanizing and decivilizing rhetoric of savagery, executive authority goads the citizenry to dissociate themselves completely from an alien identity or estranged population that is marked as barbaric, irrational, aggressive, and coercive. (Ivie, *Dissent* 107)

It is often assumed that such marking of the other would rely heavily on rousing emotions in the audience.

> The basic principle is always the same: to manufacture emotion. In other words, arouse fear, mistrust, and resentment and then provoke a reaction of vigilance, pride, and revenge. The propaganda machine is first and foremost a device for fabricating public emotion as dictated by political leaders whose words it relays and amplifies. (Semelin 73)

Warren's testimony shows how misleading those assumptions can be. Warren advocated a policy that only makes sense to people who imagine "the Japanese" as a dehumanized, decivilized, untrustworthy, and essentially treacherous hive mind, but he didn't do so with a savage rhetoric oriented toward manufacturing emotion. California attorney general Earl Warren and others claimed to be acting on the basis of facts and data, attributed emotionalism to their opponents, and even asserted that their stance was grounded in compassion for "the Japanese." It was dehumanization, and it was demagoguery, and Warren later regretted his role, and that's an interesting point. Why could he *later* see that race-based imprisonment was the consequence of panic and racism, but not see it at the time? The answer is that Warren didn't realize he was engaged in demagoguery because it didn't have the surface markers of emotionalism we wrongly assume define demagoguery. He didn't fit the common definition of a demagogue, and what he was saying didn't fit the common conception of demagoguery.

Warren's role in the hearings is particularly troubling. In 1982, the Commission on Wartime Relocation and Internment of Civilians (CWRIC) created by Congress called Warren's testimony "nothing but demagoguery" (96) and said "it had no probative value" (97), and that's a fair characterization. Warren later regretted his part in the imprisonment, saying in his memoirs:

> It was wrong to react so impulsively, without positive evidence of disloyalty, even though we felt we had a good motive in the security of our state. It demonstrates the cruelty of war when fear, get-tough military psychology, propaganda, and racial antagonism combine with one's responsibility for public security to produce such acts. (149)

The CWRIC said that the "broad historical causes" of the incarceration "were race prejudice, war hysteria and a failure of political leadership" (18). Thus, like Warren, the CWRIC blamed excessive emotionalism, especially fear, for the outcome. Since it wasn't marked as such, how could he have known at the time? How can *we* know?

Pearl Harbor and the Slow Panic

In December of 1941, the Japanese government ordered an attack on US military bases at Pearl Harbor, and the attack was devastatingly effective. A commission was immediately established to determine why the attack had been so successful (generally called the "Roberts Commission" and its report "The Roberts Report" after the Supreme Court justice heading it).[1] The Roberts Commission released its report in late December, unequivocally blaming the incompetence of the commanders of the navy and army bases, who had ignored orders to prepare for precisely the kind of attack that had occurred. Despite being told to prepare for an air attack, Husband Kimmel (in charge of the navy base) and Walter Short (in charge of the army base) were more obsessed with sabotage, and therefore engaged in practices that directly contributed to the amount of damage (such as grouping planes together). Although there was no sabotage, there had been espionage on the part of members of the Japanese embassy staff, enabling them to know exactly where and when to direct the planes. The Roberts report was clear on the point that Kimmel and Short were at fault, and absolutely silent on the issue of sabotage, but there remained a popular tendency to blame fifth-column activities for Pearl Harbor, probably fueled by the prewar anti-Japanese propaganda that tended to feature elaborate plots of spies and sabotage. For instance, at least one newspaper published urban legends about Japanese pilots with American university paraphernalia (sometimes a class ring or letterman's jacket, supposedly showing they had gone to American universities, discussed more below), arrows burned in sugarcane fields, deliberately blocked roads, and so on (Carroll). These rumors made no sense, even on their face, since pilots wouldn't have needed arrows in order to find the harbor, there wasn't a road that fit the description, and so on, but they did fit prewar fear-mongering about Japanese villains and spies.

On January 29, US attorney general Francis Biddle announced that "enemy aliens" (that is, citizens of Germany, Italy, and Japan) were prohibited from specific areas (mostly on or very near military bases), giving them until February 24 to leave those areas ("Preliminary" 2). This was the first step of many toward what would eventually be mass imprisonment, and it was restricted to citizens of the nations with whom the United States was at war, and to very specific places. Since Japanese, unlike Italians or Germans, had long been prohibited from naturalizing, the burden fell disproportionately on them, and there was little or no arrangement made for where they should go or how they could dispose of property. Many people who owned property close to military bases were simply forced to sell and move to other areas; as the areas of exclusion expanded, they might be forced to move again.

The Roosevelt administration continued to debate more extreme policies, and congressional representatives from the West Coast agitated for mass expulsion from several western states, an argument formally presented in a letter to Roosevelt February 13.[2] Roosevelt issued Executive Order 9066 on February 19, 1942; that is, two months after Pearl Harbor. That order enabled mass evacuation, but the order gave no indication whether "military zones" would be entire states, or specific areas within states, and whether "evacuation" would include incarceration; it was, as Robinson says, an "unprecedented grant of authority" (*Tragedy* 93).

It's important to remember that, even prior to EO9066, the United States had, and had used, the right to imprison without trial any *individual* who aroused suspicion. The stasis for mass imprisonment of Japanese was not, then, whether suspicious individuals had the right to a trial before incarceration; that had been determined. It was whether Japanese ethnicity was in and of itself evidence of traitorous intent, and, as I'll argue, that stasis was answered by assuming what was at stake. Behavior was presented as evidence of disloyalty that was only evidence of disloyalty if one assumed it was.

In the midst of the confusion created by the vagueness of EO9066, John Tolan, a progressive California congressman, had his committee (which had been formed to discuss interstate migration triggered by the cranking up of war-related manufacturing) shift its focus to discussing the possibility of "evacuation" of various groups on the basis of ethnicity. These hearings, held in San Francisco, Portland, Seattle, and Los Angeles in February and March of 1942, were polite and inclusive affairs, with, according to the committee report, approximately 150 witnesses—representing various points of view regarding expulsion and imprisonment, including people who argued against imprisonment or evacuation. On the first day of the hearings, Tolan opened with a statement about his goals, in which he emphasized the exploratory nature of the hearings: "This committee wants to make clear that we are not here to cross-examine any witnesses or put anyone 'on the spot.' We are here as a fact-finding body" (10965). He goes on to mention the "number of worried delegations going to Washington from the Pacific coast," almost certainly a reference to the delegations of growers and ranchers agitating for mass imprisonment, and so these hearings were an attempt to get a different, perhaps less alarmist, point of view.[3] And, in fact, the hearings were impressive in their inclusiveness, civility, and evasion of grandstanding on Tolan's part.[4]

The hearings largely consisted of pro-imprisonment rhetors expressing their suspicions about Japanese, and anti-imprisonment rhetors trying to show the suspicions were unmerited and unjustified. As in the case of the debate over Mytilene, it was, paradoxically, antipunitive rhetors who argued on the grounds of feasibility, solvency, and especially unintended consequences. The opposition argument was the more rational argument, *and* it was emotional. The whole issue was about feelings—what *feelings* Americans of Japanese ancestry have about the United States, so it was rational, after all, to imagine the feelings of people who would be imprisoned, to consider issues of fairness and patriotism. Anti-imprisonment rhetors were also more engaged in the debate itself. Although the anti-imprisonment rhetors rebutted the pro-imprisonment arguments (discussed later), the reverse wasn't true. Pro-imprisonment rhetors didn't rebut the claims of their oppositions. Anti-imprisonment rhetors deliberated.

Of course racism significantly contributed to support for imprisonment, and it was racism with a long history. In his memoirs, Warren (like many current scholars) puts anti-Japanese fear-mongering in the context of such previous acts as the California Alien Land Law and the Federal Oriental Exclusion Act (148), which were in 1913 and 1924, respectively. Greg Robinson describes in detail the planning for imprisonment (*Tragedy* especially 31–33) and argues that it was strongly influenced by the deep and long historical background of anti-Japanese fear-mongering (*Tragedy* 52).[5] Similarly, Tetsuden Kashima argues that mass imprisonment "resulted from rational planning conducted in prewar meetings and discussions" (212), and all scholars of imprisonment point to the years of race baiting and fear-mongering about the Japanese engaged in by powerful media and political entities (such as the Hearst newspapers and the Japanese Exclusion League).

Advocates of mass imprisonment (and its current defenders) argued that it was not *racism* because "the Japanese" really were enemies.[6] That assertion presumes precisely what is at stake: that people of Japanese ethnicity are just as committed to the Japanese nation-state as members of its military. Treating members of the out-group as *essentially* identical and therefore interchangeable means that there is an unnoticed equivocation in the word "Japanese." That word means, at different moments: members of the military who ordered or participated in the attack on Pearl Harbor; citizens of Japan living in the United States and prohibited from naturalization by racist immigration laws; and citizens of the United States of Japanese ethnicity. This slippage was probably not cunning; it was much like Cleon's scapegoating of all Mytileneans for what some had done. Whether deliberate or not, this equivocation was consequential—people who perceive out-group members as homogeneous can confirm their perception of the out-group by remembering (or noticing) a single confirming example.[7]

While there was equivocation and even outright evasion at moments as to just what policy anti-Japanese rhetors wanted, there was considerable consistency in their arguments. The recurrent anti-Japanese topoi were:

- The myth that fifth-column sabotage significantly contributed to Axis victories in Norway, France, and Pearl Harbor;
- The notion that it is impossible to tell the difference between a loyal and disloyal person of Japanese ancestry;
- Connected to the previous topoi, the belief that Japanese are particularly prone to hive- mind behavior; that is, their schools, religion, organizations, and family structure promote a blind obedience to the emperor and his minions (such that we cannot distinguish between loyal and disloyal Japanese because they will behave disloyally if ordered to do so);
- That there might be race riots against Japanese communities, and so some kind of protective custody is necessary for their own good;
- That a Japanese invasion of the West Coast is both possible and plausible;[8]
- Finally, a relatively open argument for vengeance (albeit sometimes framed as an odd sort of "fairness" argument)—that Americans were being (or would be) mistreated in areas held by the Japanese, and would not be accorded the same consideration being given to Japanese Americans (such as being allowed to testify at hearings).

Taken together, these topoi constitute a logic of mass imprisonment, since the logical implication of them is that people of Japanese ethnicity are so *essentially* menacing that they cannot be allowed near anything—power lines, factories, harbors, forests—relevant to the war effort. That means they have to be in prison. This is a kind of dehumanizing, in that "the Japanese" is an ontologically different identity from "the American," but it does not necessarily have the linguistic markers, tone, or rhetoric often assumed to be associated with dehumanization.

Pro-imprisonment rhetors present themselves as reasonable people willing to submit to the facts (and to the military) as against people who are deluded and motivated by soft-heartedness. They sound like Cleon.

Earl Warren's "Real Logic"

Earl Warren's testimony in the print version of the hearings consists of two parts: a statement entered into the hearings but submitted sometime after, and what he said at the hearings themselves.[9] The two are similar in many ways, especially in the circularity of his basic argument. He presents data about "the Japanese" that is supposed to show they have nefarious intent, but it is only evidence of nefarious intent if one assumes the intent behind the actions is nefarious. For instance, an important part of his argument is that "the Japanese" have bought property near power lines, water lines, and harbors—hardly surprising for people who are interested in making a living through farming, fishing, or canning. His argument would appear logical only to someone who was deeply afraid of "the Japanese." Logically, it is circular (since it is supposed to be showing that we should fear "the Japanese"), with the impact of appearing to give evidence to support the major premise. It would increase the fear of someone already fearful, and appear illogical and absurd to someone not willing to accept his generalizations about "the Japanese."

Warren's argument for treating Japanese Americans differently from German, Italian, or French Americans appears to be a hedged and careful acknowledgement of the limits of knowledge, but, again, it assumes what's at stake, while contradicting the majority of his own testimony.

> We believe that when we are dealing with the Caucasian race we have methods that will test the loyalty of them, and we believe that we can, in dealing with the Germans and the Italians, arrive at some fairly sound conclusions because of our knowledge of the way they live in the community and have lived for many years. But when we deal with the Japanese we are in an entirely different field and we cannot form any opinion that we believe to be sound.

His evidence for his claim that "the Japanese" are unknowable is that some people believe it (which is the logical equivalent of saying, "This is true because people who believe it to be true believe it to be true"). This shared consensus ("we believe" is repeated three times) is carefully hedged ("fairly sound"), and self-reflectively acknowledges its own limits—the "we" for whom he speaks is aware they cannot form a sound opinion. They cannot know who the Japanese really are. Warren appears to be reasonably acknowledging of the uncertainty of his own position; it appears to be a "rational" tone.

But, in the context of his overall argument, however, that posture of uncertainty about "the Japanese" is irrational in that it is continually contradicted by his own arguments. His whole testimony (as well as his prepared statement, submitted later) is about who he knows the Japanese (the "Japs" as he calls them) to be and what they intend to do. He presents them as nefarious conspirators given to hive-mind compliance to their emperor and inherently incapable of disloyalty to Japan. His posture as a calm person carefully and reflectively looking at data is contradicted by his arguments, all of which are fallacious, circular, paranoid, and fearful. His tone is rational and his argument irrational.

The posture he adopts in this crucial passage is typical of his testimony, and exemplifies the problems with looking to affective markers or metadiscourse of vehemence to judge whether a person's argument is rational. Warren's oral testimony, as is appropriate to congressional hearings, is personal knowledge—statements of his beliefs and thoughts (he says "I believe" or "I think" approximately thirteen times, as well as other epistemic self-referentials such as "I am of the opinion" and "I take the view"). While that self-referentiality is typical of such hearings, Warren's is more careful and apparently precise than one might expect. He often presents himself as the object of knowledge, rather than agent ("I am informed" or "I have been informed") and also often acknowledges his own ignorance or uncertainty ("I have no knowledge of that" or "I would be inclined to doubt"). Even when he claims knowledge, he often relies on hedging words like "might" (8), "could" (11), "many" (16), "some" (23) "seems" (5) "perhaps" (7), and "possible" (8) as much as, or perhaps even more than, he uses what Hyland calls "boosters"—what might be thought of as words that signal vehemence and certainty about claims, such as "must" (9), "absolutely" (2), "never" (2), "none" (4), "fact" (10), "without question" (2), "sure" (1), "show" (7), "every" (18), "only" (7), or "all" (12). It's likely that the impact of the vehement claims, and assertions of certainty, would be even more persuasive in the context of so much hedging. Since his general posture is of someone who looks carefully at both sides, and hesitates to take a definitive stance, the moments of definitive knowledge would seem to be supported. His stance becomes evidence for the quality of those claims. Notice, for instance, how what is sheer fear-mongering (and the only time he uses the word "crisis") is hedged.

> We believe that there has been no time in our entire crisis when the need of clarification of the alien situation is as apparent as it is today. There are some things transpiring in our State at the present moment that are rather dangerous and we believe that there is only one way that they can be prevented, and that is by a speedy solution of the alien problem.

He claims to be speaking for the state of California—a use of pronouns that not very subtly assumes his conclusion (that people of Japanese ethnicity are not "we"). Warren's testimony begins with a standard way to frame fear-mongering (this is the worst part of a crisis), but, instead of calling for expulsion or imprisonment, calls for something that might seem more reasonable—"clarification" of the situation, a "speedy solution." There are "some" things that are "rather" dangerous. He appears not to have reached a conclusion as to what should be done, and is therefore open-minded.

Elsewhere in his testimony he identifies his position as coming from the need to "deal realistically" with the situation (11010), and identifies the opposition belief (that Japan does not have plans for sabotage in California) "is just not realistic" (11011). He appears to hedge his claims about "the Japanese."

> While I do not cast a reflection on every Japanese who is born in this country—of course we will have loyal ones—I do say the consensus of opinion is that taking the two groups by and large there is more potential danger to this State from the group than is born here than from the group that is born in Japan. (11014)[10]

The hedging words and phrases are a kind of posture of reasonableness, and apparent rejection of unreasonable animosity (he is not talking about "every" Japanese person, he refers to "potential" danger"), but, paradoxically, this hedging doesn't make his argument any more reasonable (since it still doesn't provide evidence). At the same time it actually makes the claims impervious to disproof.

The most explicitly fear-mongering section of his testimony shows the way that his presentation of himself and his opinions as grounded in data are woven into irrational fears and claims.

> A wave of organized sabotage in California accompanied by an actual air raid or even by a prolonged black-out could not only be more destructive to life and property but could result in retarding the entire war effort of [this] Nation far more than the treacherous bombing of Pearl Harbor.
>
> I hesitate to think what the result would be of the destruction of any of our big airplane factories in this State. It will interest you to know that some of our airplane factories in this State are entirely surrounded by Japanese land ownership or occupancy. It is a situation that is fraught with the greatest danger and under no circumstances should it ever be permitted to exist.
>
> I have some maps here that will show the specific instances of that character. In order to advise the committee more accurately on this subject I have asked the various district attorneys through-out the State

to submit maps to me showing every Japanese ownership and occupancy in the State. Those maps tell a story, a story that is not very heartening to anyone who has the responsibility of protecting life and property either in time of peace or in war.

The passage starts out with the frightening image of a wave of organized sabotage that would do more damage than Pearl Harbor; while hyperbolic, his use of conditionals means it's nonfalsifiable: it *could* be more destructive. Instead of going on to describe this horrific scenario, he presents himself as someone who steps back from some fearful imaginings, and moves to an understated claim ("it will interest you") that appears to be a piece of knowledge he is transmitting, again hedged ("some"). He goes from that hedging to hyperbole ("greatest danger") and an unsupported claim: why shouldn't Japanese own land near airplane factories? It's only dangerous if the proximity will be used to commit sabotage, thereby assuming what's at stake. The argument is in his major premise, not his minor one, and yet all his evidence supports his minor premise—that "the Japanese" own land.

Warren's move of relying on the personal authority of others is repeated in other places in his testimony. In his memoir, Warren explains that he testified as he did "after a conference with the law officers, who agreed unanimously" (148). In his testimony, he describes this conference.

> I had together about 10 days ago about 40 district attorneys and about 40 sheriffs in the State to discuss this alien problem. I asked all of them collectively if in their experience any Japanese, whether California-born or Japan-born, had ever given them any information on subversive activities or any disloyalty to this country. The answer was unanimously that no such information had ever been given to them.
>
> Now that is almost unbelievable. You see, when we deal with the German aliens, when we deal with the Italian aliens, we have many informants who are most anxious to help the local authorities and the State and Federal authorities to solve this alien problem. They come in voluntarily and give us information. We get none from the other source. (11015)

For Warren, evidence is identity-based—these people are reliable judges of loyalty of "Japanese" because they are in positions of political authority; that position gives them some kind of epistemic authority. They have no disciplinary expertise—they are not trained in spycraft, antiterrorism, or antisabotage; they aren't even trained scholars of Japan or Japanese culture.

Warren's "that is almost unbelievable" is almost comically tragic; in fact, he shouldn't have believed them because what they were saying was untrue. Later in the hearings, when W. . Johnson, captain of the Berkeley police, mentions that he has had an offer of help from a young Japanese man, Tolan asked if Johnson agreed with Warren that a Japanese has never "divulged any information that would be of value" (11109, a slight, but significant rephrasing of Warren's statement). Johnson replied, "That is substantially correct," and Tolan went on, saying, "They have had it from Germans and they have had it from Italians and they have had it from every other nationality, but never from the Japanese. Is that correct?" Johnson agrees, in the course of which he tells a story that shows that Japanese do actually approach the police.

> Quite true. Up to within the last few days, no information whatsoever, to my knowledge, has come voluntarily from the Japanese to the police. None whatsoever. However, just recently now, and what the motives might be I am unable to say, certain young California-born Japanese have approached us and, as I was relaxing, are attempting to lead us to believe that they are on our side and do want to aid us. So, whether they do or not we don't know. It is virtually impossible to tell. (11108–9).

He begins by saying it's true, then tells a story that shows it's false, and then seems to be saying that, even if Japanese Americans do come forward, they've done so for bad reasons. If the Japanese don't offer information, it's a sign they're evil and untrustworthy; if they do, it's a sign that they're evil and untrustworthy.[11]

Of course, as was brought up during the hearings, someone intending to inform would probably not go to the police, but to the FBI (as the Japanese American Citizens League [JACL] did), so the whole argument is absurd. When Tolan asked Masaoka, of the JACL, about this claim, Masaoka said, "I know that information has been given, but I believe it has largely been given to the Federal agencies, notably the F.B.I." (11147). Rev. Gordon Chapman, a Presbyterian minister who worked with Japanese says, "On several occasions information has been given to me by Japanese young people with the intent that I should take it up with the F.B.I. and I have done so" (11205). Sakamoto says his organization has been "'turning in' people we thought should be checked into" (11475). Perhaps the most apt response to Tolan's question is when Goldblatt says of Warren's failure to get information from Japanese, "It certainly doesn't speak very well of our attorney general's office, that is all" before going on to say that it's completely false, and that Japanese have given information (11182). When Anne Kunitani says that Japanese have reported other Japanese, Tolan says, "Then there are some fifth-column Japanese" (11228), showing the double bind in which Japanese witnesses are placed, and the nonfalsifiability of the belief in a conspiracy.

Conspiracies, as Michael Barkun points out (and as did Richard Hofstadter) have a wealth of data: conspiracists insist that "their truths are empirically verifiable" (67, see also 7). Paradoxically, that the evidence is nonfalsifiable, overwhelmed by counterevidence, or disconfirmed by reliable sources functions to enhance its credibility among those who can interpret it correctly (that is, those who read it in the light of the inferred conspiracy). Thus, both evidence *and* lack of evidence are taken as support for the claim on which their interpretation actually rests: that there is a conspiracy. Note, for instance, how Warren handles the fact that there has not been any sabotage on the part of Japanese Americans—the lack of evidence itself becomes evidence.

> I believe that we are just being lulled into a false sense of security and that the only reason we haven't had disaster in California is because it has been timed for a different date, and that when that time comes if we don't do something about it is going to mean disaster both to California and our Nation. Our day of reckoning is bound to come in that regard. When, nobody knows, of course, but we are approaching an invisible deadline. (11012)

Not only the absence of data becomes proof of the claim the data is supposed to support, but also that there is a lot of (irrelevant) data.

> I do not mean to suggest that it should be thought that all of these Japanese who are adjacent to strategic points are knowing parties to some vast conspiracy to destroy our State by sudden and mass sabotage. Undoubtedly, the presence of many of these persons in their present locations is mere coincidence, but it would seem equally beyond doubt that the presence of others is not coincidence. (10974)

Warren's hedging—not *all* of the Japanese are part of the conspiracy—makes him seem reasonable, and enables a language of balance that almost occludes how unfounded his "equally beyond doubt" claim is.

Warren was implicitly arguing for mass imprisonment, but he evaded advocating that policy explicitly in his oral testimony. Late in the oral testimony he seems to be arguing for some method of determining who is loyal and who is not among the "nationals of countries with which we are at war" and then requiring everyone near a "vital military area" to have some kind of identification (11022). In his memoirs, Warren claims that he "testified for a proposal which was not to intern in concentration camps *all* Japanese, but to require them to move from what was designated as the theater of operations, extending seven hundred and fifty miles from the Pacific Ocean" (148). He is never that specific in his testimony (although, in fairness to him, the last part could be read as endorsing such a plan), but that plan contradicts the "need" he has established through his inference of nefarious conspiracies regarding land ownership. When Warren was arguing need (in the earlier part of his testimony) he was describing the threats Japanese posed to factories, ports, water sources, power lines; if they are so dangerous, they can't simply be moved near the factories, power lines, and water sources 751 miles from the ocean; they are still a menace there. Warren's argument endorses moving "the Japanese" to an isolated area and keeping them there: in other words, mass imprisonment. Whatever Warren's explicit argument, his implicit argument was for mass imprisonment.

H. L. Strobel, who is identified simply as a "farmer" from Monterey County, is the first to advocate camps explicitly, and he presents his argument as following from previous speakers' arguments. Summarizing the previous speakers, Strobel says: "As has been stressed by speaker after speaker," the danger presented by the Japanese is that "they are free to roam around more or less" (11087). That is not actually what the speakers said; many speakers said that the Japanese were dangerous in their area (and made what amounts to an argument for "not in my back yard"), but none had argued explicitly for a plan of incarceration. Yet, Strobel's interpretation is a fair summary of the gist of all their arguments—speaker after speaker had given reasons that the Japanese were too dangerous to be in some specific region, but in doing so had used arguments that applied to all regions. If Japanese cannot be near the coast, or factories, or power lines, or forests, or dams, then simply prohibiting them from living near those things (which are all over the state) is not adequate; they are, as Strobel says free to roam. Strobel takes the logic to its conclusion.

Strobel's argument is also more openly racist than Warren's (for instance, he seems not to know that some Japanese might be American citizens, see 11088 and 11089). The Japanese should be treated differently from Germans and Italians because, Strobel says, they all look alike.

> I believe that you have a better opportunity to determine whether a German or Italian is loyal to this country than you have with the Japanese. The Japanese have a racial similarity so that it is very hard for the average man to note any difference between them when he sees them just occasionally. Unless they are all under restraint you will have no way of knowing who is who. (11092)

Yet Strobel claims to have personal relationships with Japanese; "I know lots of Japanese all throughout the State" (11091).

Strobel too relies on a rhetoric of realism, on a metadiscourse of hedging and precision. He identifies his motive for testifying as being "interested in dispelling some of the misinformation that has apparently gone throughout the Nation" (11087). He directs the committee's attention to "the fact" (11088) that citizens are inconvenienced (his characterization of Japanese imprisonment). He frames his proposal as compassionate (it's "for their own protection" and they can work "if they desired to work" and he doesn't think anyone wants to exploit the Japanese in the acquisition of land and machinery; 11090), tries to correct the tendency to "take our own particular problems into consideration too much" (11088), and uses "the most authoritative figures" (11089).[12] He has looked into the question of increasing tomato production, discussing it with a produce grower, who discussed it with someone else (11089); he gives specific numbers (45 to 60 percent of canning tomatoes, increasing acreage by 2000 acres, Japanese produce 8 to 12 percent of vegetables and 10 to 12 percent of the total). He says,

> I feel that, perhaps, we are entitled to kill our own snake, so to speak, and if there are areas within the State of California which are acceptable to the military authorities where these people might be evacuated, and for their own protection where they might be put under restraint of one kind or another with the proper supervision of the military authorities, or whatever authorities they might designate to do that job, and that if these people were maintained in these particular localities, their services could be utilized under proper supervision. They might be taken out to work, if they desired to work, in the morning, and be brought back at night. Their labor could be utilized, and I think that that would, perhaps, be as good a solution of this problem as any you might offer.

He uses hedging words like "might" (fourteen times in his three thousand-word testimony), "could" (4), "some" (17), and "perhaps" (6), rationality markers like "fact" (4) and "determine" (2), and, as in the fairly disturbing passage above, seems to think of their feelings—they could work if they so desired.

Strobel wasn't the only one to indicate concern for the feelings of "the Japanese." The claim that "evacuation" was in the best interest of Japanese was a recurrent topos (Warren 11015, 11016; letter from Orosi Citizens' Committee 11046; Curtis 11475–6; Troy 11503; Neustadt 11049–50). Certainly, by the time of the hearings, animosity toward Japanese was rising, as indicated in Strobel's testimony. But, animosity toward a group that might result in race-based violence doesn't rationally justify race-based imprisonment. To hold victims of racial violence responsible for the feelings others have about them is to exempt those others (generally the in-group) from responsibility for their own feelings, as well as for whatever actions those feelings might inspire them to do. The topos of "it's for their own good" was disputed by various speakers, including with the plausible argument that they were capable of making their own decisions about their own protection (see, for instance, Sakamoto 11467).[13]

Strobel, like Warren, doesn't make explicit emotional appeals, but he does ground his argument in his own beliefs (he uses "think" about sixteen times) and feelings (6). The emotions to which he refers are not of hate or anger or fear (the only time he uses the term "fear" is when he says there should be "no fear" about something, and something can be done "without fear"). They are, instead, claims of intuition and perception; so his evidence that his belief is right is that he feels it is right. This move, of presenting one's own conviction as evidence that the conviction is accurate, runs throughout the pro-imprisonment rhetoric. A. H. Brazil, the district attorney of San Luis Obispo, says that there are Italians of "unquestioned standing in this community whose loyalty to this country could not be questioned" (10990). His evidence that they are loyal is the tautology about not questioning; we can't question their loyalty because we don't question their loyalty. John Halford, secretary of the County Farm Bureau, grounded his argument in feelings.

> The feeling is very widespread that all Japanese, whether foreign or United States citizens should be hastily taken care of in some manner, whether concentrated within the State or removed entirely from the State. There seems to be a very decided feeling along this line. It is my opinion that something should be done very speedily to change the present alien situation, in order that public feeling should be allayed. (11005)

The Japanese are not part of the public feeling, and public feeling about them is sufficient proof of who they are. Robert Taylor, chairman, Oregon Agricultural War Board, reads a statement of the "Clackamae County War Board."

> The members of the Clackamae County War Board have talked to many citizens concerning this problem, and so far as we can ascertain, the general feeling is that American citizens do not wish to be unjust, and wish to give due credit to the loyalty of those who may be loyal; but experience has shown that it is very difficult to differentiate between the loyal and disloyal, and it is the general feeling that all Japanese should be evacuated, as a matter of safety. (11383)

Those who described the Japanese as essentially treacherous projected and universalized their racism; as one speaker said, "all are agreed" it is advisable to move the groups in question "to live where no sabotage is possible" (Steiner 11558).[14]

Yet, the pro-imprisonment rhetors seem oddly unreflective about their own feelings and beliefs. It's surprising how many speakers argued for mass expulsion or imprisonment—in the sense that only mass expulsion or imprisonment could solve the "ill" they were describing—who, when pressed for a plan, deferred. Danger of sabotage was the argument used for why Japanese could not be anywhere near the California redwood forests (11064); any other forests (11371); fish-canning factories in Portland (11315); oil industries in the Columbia River area (11317); water treatment plants in Portland (11330) and Washington (11523); most of Oregon (since the wood-frame houses and timber forests could be set on fire (11324, 11365–6); power lines (11062); the entire state of Washington (11399, 11420, see also 11501–2). If one takes these various arguments together, then Japanese could only live somewhere with no forests, water supplies, power lines, factories, airstrips, canneries, wood houses, oil wells, or refineries—i.e., nowhere.[15] But, with a few exceptions (such as Strobel), speakers deferred when it came to being explicit about what was implicit in their argument. As one speaker said, "I think the case should be more of a Federal problem to be solved by some referee appointed by the Federal Government or some board" (11102, see also 11088, 11158, 11505, 11172, 11311, 11403).

There is, then, an important evasion of rhetorical responsibility in rhetors' testimony: they make a "needs" case for which the only possible "plan" is forcible internment in guarded camps, and yet they either equivocate at the moment they could advocate such a plan, or they disavow such an option.[16] Rhetors can make an argument with clear policy implications while denying the implications.[17]

Obviously, not every rhetor who identifies a need is obligated to lay out a plan, and it's quite responsible for a rhetor to identify the limits of her expertise, and defer the details of a plan to someone more informed. But there is something significant in how this deferral of rhetorical responsibility functions in the hearings: rhetors do not say that the plan should be worked out democratically, or even by elected representatives, but by the military or government. To fight a war against fascism, rhetors advocate fascistic methods of deliberation that, by the logic they have established, will necessarily result in a fascist policy. Robinson notes FDR's complete lack of concern for the consequences of his actions in regard to Japanese Americans (*By Order* 245), and one can see the same absence of care in Warren. Warren acknowledges that Japanese Americans were being exploited, and that it is a consequence of having "no procedure set up here for [the] handling of enemy property" (11023, an interesting slip, since the discussion is about property owned by American citizens of Japanese ancestry). He expresses liberal sentiments, such as, "I don't believe that people should be permitted to exploit even our enemy aliens. I think there should be some Federal agency that would supervise those matters to see that no one is taken advantage of by designing people" (11023). But he does no more than indicate he has the right feelings. He has given no thought to the issue and how it might be solved; he only discusses the point because Tolan has pressed him to do so. The plan he advocates—mass and immediate "evacuation" necessarily entails exploitation, unless his plan details how such exploitation is to be prevented. Instead of presenting such details, Warren bemoans an inevitable consequence of his own plan, with a vague statement that he thinks someone else should prevent that consequence.

This strategy of displacing responsibility enables rhetors to advocate policies while refusing to take responsibility for them, or even for the consequences of their own rhetoric. If Japanese are expelled from an area, they have to do something with their possessions—that is the inevitable consequence of expulsion. If the government does not agree to take guardianship of the property, Japanese property owners will be exploited. As long as Warren was not advocating government guardianship as avidly as he was advocating expulsion, he was advocating exploitation. That he thought exploitation was bad and hoped someone else would do something to prevent it doesn't change the logical consequence of his advocacy.

I'm here using "logical" as a description of the relationship of claims, not Warren's state of mind. Discourse that uses rationality markers—metadiscourse heavy in logical connectors, attitude markers that suggest being calm and in control, and claims of "facts" and assertions of evidence—can *seem* to be "logical" if the cultural assumption is that being logical and being emotional are mutually exclusive. If they are, then a highly emotional state implies the lack of a logical argument.

Such an assumption conflates "an argument that appeals to logic" and "a logical argument." An argument that has rationality markers might be the former and not the latter. The cognitive shortcut enabled by conflating the two very different concepts enables a kind of demagoguery that can, at least in the moment, evade recognition as such because it doesn't have the kind of metadiscourse and surface characteristics we are tempted to assume inevitably mark demagoguery. That is, our common sense perception of what demagoguery is (a man pounding on a podium screaming abusive epithets) is part of what enables demagoguery to succeed. The policy that Warren was advocating was hateful and racist—logically coherent only if one presumes that Japanese are a race substantially different from "whites" and essentially incapable of loyalty to the United States, but he used a language of balance, appeared to eschew paranoia and extremism, identified his position as realistic and factually grounded, hedged his claims, and espoused feelings of compassion; he explicitly bemoaned the aspects of his own plan that would create hardship (albeit without articulating an effective way to ameliorate them); he provided data. The policy was hateful, but his persona was not.

The Sabotage Myth

Probably the most alarmist and alarming topos was the sabotage myth, and it is also a fairly complicated topos to discuss simply because its exposure as a myth appeared to have no impact on its suasory power (and it is sometimes still invoked to defend imprisonment).[18] Briefly, the terrifying speed and effectiveness of the Axis victories in Western Europe were not the consequences of sabotage,[19] and, as was pointed out repeatedly in 1941 and 1942, there was no sabotage in Pearl Harbor. Knox's January statements to the press that mention the fifth column refer to the gathering of information regarding defenses (and lack thereof) in which members of the Japanese consulate in Hawaii had engaged. So, even the espionage had not been on the part of the kind of people who would be imprisoned by the plans under consideration by the Tolan Committee.

In Tolan's "Fourth Interim Report" (May 13, 1942), there are telegrams to Tolan from Henry Stimson (secretary of war), Frank Knox, and R. A. Vitousek (chairman of the Honolulu Citizens' Council), all of whom are clear that there was no sabotage. Vitousek sent along affidavits which, he says, "show there was no sabotage in the nature of cutting marks in the cane pointing the way to Pearl Harbor, and also shows [sic] there was no blocking of roadways in the vicinity" (49). As mentioned earlier, the unequivocal conclusion of the Roberts Commission was that the disaster at Pearl Harbor was the fault of Admiral Kimmel and General Short, whose behavior was "a dereliction of duty." As the report says, "These errors of judgment were the effective causes for the success of the attack" (21). Kimmel and Short had been repeatedly warned to be prepared for precisely the sort of attack in which the Japanese engaged, and, as Gordon Prange et al. say, such a warning shouldn't even have been necessary to a person at all familiar with Axis strategies (*Pearl Harbor* 376). Short, in particular, simply chose to ignore the warnings; as Prange et al. say, he "acted upon his own estimation of the situation … and he followed his interpretation of orders, selecting what portions he would carry out, instead of obeying those orders in toto" (382). The Roberts report details the espionage, and makes no mention of sabotage.

Yet, like Blix's 2003 UN briefing that documented Saddam Hussein's cooperation (but was reported in American media as saying the opposite of what it said), the Roberts report was cited in support of a position it actually contradicted (see, for instance, the Portland City Council resolution calling for internment of "all Japanese nationals and persons of Japanese descent" 11388). It isn't clear to me whether few people read the report (although it was published in full in newspapers), if they unintentionally misread it, or if the misrepresentation was deliberate.[20] Robinson points out that Roosevelt never explicitly rejected the sabotage narrative, although he knew it to be false, and General John DeWitt, of the Western Defense Command, was certainly willing to lie about it. That is, various members of the elite deliberately allowed the misreading, and may have promoted it.[21]

The Roberts report being released after a long history of what Kashima calls "improbable tales of Japanese-American spies and saboteurs" (212) may have contributed to the sabotage myth. For instance, in December, an article by Wallace Carroll, a UP reporter, includes rumors that were, even on their face, absurd to anyone familiar with the geography of army and navy bases, such as reports of arrows cut in sugarcane fields to direct pilots (the arrows would have been harder to see than the rather large harbor), and Japanese truck drivers who "drove from side to side of the road from Honolulu to Hickam Field to delay American pilots who were frantically trying to reach their planes." Somehow that narrative was also combined with one about Japanese farmers deliberately blocking the road (the road to what—the army or navy base—wasn't always consistent). In addition to these myths, other legends were repeated during the hearing, with an insistence that they were "facts." Ward lists specifics.

> I think the disclosure of the arrowhead marks in the sugarcane field at Pearl Harbor, the obstructing of the highway by Japanese vegetable trucks when officers were trying to reach their stations, and the fact that rings from Honolulu and from the Oregon State schools were found on fingers of some dead Japanese aviators, have awakened many Americans to what many of us have apprehended over a number of years. (11262)[22]

These rumors were not treated as such, despite there being no mention of them in the official reports; as one witness says, "That is factual, that is history" (11109).

Tolan was particularly drawn to the myth of "trucks blocking the road," and brought it up multiple times, with sometimes cringeworthy hyperbole, as though it were a demonstrated fact, in order to refute perfectly reasonable arguments.

> They had probably the greatest, the most perfect system of espionage and sabotage ever in the history of war, native-born Japanese. On the only roadway to the shipping harbor there were hundreds and hundreds of automobiles clogging the street, don't you see? (11181)

The city manager of Alameda told the committee:

> At a certain golf course in California where they make reservations for Sunday golf playing, it is frequented by a large number of Japanese who hold reservations for every Sunday morning. Some of these Japanese, part of them at least, are American citizens. On the morning of

December 7 there wasn't a Japanese that showed up on the golf course to claim his reservation and play golf that morning. Now you can draw your own conclusions, but that is a fact. (11111)

It wasn't a fact. It is a perfect urban legend—an unsourced story about an unnamed golf course—much like the stories of Jews not showing up to work in the Twin Towers, Muslims who warn girlfriends with children about going to the mall, "Eleanor Clubs" that radicalize African American servants, or other urban legends used to justify policy decisions. It's impossible to know whether the rhetor's use of the word "fact" suggests—at some deep, dark level—that he knows the falseness of the story of Japanese inattendance at the golf course on the day Pearl Harbor was bombed. But the story is a rumor, not a fact.

Tolan was certainly persuaded of the sabotage myth. Throughout the hearings, he was, on the whole, polite to witnesses, establishing an expressive public sphere, in which people were free to make their statements without being challenged. The striking exception is that he pressed anyone who seemed not to take seriously the issue of sabotage. When one witness argues that the Japanese are loyal, Tolan says to her, "So far, there are no cases on sabotage; that is, generally speaking. Well there weren't any in Pearl Harbor, either, were there, until the attack came? There wasn't any sabotage; it all happened at once" (11387; see also 11409). On the second day of the hearings (and after the executive session with DeWitt), Tolan refers to the "authentic pictures during the attack showing hundreds of Japanese old automobiles cluttered on the one street of Honolulu so the Army could not get to the ships" (11141).[23] It's worth pointing out that there neither were nor are such photos because such blockage never happened.

There is a photo of cars blocking the gate to one of the bases—the cars belong to servicemen and others who worked on the base who abandoned them in order to get to the base quickly. But, it's clearly the entrance to the base, not Honolulu, and Honolulu is not on the route between the army and navy bases, so, if that is the photo Tolan was shown, he was being deliberately misled. While dark corners of the internet have defenders of internment who also refer to such photos, even the most conspiratorial of sites don't provide them; while Tolan may have been shown a falsified photo, repetitions of this rumor exemplify what Michael Barkun describes as important to the persuasiveness of conspiracy narratives: "repetition substitutes for direct evidence as a way of determining veracity" (13). Someone (perhaps DeWitt) showed Tolan a photo, and persuaded him of a nonfalsifiable claim (that there was more sabotage than any officials would publicize). Tolan uses a classic *argumentum ad ignorantiam* to support a claim that is, by its very nature, neither supportable nor falsifiable: "The sabotage at the time of the attack of Pearl Harbor and the disloyalty of the Japanese there was so widespread that the details have never as yet been fully given to the public" (11153). Barkun argues that conspiracy ideas often rely on stigmatized knowledge, such as narratives and texts rejected as forgeries by mainstream culture or discarded by experts; this claim about the nonpublic evidence of sabotage functions in a similar way. Stories of Japanese airmen with college rings and arrows burned in sugarcane fields weren't part of the official explanations (e.g., the Roberts report), but they were repeated by Wallace Carroll in newspapers, and they did fit with anti-Japanese rumors promoted for years by various West Coast media outlets (described by Roger Daniels).

Warren admits during testimony that there had been no sabotage and no fifth-column activity found in California up to that time.

> But I take the view that that is the most ominous sign in our whole situation. It convinced me perhaps more than any other factor that the sabotage that we are to get, the fifth column activities that we are to get, are timed just like Pearl Harbor was timed and just like the invasion of France, and of Denmark, and of Norway, and all of those other countries.[24] (11011-2)

An expert on Norway would later refute the myths about Denmark and Norway, but there is no indication that Warren (or anyone else) stayed around to listen to other people testify.

Agency by proxy is also perception by proxy—one adopts the perception of the oracle, thereby becoming a perceptive person (a relationship I'll argue is central to the kind of elite oracular rhetoric in which Madison Grant engages). While others might find the situation puzzling or random, true members of the in-group can see the order behind it.[25] Seeing order in the particular series of missteps, luck, and chaos that was the Pearl Harbor disaster is a reassuring one. After all, "a conspiracist worldview implies a universe governed by design rather than randomness" (Barkun 3). The narrative that the Roberts report tells is one of military incompetence. If something like Pearl Harbor can happen once, despite career military officers being given appropriate orders and warnings, then something like it could happen again. The public cannot prevent such an outcome, and, as has been shown, when people feel out of control they are much more likely to see patterns and believe conspiracies.[26]

The uncomfortable narrative offered by the Roberts Commission (or any other narrative that blames the American military) means that members of the in-group contributed to the in-group's failure, a fact that frustrates the ability to believe one's in-group is always and necessarily better (for more on this point, see Proulx and Heine, "Meaning and Threat Compensation"). Blaming spies and saboteurs implies a much more comforting narrative than acknowledging in-group incompetence; it suggests we can prevent such disasters from occurring again by engaging in intracommunity cleansing, by purifying our communities of out-group elements (something for which various groups had been agitating since the nineteenth century).[27] Blaming Japanese-American saboteurs also raises the possibility of materializing an abstract loss and threat into a body onto which vengeance can be enacted.[28] It thereby can feel as though a potentially out-of-control situation can be brought back into control. Daniel Sullivan et al. argue that people are motivated to perceive themselves as controlling their environment yet realize that their lives can be negatively affected by myriad diffuse and capricious hazards. To minimize the threat that this realization potentially poses to perceived control, people narrow the multifarious sources of potential misfortune to a focal individual or group that can be effectively controlled, managed, or (at minimum) understood. To the extent that an enemy is perceived to be an influential source of misfortune, enemyship allows people to maintain a sense of personal control by perceiving their overall environment as containing less randomly distributed risk. Thus, perhaps counterintuitively, the narrative that someone is out to get us is a more comfortable narrative than "accidents happen" or "people screw up."

As Kashima points out, the FBI and other agencies had not been caught flat-footed by Japan's entry into war, but had been gathering information on suspected aliens for several years (beginning as early as 1938); even before Roosevelt issued Executive Order 9066, "the Justice and War Department interned 31,275 persons, of whom 17,477 were of Japanese ancestry" (Kashima 4).[29] The relative ease with which Japanese were imprisoned, and the great latitude given to courts to determine their fates, are both important considerations for then and future defenses of internment. It was extraordinarily easy for various parts of the government to imprison suspicious citizens: why imprison unsuspicious ones?

The arguments on this stasis, particularly by people who argued against mass evacuation of Italian or German aliens, were sheer racism: "It is impossible to deal with them, particularly the Japanese, individually" (10997). The spokesman for the Joint Immigration Committee says, "There may be Japanese who are loyal to this country, yet there is no way of proving that loyalty" (11070). Strobel says "It would be almost impossible for any man or for any agency to determine the extent of the loyalty of any Japanese to our country" (11091; see also 10995, Warren 11015; Riley 11304; Multnomah County Labor Committee 11384; American Legion Resolution 11435). According to the Los Angeles chief of police, the Japanese are distinguished by "racial characteristics, that of being a Mongolian, which cannot be obliterated from these persons, regardless of how many generations are born in the United States" (10988).

Warren characterizes "the Japanese" as homogeneous, "very closely organized" (10974), and members of "Japanese organizations covering every branch of life" (10975) that have interlocking memberships, so that "the actions of individual Japanese have been in the past very largely controlled by the organizations to which they belong" (10975).[30] Warren says, "If the leadership of the main Japanese organizations fell into the wrong hands, it is quite conceivable that some, though certainly not all, of the Japanese organizations could be utilized for carrying on a program of sabotage and fifth-column activity" (10975). His evidence for this perception of the lockstep nature of Japanese organizations is 1) an uncited reference to something in the public press saying that representatives from twenty-seven hundred Japanese organizations were to meet in Japan in November 1941; and 2) that a petition protesting certain practices regarding produce was signed by Japanese growers associations from all over the state! That these organizations are inherently military is supported by his quoting from several unnamed Japanese newspapers that Japanese organizations had sent tinfoil and money to Japan for its war against China.

This line of argument is typical of out-group thinking—members of the out-group are thought to be incapable of autonomy and independent judgment; their falling in line with what their authorities tell them means they are mindless automatons (but our doing the same means we are independently thinking all the same things).[31] And, as is typical, precisely the same kind of behavior is seen as positive in the in-group. Unanimity in the out-group shows mindless obedience; yet, the considerable unanimity pointed to in the in-group (such as the nearly identical statements on the part of various groups) is a virtue. The unanimity of police organizations and white growers' groups is not a sign of homogeneity or hivemindedness; it's proof that their beliefs are true. That Japanese appear to disagree is not proof that the univocality perception is wrong; it just shows how clever they are. So, there is another instance of the damned if you do and damned if you don't quality of the pro-imprisonment position.[32]

That many of the rhetors who made the argument for mass imprisonment did so with disavowals of mass imprisonment, expressions of concern for the victims, or an apparent lack of intention, does not change that it was a logic of mass imprisonment. When rhetors like Warren argue for the necessity of evacuation or incarceration to "protect" the Japanese from hostile crowds, they ignore the extent to which they have rhetorically created those crowds.[33] Mass incarceration without trial remains a tragic example of holding a group responsible for the fear others feel about them, rather than holding the fearful (or fear-mongering) responsible for their own fear; the hearings are a horrifying instance of rhetors disavowing responsibility for the arguments they make.

"I Don't Think That Is Real Logic"

As mentioned earlier, the major arguments for mass imprisonment were directly refuted by speakers at the hearings; this wasn't an enclave or echo chamber. Warren's argument that the absence of sabotage is proof that sabotage is planned is, as one witness points out, illogical: "Attorney General Earl Warren said that because so far there hasn't been a single sign of fifth-column activity that is a sign that there is fifth-column activity. But I disagree with that. I don't think that is real logic" (11155).[34] Several witnesses refuted the sabotage argument. Anne Kunitani, for instance, says,

> Mr. Tolan pointed out frequently this morning and this afternoon, that he heard of Army trucks in the road. I don't know where Mr. Tolan got that information. I don't know whether that is true or not. I can only go to the Roberts report, which was the only official United States document put out, as to what happened at Pearl Harbor, and why things happened as they did. I think if you gentlemen look into the Roberts report again you will find that no mention was made of sabotage on the part of Japanese-Americans. They pointed out that the 200 members operating out of the Japanese consulate were the most active participants in fifth column activities in Hawaii. (11226)

Sparkman, one of the committee members, replies, "The Roberts report did not deny the idea of sabotage and fifth-column activity. It simply didn't mention it" (11226). Sparkman's argument is absurd. Since the Roberts Commission report covered the major contributions to the losses at Pearl Harbor, its failure to mention sabotage means either there was none or it did not contribute. Eric Bellquist, political science professor from Berkeley, and an expert on Scandinavian countries, submitted a prepared statement which, among things, specifically refuted the myth of fifth-column activities in Norway (11245).[35]

Speakers against mass evacuation and racist treatment against Japanese were eloquent, well grounded and reasonable. Hito Okada pointed out the bizarre logic of the argument that the Japanese had to be imprisoned to protect them from racist rioters by noting that the Chinese should also be removed; after all, he says, most people can't tell the difference. Mike Masaoka, of the Japanese American Citizens League, provided statistics showing that a plurality of Nisei are Protestant, thereby refuting the argument that Japanese are unreliable because their religion requires that they worship the emperor (see also 11569–70). Masaoka mentioned the number of Japanese Americans serving in the military and rebutted the claim that the Japanese purchased the land around Lockheed after the plant was put in place (see also 11225). The argument about the significance of dual citizenship was effectively refuted by several witnesses who pointed out that the granting of this citizenship by Japan was done against their will (11224, 11473). Pastor W. P. Reagor presented fourteen hundred signatures of Japanese Christians (11196); Frank Herron Smith testified to large numbers of Japanese Christians (11207–8; see also 11355), something also noted by Hito Okada. When Sparkman pushes Okada for details about the Japanese religion, Okada responds, "I couldn't answer that because I am a pretty good Methodist" (113550). Louis Goldblatt's testimony was particularly powerful.

> No matter how great our resources, no matter how strong our man-power, this country of ours can never withstand the pressure of internal conflict arising out of this policy of hunting down saboteurs and spies by race, nationality, or creed. During a period of hysteria there are al-ways those who think they can save their own skins by joining in the persecution of another minority group. When it comes their turn to be kicked around it is too late to reconsider.

> The great need of America is the unity of its people. Much damage has already been done to this unity by such practices as discrimination against Negroes and minority groups, the refusal of officeholders to drop their political bias and work for the general welfare, and the rejection by employers of all offers of labor cooperation. If to these is to be added a policy of demarcation of Americans by race and nationality, national unity will be nothing but a tragically empty phrase. (11188)

Goldblatt's dissent is the kind that Ivie praises—it "is a double gesture of non-conformity and solidarity, difference and identification, division and consub-stantiation" (*Dissent* 109). "Dissenting from war," Ivie says, "means nothing less than communicating a bond of humanity to mitigate factious relations between disputing parties" (*Dissent* 101). Advocates of imprisonment were proposing to bring the war home (although accusing the Japanese of doing so) by declaring war on Americans of Japanese ancestry, and Goldblatt's testimony was an elo-quent attempt to remind his listeners that they were proposing violating basic principles of the American tradition. He tried to undermine the very distinction of "us" and "them."

Goldblatt raises a point made by several other rhetors that the proposed treat-ment of the Japanese was not a military necessity and would, on the contrary, hurt the military effort. In addition to the loss of productivity (something to which many of the agricultural groups responded by saying the "white" farmers could increase production), the racist treatment of Asians contributed to Japanese propaganda efforts (see, for instance, Fisher 11199; see also 11428). When asked how one could tell if a Japanese person was loyal, Steiner replied, sensibly: "I would think that that same question would need to be asked concerning all of us. That is, how do we know that I am loyal or that anyone is loyal? . . . We must know it by their actions, by the company they keep, the organizations to which they belong" (11560). These were all reasonable arguments.

Yet these arguments seem to have little impact. Too much testimony concerned whether this imagined group of "Japanese" was, as a whole, trustworthy, something that was answered in terms of whether various individuals felt trust toward that imagined entity. And the answer was, not surprisingly, they feared the hobgoblin their own fear had created. That some rhetors presented these feelings of mistrust as balanced and considered judgments grounded in data doesn't change the fact that they were tautological and nonfalsifiable stereotypes about a group. James Crosswhite argues that the "power to signify is rooted in our 'referring' ourselves toward beings, to the world, toward others and ourselves" (297). The language of mass imprisonment didn't include interlocutors for whom "Japanese" did not refer to cartoon villains, nor even people who were being honest with themselves about what they were advocating.

Since it isn't even clear what's being argued, no policy can be effectively debated, and, in Tolan's hearings, one sees interlocutors discussing different (and sometimes mutually exclusive) policies. To criticize the interlocutors for ambiguous reference isn't to endorse any kind of linguistic realism, but just to point out that people could keep from thinking about what they were advocating, or even shift among policies when it was convenient; the ambiguity enabled what Hannah Arendt famously called "thoughtlessness" (Life of the Mind) and prevented effective debate. As Crosswhite points out, topoi become ideologies through epideictic oratory, which has the consequence (or perhaps function) of the "converting of temporary and limited agreement into something that appears to be universal and necessary" (73). The topoi of mass imprisonment became ideology because crucial and highly problematic beliefs were protected from examination.

These topoi enabled people to focus the generalized anxiety inherent in American entry into the war, gave the public a pleasurable way to explain their situation (one that was grounded in prewar consensus about race, citizenship, and loyalty), reduced uncertainty through increasing group identification, enabled the dismissal (not even refutation) of the most compelling arguments against mass expulsion and imprisonment, and, finally, resolved the cognitive dissonance created by what purported to be a democratic and law-abiding country using racist and totalitarian strategies in what was supposed to be a war against racist totalitarianism.

The goal of rhetoric, Crosswhite argues, is not "to strip arguments down to their epistemological bedrock and assent only to those that yield unassailably certain results" (299). Many advocates of racist policies felt fear and anxiety (they also probably felt certain that those feelings were not in them, but in the things they feared), and people arguing against those policies were not less prone to feelings (they felt affection, compassion, and different fears). The argument about "the Japanese" couldn't be solved by trying to find epistemological bedrock—there was none. But what Crosswhite calls deep rhetoric would have helped.

> The more arguments we develop on the different sides of an issue, the clearer we become about how many perspectives and choices there are, about what guidance is available for making our choices, and about what commitments may be involved. This kind of transparency, the "seeing" of the relevant facts and concerns and the possible arguments, transforms the rhetorical situation. (299)

Warren famously later said, "Whenever I thought of the innocent little children who were torn from home, school friends, and congenial surroundings, I was conscious-stricken" (149). Martha Nussbaum has argued that there are three "thoughts" that structure the kind of compassion that enhances political deliberation: "the thought of seriousness," "the thought of nonfault," and "the thought of similar possibilities." Her argument is that compassion for the suffering of another means that we take their suffering seriously, that we think they do not deserve the suffering, and that we can imagine the sufferer as similar to ourselves. The shift in Warren's perspective from the one he held during the oral testimony before Tolan's committee and the one he expressed when conscience-stricken is captured by Nussbaum's three thoughts.

At the end of Warren's testimony, when he describes what he is advocating (which is, at that point, required identification to be in military areas) as trivial, he isn't taking the logic of his own argument—or what is really being advocated—seriously. Warren minimizes the implications of the kind of argument he and others are making, thinking only of himself and other members of his in-group as potentially suffering (the suffering about which he is concerned is the nonproblem of Japanese invasion). His descriptions of nefarious land-buying practices, Japanese educational methods, and so on are all attributions of fault. He wasn't thinking of the "innocent little children" who would actually be affected by the policies. Finally, he wasn't imagining what he was advocating. The slippage in which he and others engage at the rhetorical moment of taking responsibility enables him not to think, imagine, or feel what treating "the Japanese" as essentially treacherous really meant. In-group members' fears serve as premises, but not objects, of argument. The tragedy of the public discourse over mass imprisonment of Japanese Americans was that equivocation, deliberate fear-mongering, and even an expressive model of discourse meant that the real commitments at play in the decisions were left obscured and unquestioned, so that what should have been the object of argument became the basis.

4

When the Choir Claims to
Have Been Converted

One would almost expect that anyone writing on "The Passing of
the Great Race" would try to prove first that it is a distinctive Race;
second that it is Great; third that it is Passing. No such necessity
oppresses Mr. M. Grant. He assumes them all, not even trying
to show why, if it was a "Great Race," it could not protect itself.
—Bolton Hall

I n the previous chapter, I used Earl Warren's testimony before the House Select
Committee Investigating National Defense Migration to illustrate one kind of
demagoguery of the elite: in which an elite engages in demagoguery while adopting a controlled, calm, rational, and evidence-based posture. Warren's immediate
audience—the members of the committee—were also elite, but his evidence was
fairly straightforward, and his arguments (e.g., these patterns of land ownership
show this intention) were, although fallacious, easy to understand.

This chapter will consider another kind of demagoguery of the elite, in which
a member of the political elite engages in demagoguery while adopting the same
posture that Warren did, but with an argument that is obscure and obfuscating.
Madison Grant's *Passing of the Great Race* (1916) has many of the surface features
of scholarly and academic discourse—hair-splitting taxonomies, metadiscourse
of precision, rationality markers, a rhetoric of realism, evasion of self-mention
(thereby implying objectivity), and unfamiliar words that appear scholarly to
the layperson (though they aren't). Anyone familiar with the fields from which
Grant is drawing authority—such as cultural anthropology—would recognize
that the book was not grounded in current scholarly consensus, was not practicing
appropriate citation methods, and was not accurate. In fact, as others have noted,

Grant's argument doesn't quite make sense, and the relationship of his "data" to his claims (let alone the relationship of his claims to his argument) is obscure.[1] The gist of his argument was (and is) attractive to racists, even, oddly enough, when the details of his argument condemn people like them (non-Nordic whites). So, what does Grant's book *do?*

As mentioned in the introduction, it is conventional to attribute significant political and historical impact to *Passing of the Great Race;* Timothy Ryback calls it "an American Bible" for Hitler, saying it "opened Hitler's eyes to new perspectives" (96) and "compelled" Hitler "to think not only geographically but also temporally, and not merely in decades but in centuries and even millennia" (97).[2] Of course, as Ryback makes clear, *Passing* did not convert Hitler to racism, it was not the only racist book that Hitler read and admired, and Hitler's "embrace of Grant's work was noticeably selective" (104); hence Ryback's use of the word "compel" is perhaps hyperbole. But, as mentioned before, Ryback is far from alone in attributing suasory power to the book—many other readers did (and do) as well. That paradox—a book that confirms a worldview that is described as rhetorically moving—raises several questions. What rhetorical impact does a book like this have? And, if a book like this does nothing other than confirm what people already believe, why would those people describe the book as moving them and changing their beliefs?

The approval of an argument that can't possibly have been understood in any detail is ironic, since one of the common claims of white supremacists is that Grant's critics were politically, even racially, motivated. It may be that they were, although their criticism that Grant's evidence was nonexistent may have been equally important. There can be no doubt that Grant, and his defenders, were (and are) politically motivated. In a connected irony. Grant's book was cited by people who were themselves cited (such as Lothrop Stoddard, C. S. Cox), and he and his "disciples" (as Spiro appropriately calls them) had demonstrable impact on legislation regarding eugenics, sterilization, and immigration. He was able to have that impact, and his book was read by powerful people, because he was himself part of the power elite. An equally flawed book by a "non-Nordic" would never have had the positive reception that *Passing of the Great Race* met. Thus, the powerful impact of his contradictory and even incoherent book complaining that his "race" was passing actually demonstrated the considerable political and cultural power members of his group continued to wield, thereby showing that every aspect of his book was false.

Grant's book is demagoguery, but not because his motives are bad (he probably sincerely believed he was doing the right thing) or because his rhetoric is emotional (it isn't) or because he was a populist (he wasn't). He reduces complicated questions about immigration, crime, segregation, poverty, and political control to a determined, ontologically grounded (although incoherent) narrative about race with policy implications so obvious that anyone who disputes them can be dismissed as biased. He engages in scapegoating, projection, binaries, and the various other characteristics of demagoguery, but he does so in a way that looks expert and is boring. As such, it is an elegant example of how that kind of demagoguery works, and, I will argue in this chapter, how it's possible to identify demagoguery even in a text that is just shy of comprehensible.

Madison Grant's Argument

Grant's overall argument is "when immense periods are studied and compared . . . the lesson is always the same, namely, that race is everything" (87). The book is primarily about the three white races, and their achievements—primarily attributable to the Nordics' invasion of some country, intermixing with the natives, creating a great civilization, and then lapsing into a muddy swamp of disease and inactivity. This is simply another version of the course of empire narrative, which appears in such different sources as Edward Gibbon's *Rise and Fall of the Roman Empire,* Thomas Jefferson's obsession with the "yeoman farmer," or painter Thomas Cole's famous 1830s Course of Empire series. This narrative posited that civilizations begin clean and manly, become increasingly complex and decadent, and then collapse because of contamination from some outside force. Still popular (e.g., Huntington on non-Protestant religions in the United States), the notion is that an empire that wants to maintain hegemony must remain pure and manly. In regard to Greece, for instance, Grant says:

> The first result of a crossing of two such contrasted subspecies as the Nordic and Mediterranean races, has repeatedly been a new outburst of culture. This occurs as soon as the older race has imparted to the conquerors its civilization, and before the victors have allowed their blood to be swamped by mixture. This process seems to have happened several times in Greece. (146)

The Nordics burst out of Scandinavia, settle in an area, fuse with the inferior culture, raise them up, then are seduced by the easy women and easy culture, their pure blood dilutes, and the civilization collapses (sometimes through conquest by the latest instantiation of Nordics).

Grant's second theme—that good and upright men are seduced by Other women into transgressing boundaries, thereby forfeiting their power and inviting punishment—is also a very old story. The association of "purity" with strength, and "mixing" with weakness, is the schema that Mary Douglas famously argued was behind various dietary requirements in Scripture, and in cultural practices that might be universal. Neither new nor unusual (a fairly straightforward version of the tragic "going primitive" narrative discussed later in the chapter), the claim that pure men are degraded by sexual contact with the Other would have been familiar to readers of racialists like Arthur de Gobineau or Houston Chamberlain, as well as to readers familiar with the large body of literature, sermons, and polemics about "white" men who were seduced by Other women into slovenly, sinful, loose-living.[3] It's a sexualized terror of hybridity.

But, it's important to point out that the book is not logically an argument for racial purity, especially not for a white/nonwhite binary. Nordics intermarrying are the cause of the civilization *and* its fall, so hybridity can be good. The benefits of hybridity are also demonstrated in Grant's origin story of the Nordic race (since it came from the Alpine, there must have been a time when they were mixed), his history of Europe (which, as he says, has had mixtures for centuries), and the failure of the "pure" Nordics to create a civilization (it only occurs under conditions of hybridity). This is an important point, especially for thinking about what people mean when they say they were changed by reading the book. Even were his narrative right (it isn't), it wouldn't prove his claim (that we should maintain Nordic purity). In Grant's narrative, not only is hybridity actually beneficial, but this is not an argument for "whites" to stick together. After all, when civilizations collapse, it is not because "whites" have been overtaken numerically by nonwhites, but because Nordics have intermarried with the lower races of whites, such as Mediterraneans or Alpines.

The danger to the "great race" is not from nonwhites, but from the other two kinds of *whites*. As the Nordics weaken, the lower white races gain political power—precisely the process Grant believed he was watching in the rise of Irish, Italian, and Jewish political machines in the Northeast. Jonathan Spiro notes that Tom Buchanan in *Great Gatsby* has been reading a book that is almost certainly a sly reference to Madison Grant and his disciple Lothrop Stoddard ("this man Goddard"). Buchanan summarizes the book: "The idea is if we don't look out the white race will be—will be utterly submerged. It's all scientific stuff; it's been proved." But Buchanan is part of the mongrelized besieger class, not the besieged, and he has misread the book. Buchanan's reading represents a common misreading of the book, and it is a common misreading. (Theodore Bilbo and E. S. Cox—discussed in the next chapter—similarly misread the book.) So, the book's biggest impact comes from misreading. It is "influential" and "compelling" at bringing people to a conclusion it doesn't draw, and that is at odds with its argument and evidence.

Granted, it's an easy book to misread, since the author contradicts himself, equivocates on crucial terms (such as race), rejects and relies on the same claims to make his case (such as whether Caucasian is a race), and has a citation practice that makes it difficult (sometimes impossible) to determine the sources for his information. Thus, contradictory readings of the book can always be supported by a quote or two. The main thesis is easy enough to summarize, as it was even in its time a clichéd narrative (although nineteenth-century advocates of it didn't use the term "Nordic"). According to Grant, a particular kind of European "race" was the origin of all the best achievements in human history; when members of that race allowed their culture (or race) to become impure, the civilization collapsed. When purified, they would rise again. But Grant's argument is hopelessly entangled.

For instance, Grant never gives a clear definition of his central term: race. The closest that he gets to a definition is:

> It will be necessary for the reader to strip his mind of all preconceptions as to race, since modern anthropology, when applied to history, involves an entire change of definition. We must, first of all, realize that race pure and simple, the physical and psychical structure of man, is something entirely distinct from either nationality or language, and that race lies today at the base of all the phenomena of modern society, just as it has done throughout the unrecorded eons of the past. (xvii)

Grant here positions himself against the reader, who has preconceptions as to race, suggesting that Grant himself has no such preconceptions. He invites the reader to become the sort of person whose beliefs are not based in preconception. But, what exactly is this new and more precise definition? Neither new nor precise. The idea that race is not determined by either nationality or language, and that it involved both internal and external qualities, was already common enough in 1896 (twenty years before Grant published his book) such that Henry Cabot Lodge could refer to it in an anti-immigration speech (2819).[4] That is, Grant's definition or race confirms preconceptions while claiming to be a rejection of them. It thus makes the same move so interesting in positive reviews of Grant—claiming that something is new when it isn't, and that something is free of prejudice when its main function is confirming prejudice. More importantly, that really isn't a definition of race, but a description of how people should think about it.[5]

Skull shape is important to his argument, and it too is troubled. He says that, "skull shape, eye color, hair color, and stature are sufficient to enable us to differentiate clearly between the three main races of Europe" (26), but skull shape can't be used with other races; it "is of little value in classifying the Amerinds," (20) since they seem to have all types, and it is entirely to be ignored in regard to Africa, since everyone in Africa has long skulls (20). Because Asia has a similar distribution of

WHEN THE CHOIR CLAIMS

skull types to Europe, Grant speculates that "Thibet and the western Himalayans were probably the centre of radiation of all the round skulls of the world" (20). Yet, when the similarities between European and African skulls comes up, suddenly having identical skulls "is no necessary indication of relationship" (21).[6] It's useful evidence if it supports his argument, but irrelevant if it doesn't.

Grant's acknowledgment that physical characteristics do not consistently signify race strongly vexes his argument. While the title of chapter 4 is "The Physical Basis of Race," if race is based in physical characteristics, how is it that people with different physical characteristics have the same race? Throughout *Passing of the Great Race*, Grant admits that individuals within a "race" do not all have the same physical and psychical structure, that people with the same physical structure do not necessarily have the same "race," that hybridity is the norm, and that the very notion of an evolving race necessitates a period of racial hybridity as one "race" develops from another. "Race" cannot be a stable and immutable ontologically grounded category in a narrative that depends on evolution. But Grant tries to have it both ways—races are immutable and are signified by the same physical characteristics, *and* physical characteristics don't consistently signify stable categories—in one sentence.

> Every human being unites in himself the blood of thousands of ancestors, stretching back through thousands of years, superimposed upon a prehuman inheritance of still greater antiquity, and the face and body of every living man offer an intricate mass of hieroglyphs that science will some day learn to read and interpret. (31).

The evolutionary narrative requires that there was a time when the current taxonomy was not present, but his political narrative requires that the current taxonomy (and hierarchy) is eternal. That is, for Grant, race is both mutable and immutable.

The grounding of social values in nature gets Grant into the common contradiction of needing to pass laws in order to prohibit behavior that is supposed to be unnatural. He says,

> Race feeling may be called prejudice by those whose careers are cramped by it, but it is a natural antipathy which serves to maintain the purity of type. The unfortunate fact that nearly all species of men interbreed freely leaves us no choice in the matter. (193)

Were race feeling really natural, then men would never "interbreed" because they would feel too much antipathy; after all, we don't have to pass laws to force people to submit to gravity. Grant's use of the term "natural" doesn't mean that it is a law of nature, but a characteristic in our nature, which can be resisted, much like Christian explanations of original sin. But, instead of acknowledging that his feelings about race mixing reside in him, and are *his* feelings, he asserts an ontological grounding for them, as though they are in nature.

In the midst of this narrative of the benefits of hybridity, Grant intersperses claims that it is always disastrous. Despite his lovely maps of Europe showing the various white races coexisting in Europe for a thousand years, he says,
Where two distinct species are located side by side history and biology teach that but one of two things can happen; either one race drives the other out . . . or else they amalgamate and form a population . . . in which the lower type ultimately preponderates. (69). Yet his maps show coexistence. In one of few places where he relies on genetics, he says,

> Whether we like to admit it or not, the result of the mixture of two races, in the long run, gives us a race reverting to the more ancient, generalized and lower type. The cross between a white man and an Indian is an Indian; the cross between a white man and a negro is a negro; the cross between a white man and a Hindu is a Hindu; and the cross between any of the three European races and a Jew is a Jew.

Since a higher and lower race always result in lowering the race, how did the "higher" race of Alpine arise from the "lower" race of Mediterranean, or the "higher" race of Nordic arise from the "lower" race of Alpine? If his narrative is right, then his central claim about hybridity is wrong. If his central claim is right, then his entire book is wrong.[7]

This notion of mixing always bringing decline was a common assertion among supporters of segregation and restrictive immigration, although it had already been refuted by Franz Boas in 1884. His "Half-Blood Indian: An Anthropometric Study," in Michael Little's words, "demonstrated that the stature of hybrids was greater than for either parent, that facial measurements were intermediate, but tended toward one parent or the other, and that fertility of Native American–European unions was equivalent to full Native American unions" (58). But, of course, Boas had also already shown the head shape data didn't prove what Grant said it did, and that had little impact on Grant or his acolytes.

Superficially read, Grant could *look* perfectly reliable, as his text has all the markers of scientific discourse. He never uses the first person, often hedges his claims, and provides an overwhelming amount of data. To take a passage, selected at random:

Similar expansions of civilization and organization of empire, followed the incursion of the Nordic Persians into the land of the round skull Medes, and the introduction of Sanskrit into India by the Nordic Sacae who conquered that peninsula. These outbursts of progress, due to the first contact and mixture of the contrasted races, are, however, only transitory and pass with the last lingering trace of Nordic blood.

In India the blood of these Aryan-speaking invaders has been absorbed by the dark Hindu, and in the final event only their synthetic speech survived. (191)

The passage, coming just after an explanation of a discussion of ancient Greece, appears to be detailed and precise. There is a range of abstraction from very high (the claim about "expansions of civilization") to much more specific (the apparent precision of "Nordic Sacae"); it looks like a paragraph proving a claim. But it's actually a fairly strange passage, and the relation of the specific to the general is somewhat murky. The two paragraphs are entirely unsupported and without mention of any archeological, linguistic, or anthropological data that would suggest Grant's narrative is accurate. He does not even mention any other authorities who tell the same narrative. (In the second edition of *Passing of the Great Race*, which was supposed to respond to criticism that the book lacked sufficient evidence, Grant removes commas from the paragraphs quoted above, but leaves them otherwise unchanged.)

Grant's relationship to authority is surprisingly complicated. For instance, as part of his argument that the Nordics are responsible for the rise of significant human accomplishments, he posits a circle: Alpines originated in the Caucasus, went west, and, in some vague way, led to Nordics, who went east and back down through the Himalayas and Caucasus. He says,

As mentioned above, the grasslands and steppes of Russia extend north of the Caucasus Mountains and the Caspian Sea to ancient Bactria, now Turkestan. This whole country was occupied by the Nordic Sacae and the closely related Massagetae. At a very early date, probably about the beginning of the second millennium B.C., or perhaps even earlier, the first Nordics crossed over the Afghan passes, entered the plains of India, and organized a state in the Penjab, "the land of the five rivers," bringing with them Aryan speech among a population probably of the Mediterranean type, and represented today by the Dravidians. The Nordic Sacae arrived later in India and introduced the Vedas, religious poems, which were first transmitted orally, and which were reduced to written form in Old Sanskrit by the Brahmans at the comparatively late date of 300 A.D. From this classic Sanskrit are derived all the modern Aryan languages of Hindustan, as well as the Singalese of Ceylon and the chief dialects of Assam. (223)

This is the narrative version of the map he gives (in all four editions) showing Nordic movement eastward and then southward, and it is the foundation for his claims about Nordic superiority. If the movement went the other way, then either Nordics do not antedate Alpines, or they are not responsible for the Persian and Indian civilizations. In later editions, in which he tried to respond to criticism of his lack of evidence, he gave footnotes for the passages with this narrative (somewhat shorter than in the first edition). The footnotes for page 172 cite Ripley's *Races of Europe,* the parts in which Ripley asserts rates of occurrence of blonds and brunettes in the relevant parts of Russia (346–8, and 352ff.). Grant's other citations are similar. They do not support his narrative of Nordic movement west to east and southward; at best, they support the claim that people with fair hair live there (meaning, possibly, a movement of east to west, or south to north, or even random development).

Yet Ripley, the authority on whom Grant relies most heavily, does not support Grant's obsession with (and prizing of) purity. Ripley also uses terms that Grant rejects as meaningless (such as "Teuton"), and explicitly rejects the argument that is so important to Grant, regarding "purity" of races in America. Ripley quotes with approval Huxley's comment regarding "the serene impartiality of a mongrel" (456), adding that, "We have no monopoly of inheritance" in any race. Europe is no better: "Intermixture, migration, the influences of environment, and chance variation have been long at work in Europe. The result has been to reduce the pure types, either of blond or brunet, to an absolute minority" (66). That Grant disagrees with his major authority is not necessarily a problem, if he has evidence from another authority with which to refute Ripley, or even some basis for his argument other than argument from authority, but he has neither. Grant's text is primarily a narrative argument, and it is made by assertion. Hence, that his arguments from authority fail to support his claims means that we have nothing other than his word that what he is saying is true; it is oracular.

As critics noted at the time (discussed below), Grant's book was largely a rehashing of Arthur Gobineau (especially his 1853 *Essai sur l'inégalité des races humaines*) and Houston Chamberlain's *Foundations of the Nineteenth Century* (1899). Yet, just as Grant's book doesn't quite support Buchanan's claim (or, as will be argued later, American segregation laws), so Gobineau didn't quite support Grant (or Chamberlain). As the *International Encyclopedia of the Social Sciences* says,

What Chamberlain, supporter Robert Knox, and others failed to acknowledge was Gobineau's insistence that the Aryan ideal had been
overtaken by history. They also overlooked Gobineau's less than flattering condemnation of white Americans as "an assortment of the
most degenerate races of olden-day Europe," as well as his resistance to
American treatment of slaves and Native Americans, and his argument
that racial mixing, and specifically black blood, had produced artistic
mastery. (336)

Chamberlain's two-volume *Foundations of the Nineteenth Century* has many of
the characteristics that James Darsey identifies as part of the "prophetic tradition," especially the author's presenting himself as someone who has had direct
access to the Truth, and who, like a prophet, speaks for God, without supporting
data (nobody asks Isaiah to support his claims). *Foundations* is largely a broad
assertion, with little or no data; the reader adopts Chamberlain's point of view or
rejects the argument (or, as in the case of Redesdale's famous introduction to the
book, endorses the assertions with which the reader already agrees before reading
the book, and rejects the ones with which the reader disagrees).

Such a posture wasn't unusual in the nineteenth century for the "human
sciences," especially since Chamberlain's book wasn't scientific, and wasn't pretending to be, but was more in the "natural philosophy" tradition (of Gobineau
or perhaps even Hegel). He was trying to describe, as he says, the unitary vision
enabled by art, rather than science.

> The mastery of such a task, scientifically, is impossible; it is only artistic
> power, aided by those secret parallels which exist between the world
> of vision and of thought, by that tissue which—like ether—fills and
> connects the whole world, that can, if fortune is favourable, produce a
> unity here which is complete, and that, too, though only fragments be
> employed to make it. If the artist does succeed in this, then his work has
> not been superfluous: the immeasurable has been brought within the
> scope of vision, the shapeless has acquired a form. (lix–lx)

Chamberlain claims this process is not the creation of new things; it is an almost
mystical perception of what is really in the world: "Before be reasons, he must
know: before he gives shape to a thing, he must test it. He cannot look upon
himself as master, he is but a servant, the servant of truth" (lxi). Chamberlain's
"method," then, is to look at the "immeasurable world of facts" and infer the "se-
cret parallels which exist between the world of vision and of thought" in order to
"produce a unity" (lix). Chamberlain's ontology is foundational (there is a reality

external to human perception) and his epistemology is simultaneously naïve realism (there is not any particular difficulty perceiving the facts) *and* Romantic, in that one perceives the true meaning of the facts through an internal vision. It is a kind of sloppy (if common) Kantianism.

Thomas Hylland Eriksen and Finn Sivert Nielsen, in their *History of Anthropology,* argue that, after Kant,

> knowledge no longer consisted of mental images that reflected reality as it is in itself more or less adequately, but of mental *judgements* based on criteria that are subjective (they exist only in the mind), but also objective (they are universally present in every knowing mind). (16)

For those in the natural philosophy tradition, such as Chamberlain, this process meant that taxonomies of race exist simultaneously in the world and in the mind of the person perceptive enough to recognize them. C. Loring Brace has pointed out the importance of this Romanticist approach to anthropology, especially in Ripley and his followers. Brace quotes a passage in which Ripley makes a kind of rhetorical retreat to races as "types" that ends with Ripley's insistence that types do and do not exist: "Rarely, if indeed ever, do we discover a single individual corresponding to our racial type in every detail. It exists for us nevertheless" (112, qtd. in Brace 27). Brace glosses the quote: "Needless to say, this is not science but a peculiarly American form of Romantic faith bolstered by an admiration for what was perceived as continental sophistication" (27).

This approach to science isn't a method, but a rhetorical posture. Such practitioners present themselves as someone who can perceive "racial types," despite that they exist only as ideas (so it's a kind of neo-Platonism). And, since these practitioners are making claims about all of history, they are one privileged to see the world in what McClintock calls "panoptical time"; that is, "the image of global history consumed—at a glance—in a single spectacle from a point of privileged invisibility" (37). McClintock is not describing Ripley or Chamberlain specifically, but the pro-imperialist authorities on race, including them, whose rhetorical stance was as if from the center of Bentham's imagined Panopticon (made famous by Foucault). The Panopticon, a set of prison cells arranged in a circle with the jailer at the center, enabled the jailer to see all inmates at once, a view not available to any of the inmates. The fantasy of the oracular voice in the natural philosophy tradition was that some men, by virtue of their position, can see into the very souls of others—the world and all time are laid bare to their vision—in ways that others cannot see into them. For Chamberlain, Ripley, Grant, and other racists, that epistemological position is constituted by race. Thus, an Aryan like Chamberlain or a Nordic like Grant could generalize about all other races because his race gives him that position in the center of the Panopticon—other races are trapped in the cells. Race is an epistemological position.

Grant took large parts of his argument from Gobineau, as well as Chamberlain, and cited them both to support his position, but, of the various books on which Grant relies (sometimes, as Spiro points out, to the point of plagiarism) the most influential is probably William Z. Ripley's 1899 *Races of Europe*. Ripley, although a Romanticist, has a different style, one closer to that described by Gross et al.: "The objectivity and efficiency of scientific prose have a single purpose: to lay bare for close scrutiny the arguments that scientists make in establishing new facts and explanations about the material world" (216). Like Warren, Ripley presents his evidence in ways that enable the reader to find the sources of the evidence, and Grant does no such thing.

One can see the difference by comparing two extremely similar passages (in fact, Grant may be paraphrasing Ripley at points). Ripley's two-page discussion of the ethnic makeup of the area around Rome cites well over a dozen authorities in the six footnotes. Grant's discussion of the racial makeup of Rome provides no citations at all. It also has no evidence, and it is circular.[8] After asserting that the Roman state is an example of the benefit of mixing Mediterranean and Nordic blood, he says,

> To what extent the Mediterranean race entered into the blood and civilization of Rome, it is now difficult to say, but the traditions of the Eternal City, its love of organization, of law and military efficiency, as well as Roman ideals of family life, loyalty, and truth, point clearly to a Nordic rather than to a Mediterranean origin. (139)

Rome's excellent qualities must have had a Nordic origin, because only if they came from Nordics is his argument that all good things come from Nordics true. Or, to put it more bluntly, Grant's thesis is the only support for an example that is supposed to support his thesis—like Warren's use of land ownership patterns, a very straightforward example of circular reasoning.[9]

The oracular posture polarizes audience response to acceptance or rejection. Grant's data can't be investigated by the reader because it doesn't make sense. The data functions, not to support the claims about race, but to support the implicit claims about Grant: that he is a knower, who can see beyond the contradictory and complicated world to the clear and foundational taxonomy behind it. This is a slightly different rhetorical relationship with the audience from the one Warren establishes, in that the audience could see Warren's maps, and could see for themselves that "the Japanese" did own a lot of land near power lines, water lines, and factories. Grant's readers are instead left with passages like:

The Hallstatt iron culture did not extend into western Europe, and the smelting and extensive use of iron in south Britain and northwest Europe are of much later date and occur in what is known as the La Tene Period, usually assigned to the fifth and fourth century B.C. Iron weapons were known in England much earlier, perhaps as far back as 800 or 1000 B.C., but were very rare and were probably importations from the Continent.

Even in context, it is not at all clear what the significance of these details is for his overall argument, nor who calls it the "La Tene Period," what the Hallstatt iron culture was, or what the adverb "earlier" refers to.

Expert discourse is often obscure to laypeople, and the obscurity of the language can seem to push the lay audience into an either/or position: either they accept the authority of the expert, and infer that the claims make sense; or, they reject the authority of the expert, and reject the argument. Grant's rhetoric precludes any assessment of the relationship between claim and evidence. As with conspiracy rhetoric (with which expert discourse has much in common), the very obscurity of the argument seems to enhance its credibility, and something like that appears to happen with people who are impressed with Grant.[10] The obscurity of Grant's language might, by a layperson, be mistaken for legitimate intradisciplinary precision—a posture that makes it difficult for a layperson to assess his argument. If one doesn't know what the Halstatt iron culture is, or why its extension into Western Europe matters, it might seem that one can't determine whether Grant has adequately supported his conclusions. But Grant's argument exemplifies how one need not know what he means by his terms (such as "Sacae-Nordic") in order to know that his argument is invalid; his problems were rhetorical, and can be exposed through rhetorical analysis.

Problems with Grant's Argument

While Grant made many discipline-specific errors, the major flaws in his argument—that it was internally inconsistent, relied on problematic data (to the extent that it had data), failed to define the most important terms or use them consistently, failed to support its claims—could have been inferred by looking at his overall argument. In addition, the major flaws in Grant's argument were noted by Grant's contemporaries when the book was first published in 1916.[11] My favorite critique is probably Bolton Hall's short review in the July 1918 issue of *The Public*, which says,

> One would almost expect that anyone writing on "The Passing of the Great Race" would try to prove first that it is a distinctive Race; second that it is Great; third that it is Passing. No such necessity oppresses Mr.

M. Grant. He assumes them all, not even trying to show why, if it was a "Great Race," it could not protect itself. (Hall 340)

Reviews at the time, both critical and favorable, noted how difficult it was to follow Grant's evidence. A critical review in the *Nation* says, "It is difficult to keep pace with Mr. Grant's quick changes of reasoning" (noting a passage in which Grant contradicts himself about mountaineers, "Shamanthropology"139). An anonymous review in the *Spectator* called the book "pseudo-scientific" and said, "We cannot help thinking that Mr. Grant has let his theories and a few skull measurements carry him away into the realms of fantasy" (386). A very short and somewhat unenthusiastic 1918 review ("The book . . . has some interesting features") in the *International Journal of Ethics* points out two errors—one in which Grant ties the origin of iron to two different cultures and dates (about eight hundred years apart); and a second fairly technical one regarding the dates of a culture (295). An anonymous reviewer in the *Journal of Geography* quotes two passages, the first to the effect that, in Grant's words, "It is race, always race, that produces genius" (from page 86) and the second passage (from 152) explains that the Nordic type's development required certain climatic conditions. So, as the reviewer says, "In short, the author considers that race is everything and then holds that race gets its essential qualities from geographical environment" (207).

Other reviews went into more detail about the issues with the book. For instance, Isaac Berkson's *Theories of Americanization* (published in 1920) carefully explains the problem with Grant's equivocation on the term "race," an equivocation common both then and now. Berkson says there are two ways to use the word "race": one to mean ethnic group, and another to mean people whose outward appearance is similar, but who may actually have different origins (82). In a long footnote Berkson argues that Grant's book is an "excellent" illustration of the "error of double and equivocal usage" (82, quoting as an example a passage from Grant's book).[12] A review of another book, *Germany's Ethnic Pathology*, says that the book is "based on some fallacies from Madison Grant's 'Passing of the Great Race' evidently accepted as facts" and goes on to say,

> This is merely another sad illustration of how really mischievous inaccurate and biased books of this nature may prove among people not directly and reliably acquainted with Anthropology. Few dilettante products of recent times have caused more popular confusion than the "Passing of the Great Race." (92)

One of the more famous negative reviews of *Passing* was Franz Boas's January 1917 review in the *New Republic* called "Inventing a Great Race" in which Boas compares the argument of the book to contemporary anthropology. Boas points out that the book is "practically a modern edition of Gobineau, and a reflex of the opinions of Chamberlain" (305). The data "are based on dogmatic assumptions which cannot endure criticism" largely because they are based on a conflation of heredity and race, whereas "the hereditary lines that are present in every single race are very diverse" (305). Grant, according to Boas, ignores the extent to which the traits that are crucial to Grant's classifications (such as height and head shape) had already been shown to be strongly influenced by environment. Boas notes Grant's inconsistencies—"it would lead us too far to enter into the numerous inconsistencies in the treatment of this subject" (305)—and mentions a few: that Grant sometimes "considers the form of the head as of fundamental classificatory value, in others he treats it as irrelevant" (305), that he does the same with height and environment (both of which sometimes matter and sometimes don't). Grant, correctly, according to Boas, insists that language and nationality are not importantly related, but then Grant "falls back repeatedly upon the assumption of identity of race and language" (305). Grant's narrative has some truth, Boas says, but is "mainly built up on assumptions that have been selected, as it would seem, solely because, if true, they might demonstrate the superiority of the northwest European type" (306). Boas says, "We cannot follow in detail the reconstruction of the history of the European races," which is more or less my reading as well. It sounds impressive as one is reading it, but is almost impossible to formulate. Grant's discussion of the Aryan language is based on outdated notions about language falsified by "even the most rudimentary knowledge" of the various relevant linguistic groups, and is therefore meaningless. Boas, as an anthropologist, should have more credibility than Grant, an amateur, and yet his criticism was rejected because of his being Jewish: a Jewish anthropologist is inherently less credible about anthropology than a WASP amateur.

Douglas Walton's summary of scholarly discussions of the appeal to authority (and whether it is fallacious) emphasizes that the fallacious/nonfallacious argument about the move hinges largely on whether one sees the appeal to authority as something that ends the discussion. That is, it's fallacious to assume that any interlocutor appealing to an authority means the conclusion has been reached. If I cite Antonin Scalia to support a claim I make about the meaning of the third amendment, my interlocutor might challenge Scalia's credentials, the relevance of his claim to the one I'm making, or otherwise rebut my attempt to end the argument in a quote from him. At that point, for argumentation to continue, I'm obligated to do one of several things: support my implicit claim that Scalia is a credible expert; support my explicit claim by finding another expert who makes the same argument as Scalia; retract or modify my claim; or find different support for it.

Walton argues that an appeal to authority shouldn't be seen as necessarily ending an argument because we can argue about whether someone really is an authority. Often there is evidence that we can consider—does the evidence confirm or contradict the authority's claims (*Appeal* 51)?[13] The second method is to look for consistency within what the authority has said on the subject: "The authority may have made other pronouncements on the same subject, statements that may either support or be inconsistent with the opinion currently in question" (*Appeal* 51). If the authority has contradictory evidence or contradictory arguments, that does not mean the claims are false, but that, rhetorically and logically, the appeal to authority is inadequate. If my interlocutor points out that Scalia's stance on the third amendment is too muddled to be able to characterize consistently, that does not necessarily mean everything else I say is wrong, but it does mean that I need to provide some additional support. If I refuse to support my claims, we are no longer in the realm of argumentation; I am asking that my word be accepted on the basis of nonfalsifiable reverence.[14]

And this is why the presence of criticisms that identify the major problems in Grant's era matter for how we assess his argument. The reviews challenged Grant with what Walton calls "an inconsistency of commitment"—that is, having made incompatible claims. And Walton says what should happen under those circumstances.

> If an inconsistency of commitment is challenged by the other party, the party who has been challenged needs to resolve the issue one way or the other. A participant may need to retract commitments. It is taken to be an indicator of rational argumentation in a persuasion dialogue if a participant makes a decision to retract one of a pair of inconsistent propositions she had previously been committed to, once the inconsistency of commitments has been pointed out by the other party. (*Witness* 167)

Grant did add sources in later editions, and he did make some revisions, but his sources and citations didn't solve the logical problems, especially not the major ones. He was aware of the criticism, but didn't respond rhetorically; instead, he tried to get Boas fired. Grant wasn't engaged in argumentation.

Grant's rhetoric was oracular, and the important impact of his book on readers was not that he moved them to believe specific claims about races (to which many readers who praised the book didn't assent) but that he confirmed the perception that their preferred racial hierarchy (about which they didn't necessarily agree with Grant) was both eschatologically and ontologically grounded. The pleasure of Grant's book comes not from specific propositions (most of which were incoherent) about the passing of any supposed race, but from his confirmation of a pleasing epistemology, eschatology, and ontology. Thus, like Cleon, Warren, or the Supreme Court justices, all of whom presented themselves as sources of authority because they, unlike their opponents, were submissive to the authority of reality, so Grant models an intellectual authority and submission at one and the same moment.

Positive Responses to Grant

If the argument was so flawed, and rejected by experts in the discipline from which Grant was drawing, why did it have such a positive reception? The positive reception among racialist science is puzzling since, as Spiro says, "almost nothing in *The Passing of the Great Race* is new" (157); it "is a compendium of the work of other scholars, and almost every paragraph can be directly traced" to other racialist authors (157). Even positive reviewers noted its lack of originality: "The book contains little with which the specialist in all these fields is not already familiar" (Hyde 24). The very positive anonymous review in the *Journal of Heredity* says that "the book contains little with which specialists are not familiar" ("The Great Race Passes" 34). William Gregory's review of the second edition says in regard to the first, "No doubt those who were familiar with Ripley's *The Races of Europe,* were not altogether unprepared for these conclusions" (135). Others noted that his "theories of race" (*Theosophical Quarterly* 385) and "conclusions" (Nye) came from elsewhere.[15]

Yet, even reviewers who noted that the argument was not new also claimed it was. Hyde called it "novel." H. F. Osborne, in the fawning preface to *Passing,* says "European history has been written in terms of nationality and of language, but never before in terms of race," and he describes the argument as "wholly original in treatment."[16] One reviewer (G. H. B.), in *Journal of Race Development,* approvingly quotes Osborne's assertion about newness from the preface, explaining that *Passing* "presents a new phase of the old quarrel between the rival claims of 'heredity' and of 'environment.' . . . It is heredity, says the author, that is, race, which is the great factor in determining the progress of nations" (153–4). Notice the easy equation of "race" and "heredity," the conflation criticized by Boas and Berkson, and intermittently contradicted in Grant (since some racial characteristics are inherited and some are produced by environment). This same easy equation is made by the anonymous reviewer in *Bookseller* (November 15, 1916), who says, "The story of the world's life is here written from the point of view of race—of heredity, rather than environment" (724). Some reviewers assumed Grant had scientific expertise. The November 1916 review in *Bookseller* says the book has "a sure foundation in science" (724). Elsewhere, reviewers claimed scientific expertise and grounding that neither Grant nor his book had: "In the field of anthropology he has followed the latest authorities" (*Journal of Heredity* 34).[17] And John Corbin, in the bibliographic notes for his book, uses an appeal to authority to argue that Grant must be right: "For the general accuracy and soundness of his conclusions Professor Osborn is sufficient authority" (344). Thus, Grant's argument must be true because an authority has said so. Yet, what conclusions does Corbin mean? Corbin says that he disagrees with Grant's claim that the Greeks maintained their purity. Corbin says it is "incontrovertible" that "the Nordic and the Mediterranean races mingled to produce Greek genius" (344). The first two times I read the book I also read Grant as claiming purity for the Greeks, because there are places where he seems to make that claim (they were "unmixed" around the siege of Troy, 145) but Grant also explicitly says they were mixed (145). I mentioned earlier Ryback's summary of Grant's book, in which he says that the Nordics originated in Scandinavia. That's also how I initially read the book, but, in fact, Grant's claim is that the Nordics arose in the Baltic region (152).

Walter Woodburn Hyde's generally positive review has the same contradiction as Grant's book—that everything is race except when it isn't. Although he says that "race alone is the real basis of modern society" (19), when he has to explain why the Nordic race is dying out, he appeals to environmental causes: "By nature [the Nordics] are adjusted to certain environmental conditions. . . . Away from this environment . . . they pine away and cease to breed. It was not only malaria but sunlight which caused them to disappear after the great classical period; there the Mediterraneans, naturally acclimatized, have finally caused them to disappear" (23). One might infer from his argument that the Mediterraneans are the fittest for that environment, as well as for the urban environment: Nordics "are less adapted to urban life than the Mediterraneans." He even reproduces Grant's deeply problematic argument that Nordics are prone to alcoholism and consumption: "They are furthermore suffering by selection through alcoholism—a peculiarly Nordic vice—and disease, especially consumption" (23).

One of the more puzzling sorts of claims is in Hyde's review. He says, "The author's literary brilliancy, force, directness, and clearness of exposition, courage to state novel and startling positions—all make it a masterly production" (24). Hyde here has three claims, each of which is worth considering. First, that the text is clear. As Spiro says, before quoting a long and largely unintelligible passage chosen at random, "Passages like the following, to pick one at random, may be pedantic nonsense, but they certainly give the impression that the author is in command of his facts" (146). The prose has an odd quality of looking as though it is meaningful, but is filled with unexplained terms and unclear relations; it is far from clear. Or, as Hyde says, "Great masses of facts are compressed with almost epigrammatic brevity into a few pages" (24). Second, Hyde, like many readers and reviewers, says that Grant's argument is novel, even startling, *and* admits that it isn't new at all (24, previously quoted). Third, Grant is courageous for saying these things; yet it hardly takes any courage for Grant to tell his readers what they already believe and what justifies the current hierarchies.

This puzzling insistence that a text that is neither new nor courageous is both shows up in regard to other xenophobic, racist, and homophobic texts. Nazi and neo-Nazi autobiographies are conversion narratives, in which the protagonist begins as a good liberal, and is forced, by the overwhelming evidence, to realize the truth of anti-Semitism, racism, homophobia, and so on. One sees this in texts ranging from Hitler's *Mein Kampf* to David Duke's *My Awakening*, a bildungsroman, in which the protagonist, once converted, takes on the difficult work of speaking the truth to others. In fact, of course, there was no such conversion; nor do the racist and homophobic views advocated by these individuals amount to extraordinarily brave acts of conscience. Rather than the audience being brave to agree with the brave author, a more accurate description of audience response is what Hyde says about reading Grant: "The chief impression on the reader is one of satisfaction." The book is *satisfying* to a certain kind of reader. Hyde admits "One feels that in the present unstable condition of many problems of anthropological science the book is too simple, too satisfying" (24–25).

Even positive reviewers acknowledged that the evidence was problematic. Nye says that "the thesis of the Nordic race . . . over the Alpine . . . and the Mediterranean . . . is derived from evidence falling short of scientific demonstration" (377).[18] Although the second edition was supposed to provide more evidence, it did not; even positive reviewers admitted that "the author rarely if ever discusses disputed points" and, while he now has a bibliography, "nowhere does he insert a footnote or give a reference to the source of his information" (Woods, *Science* 419).[19] Nye noted problems with two of Grant's premises (the "strict immutability of somatological or bodily characters" and the notion that the Nordic race "contains the most desirable traits"), but all of these criticisms go to Grant's argument that the Nordic race is the best within the "white" races (377). While Nye notes that Grant's conclusions are similar to various others, he still claims that this is a "new scientific method" (378), a confusing claim, since he had said that the "method" was based on faulty premises and lacked evidence.

Some insisted that, despite the poor evidence, the book was true, albeit for reasons other than the ones Grant gives. Woods, for instance, admits that Grant's evidence is weak; he says the argument is true because it is supported by statistical evidence (419). Yet Grant doesn't use statistical evidence. The anonymous review in the *Journal of Heredity* acknowledges that "in the field of genetics the author makes some misstatements" (34). Gregory's review of the second edition admits that "in the earlier editions of this work even the favorably disposed reader could not escape the impression that it was an *ex parte* statement of the case" (135). In short, positive reviewers praise the thesis, but not the argument, and endorse the conclusions but take issue with the evidence that is supposed to ground the conclusions.

Nye is clear that the main virtue of the book is not the quality of its argument (which is flawed) but its political utility: "If it aids in securing in our population a sentiment whose aim shall be the attaining of as large a proportion as possible of persons whose traits are of the greatest value to our social order, it will have performed a valuable service" (378). The review in *Theosophical Quarterly* also praised the book because it is useful for Theosophists' political agenda: the book "is one of the best arguments against the validity of democracy which I know" (385, 386). Woods's positive review notes the political utility of the book (the evidence of which he has criticized): "This is a book that will do much to widen the rapidly expanding interest in eugenics and help to disseminate the ever-growing conviction among scientific men of the supreme importance of heredity" (420). That is, positive reviewers were quite open about the fact that they approved of the book (even when they disputed the evidence) because they found the conclusions politically useful. That admission—this is true because politically useful, even if argumentatively flawed—troubles the tendency reviewers have to claim that *they* are motivated by the truth, and the opposition is politically motivated.

As mentioned earlier, defenders of Grant dismiss critics as ethnically motivated. Frederick Adams Woods, a "Nordic," who published "A Review of Reviews" in the *Journal of Heredity* (a pro-eugenics journal) says,

> In closing this too brief review, which is really more of an objective analysis of the book's reception, it is interesting to summarize the matter. Nearly all the reviews published in scientific journals or in the leading newspapers were either favorable or moderately favorable. The distinctly unfavorable were either important British reviews, which were apparently actuated by war-emotion, or were published in American newspapers and magazines and signed by persons of non-Nordic race. (95)

Woods asserts that this reaction on the part of the critics comes from the tendency men have to "resent an injury to the group" (95). Yet, it's interesting that Woods doesn't draw the logically connected conclusion about his own reactions—most of the favorable reviews were signed by reviewers with "Nordic" names. If people are motivated to defend their race, then the "Nordic's" favorable review of the book is just as much a manifestation of this sense of racial feeling as negative reviews by non-Nordics.[20]

This is, of course, a manifestation of the epistemological privilege of whiteness, that, because whiteness is unmarked, it is invisible; it is the perspective of no perspective, and, hence, synonymous with objectivity. This is an example of the assumption that whiteness provides an objective viewpoint.

> Whites are taught to see their perspectives as objective and representative of reality. . . . Within this construction, whites can represent humanity, while people of color, who are never just people but always most particularly black people, Asian people, etc., can only represent their own racialized experience. (DiAngelo, "White Fragility" 59).

Grant's epistemic authority doesn't come from citing other authorities, providing evidence that the reading can follow to his conclusions, or having an internally consistent argument: he has epistemic authority to the extent that the reader already agrees with him and is impressed by his insight.[21]

For a sympathetic reader, Grant's inconsistencies, incoherence, and fallacies might enhance his rhetorical effectiveness. His equivocation regarding "Nordic," for instance, in his text and in his maps means that anyone who does not have absolutely black hair could consider themselves Nordic. He says "the range of blond hair color in pure Nordic peoples runs from flaxen and red to shades of chestnut and brown" (22), and his maps have little circles throughout Western Europe, so that, no matter where one's ancestors were from (including Italy or Ireland), one could imagine one's ancestry as Nordic. In other words, the very quality for which Grant was condemned by critics (his equivocation) was quite probably what made his argument attractive to a large number of his readers.[22]

In the first decade of the twentieth century, members of the WASP elite faced two paradoxically related challenges, both a consequence of the increase in immigration. The United States may not be a nation of immigrants, but it wouldn't be unfair to call it a nation constructed by anxiety about immigrants. The early Anglo settlements had anxiety about how to assimilate new kinds of people, with Bradford's *Plymouth Plantation* expressing anxiety about new immigrants' [the New England Puritan settlers were immigrants, after all, and they didn't worry about their own corrupting influence—immigrants always worry about the new crop] corrupting influence; by the late seventeenth century, New England Puritan ministers were performing jeremiads about how much purer the previous generation was, Pennsylvania Quakers were worrying about the corrupting influence of German immigrants, and everyone was worried about Catholics. Immigrant anxiety in American political discourse consistently relies on the same narrative: our origin was in the strength and will of a small, stable, and homogeneous group, and the values that united them; new members must be able to adopt those values, take a lower place in the stable hierarchy created in our origin, and make themselves just as homogeneous, or our community will collapse. The anxiety is that something about *this* group of immigrants—Anglicans, Germans, Catholics, the Irish, the Italians, the Jews, the Mexicans—makes them incapable of that assimilation, and they will displace us, create a new order, change the cultural values, or otherwise bring disorder to what has been ordered and stable until their arrival. This narrative is always there, and always false.

Documents from every era show very little perception of a clear and stable hierarchy, and a longing for a recent past in which things were clear and stable. Servants became masters, dissenters thrived, groups lost their hegemony, or held on to it by expanding the definition of "Christian," "white," or whatever term was supposed to identify the in-group. A new origin story was invented that erased the conflict and anxiety of previous generations and the myth of a *new* crisis was created. For instance, the narrow definition of correct in-group used by the New England Puritans (their very specific kind of dissenter, not including Baptists, Anglicans, Catholics, Quaker, let alone later groups like Methodists or Mormons) in the hands of twentieth-century fundagelical advocates of theocracy has become a vague notion of "Christian" (a category that includes groups the New England Puritans would not have considered "Christian"), but the argument remains the same: that the in-group founded our country, and if we lose the in-group identity, our country will lose its foundation. In the late nineteenth century, there was anxiety about losing the homogeneity created by the political hegemony of the white (a category that didn't include all groups that now call themselves white) Anglo-Saxon Protestant; recent jeremiads about the dangers of "Mexican" immigration (or "shithole countries") is exactly the same anxiety, but about more recent groups. The anti-Catholic fear-mongering of Samuel Morse (who also advocated a "Protestant" foundation to democracy) becomes the anti-Eastern European fear-mongering of Grant. In each case, the narrative that we are now on the brink of catastrophe because *this* group is about to destroy our homogeneity is maintained by an unacknowledged expansion of the in-group identity and fear-mongering about a supposedly "new" threat.[23]

To some extent, the scare quotes on "new" are unjustified: each immigrant wave is new in some way—a new group, a new number, and just simply new individuals. By the late nineteenth century, the United States was seeing a new proportion of immigrants, both in ethnicity and sheer numbers: "The origin of the majority of immigrants had shifted from nations in northwestern Europe to those in southern and eastern Europe, and the overall number of immigrants nearly doubled" (Petit, *Men and Women* 6). Their numbers suggested that, were they to organize, they could present a significant threat to the existing political and economic structures, with the prospect of large numbers of organized voters and organized workers—"class conflict" (meaning the ability of workers to form unions) was always framed in racialized terms.

Threats to privilege have a material menace. If Grant's group—however defined—lost political and economic power, there would be material consequences for them. It's interesting to note that Michael Mann has argued that people will go to more trouble to retain existential privilege. Mann has argued that elites support authoritarian and even fascist regimes because of highly irrational calculations of threat, in which threats to property and privilege inspire more panic than threats to profit because of two mistaken beliefs

> that collective organization was an infringement of liberty and that only the educated and refined man (i.e., not a woman) was capable of such rational calculation. Thus capitalists hated trade unions as an infringement on their fundamental freedoms and as irrational blockage to an efficient economy. (*Fascists* 63)

As Mann points out, trade unions did not actually harm profits, and, as was argued in Grant's era (and our own) immigration benefits capital by keeping wages down. Elite opposition to immigration is not about rational calculation of profit. It is about political privilege, which is largely the power to determine what is considered a political issue.

Mann argues that genocide is a kind of evasion of politics; the decision (conscious or not) to reframe policy issues as purification issues has the consequence (and perhaps the intent) of refusing to allow some group to participate in the give and take of political liberalism. It is an evasion of argumentation. Jacques Ranciere says something similar: "Politics exists because those who have no right to be counted as speaking beings make themselves of some account, setting up a community by the fact of placing in common a wrong that is nothing more than this very confrontation" (27). To simplify Ranciere's very complicated point: politics is the moment when a previously excluded group insists on being included as interlocutors in political discourse, when they no longer want to be spoken about or spoken to, and insist upon being spoken with.

And that is a far graver threat to political hegemony than infringing on profits. Part of what made the immigration of non-Western Europeans so threatening was that they would shift what was political; they would start acting like the in-group. Thus, it was not that they would fail to assimilate, but that they would assimilate quite effectively, or, as in a famous passage from Grant: "These immigrants adopt the language of the native American; they wear his clothes; they steal his name; and they are beginning to take his women, but they seldom adopt his religion or understand his ideals" (81). The mere presence of the out-group causes people like Grant to retreat: "The native American is too proud to mix socially with them, and is gradually withdrawing from the scene, abandoning to these aliens the land which he conquered and developed" (80–81). Grant's plaint is not that immigrants are drags on society, or that they remain entirely foreign, but that they are doing too well, and they impede on his group's ability to keep its privileges to themselves. He has to interact with people who do not share his religion and "values," and that insistence on being seen by him is a violation of his privilege. There are various ways, not incompatible, of interpreting this anxiety about miscegenation. McClintock says, "Panic about blood contiguity, ambiguity, and *metissage* expressed intense anxieties about the fallibility of white male and imperial potency" (47), an interpretation that suggests that Grant's anxiety about race mixing was another manifestation of anxiety about WASPs like him losing cultural and political hegemony.

Immigration threatens privilege in that immigrants might become successful, and it also threatens the narrative that the in-group has about nationhood and achievement. Success on the part of the out-group is always threatening to the in-group because it has to be *explained* in a way that is consistent with the in-group's story about itself. The in-group explains its privileges as earned and signs of their essential superiority, and the lack of privileges on the part of the out-group as one of many signs of their essential inferiority. If members of the out-group begin to attain the same achievements as the in-group, that narrative—in-group success as both earned and essentially entitled—is threatened. There are various mechanisms for legally denying achievements to the out-group. Antiliteracy laws, deliberately restrictive access to college, discriminatory voting requirements, gerrymandering, disempowering collective bargaining, redrawing the lines of in-group/out-group to include the newly successful group (as continually happens with terms like "whiteness" and "Christian"), delegitimating the achievements (as in the deprofessionalization of clerical work, artisanship, or teaching), or, finally, expelling or exterminating the out-group.

The power of WASP elites was not threatened, but their privilege of excluding non-WASPs from politics was, and so was their narrative about themselves as the foundation of Americanness, and the center of American identity. The "going primitive" narrative can, as Marianna Torgovnik argues, appear to be a respectful attitude toward indigenous cultures, since the person who goes native does so with praise for that culture, as when modernists praise the colonized for simplicity and authenticity. Something like the "going primitive" narrative was powerful in the late nineteenth and early twentieth centuries because there was what Jackson Lears has called "a crisis of cultural authority" (5)—"a spreading sense of moral impotence and spiritual sterility—a feeling that life had become not only overcivilized but also curiously unreal" (4–5). Lears argues that, although the notion that the WASP elite was losing power in America is a myth, it may have felt very much like that to some people, with a "mingling of race and class fears" particularly in response to more recent waves of immigration and labor unrest (28–39). Lears describes the belief among social theorists and literary critics that "the emergence of an interdependent, commercial society signaled the displacement of the romantic warrior by the peaceful bourgeois" (100), or, in Grant's terms, the passing of the "great" race in favor of the Alpine and Mediterraneans. As Lears says,

> Anglo-Saxon racism offered a rationale for imperialist crusades against "inferior" overseas foes and also met less obvious social and psychic needs. Racism reasserted the cultural authority of the WASP bourgeoisie. . . . In a variety of ways, racism revitalized the hegemony of the dominant WASP culture at a critical historical moment. (108)

Lears emphasizes that the WASP bourgeoisie was not, in fact, losing ground, but they felt that they were. Thus, the policies that were actually perfecting their cultural hegemony could be reframed as necessitated by self-defense.

This tragic narrative helps resolve several problems in defenses of Protestant imperialism.[24] Especially in America, condemnations of imperialism used metaphors of uncontrolled lust—the Other kind of imperialist (usually Catholic) was motivated by lust for gold and resources, raped and enslaved the indigenous peoples, instituted corrupt and oppressive governmental systems, and allowed the peoples to wallow in their superstitious customs and religions. Bad imperialism is a kind of barbaric disorder. Good imperialism, on the contrary, is altruistic, motivated by a desire to raise the peoples up, by sharing the benefits of Protestant culture and economy. It is the imposition of order.

If good imperialism raises people up through civilizing them, there has to be a limit as to how successful it can be, or one has the possibility of the colonized reaching the height of the colonizer. If the colonized are capable of achieving just as much as the colonizer, then colonialism is only defensible (if at all) for a short period. And, of course, Protestant colonialism had been in place for hundreds of years, without the colonized reaching equal status. This failure to raise up the colonized suggested that good imperialism might be just as exploitive as the bad kind (since the colonizers weren't really going to let the colonized succeed); the fact that Protestant imperialism seemed to have considerable benefits in terms of resources, and even looked much like exploitation, also suggested a distinction without a difference.

The "going primitive" narrative resolves the cognitive dissonance created by Protestant imperialism through reversing the dynamics of desire and, hence, exploitation—instead of the colonizer desiring to conquer the resisting native, a narrative that would make the colonized the victim, the colonizer is reframed as a victim of the desires of the colonized. Because the Nordic will eventually find the seductive wiles of the colonized impossible to resist, the ability of the colonized to raise desire in the colonizer is criminalized.[25] This tragic narrative, then, tells a story of ontologically grounded privilege, a privilege that is a conveniently burdensome responsibility to exploit (but not breed with) inferiors, who are then held responsible for the exploitation. Colonizers are reframed as courageous individuals gallantly resisting a group—the same narrative told (about resisting liberalism) in racist bildungsroman. If this is Grant's narrative, then it would mean that, perhaps, to the extent that this is a "new" approach, it is a new way to ground an old argument.

Grant's grand narrative and impenetrable argument legitimated an entire set of practices that were facing some criticism—restriction of immigration, white supremacy, inter- and intracontinental imperialism, and eugenics. Grant's book wasn't the origin of those practices, but he made people feel that they were respectable, intellectually defensible, and grounded in data.

As muddled as the concept of "race" is for Grant (and his disciples), he is clear and consistent in his proposition that people of a superior race are superior in every way, including in intelligence. Or, in Woods's terms,

> We may not be able to get agreement as to whether pure science or pure song be of the better worth, but it is possible to map geographically the origin of science, both pure and applied, including administration of faculties, success in business, war, and government. So far, the weights all fall tremendously to the credit of the Nordic race. (95)

Of course, they "fall" to the credit of the "Nordic" race because that "race" was defined post hoc, and given a narrative that enables it to take credit for human achievement. The circularity of this argument would not be troubling to racists, not because they would enjoy racial fawning, but because racism is an epistemology. While the ethnicity of Grant's critics proves their argument wrong, his ethnicity is, for a racist, evidence of its truth. It is perhaps not so much that Grant's ethnicity is invisible, as that it is a part of the logic of his argument. His authority comes not from citation—since he never managed an edition that clearly connected his claims and any other authorities—but from his person: his use of terms and distinctions unfamiliar to his audience (because he has invented them) could be (mis?)read as signifying deep familiarity with expert discourse.

His conclusions seem to follow, not from the logic of his argument, but from the absence of argumentation (and his failure to define the terms he has invented) such that one cannot argue against him. He is irrefutable; one either submits to his perception or rejects it all.

Robert Hariman argues that Aristotle attributes practical wisdom (sometimes called "judgment") to two sources—first, to character, and second, to a kind of training. The oracular, omniscient posture lays claims to the former; being of the right ethnicity means that one has a better character and, necessarily, one has better judgment. In short, there is a circularity to race as a form of epistemic authority that makes it difficult to intervene productively: Grant's argument is that "his race is better because he says so, and he is a member of the better race that knows such things." Membership in his race confers good judgment, and other groups have poor judgment. Race is reason.

If race is reason, people of the wrong race have the wrong beliefs. From a rhetorical perspective, this is deeply troubling, since it suggests that there is a circular and self-reinforcing kind of reasoning to racism: people of the correct race (the in-group) are reliable, because their race makes them more perceptive about the world; they can read the ontic logos. Those who dispute the superiority of that race (the in-group) thereby demonstrate that they cannot read the ontic logos correctly; they are unreasonable and lack judgment. Whoever disagrees, therefore, is either not of the perceptive race, or is a race traitor, who knows the truth and denies it in order to curry favor with the lower races.[26]

This is not simply to say that racism is a circular ideology, although it is, but that it is an epistemology as well, and the ideology is therefore never experienced qua ideology. Racism isn't experienced as a set of beliefs separate from who the person is because racism makes beliefs, identity, judgment, and perception all one moment. The conventional notion of racism—that is a feeling of hostility that causes a racist person to reframe or distort perceptions—is a narrative about how knowledge works: it assumes that one first experiences reality in an unmediated way, and *then* racist feelings distort those initially accurate perceptions. People who believe that racism works as a postperception distortion caused by feelings of hostility believe that they can know whether they are engaged in racism simply by asking themselves whether they remember initial perceptions being distorted, or whether they are aware of hostile feelings in themselves that they can remember causing such distortion. Or, as someone said to me about the controversy in Ferguson, Missouri, "At what point are you saying the interaction became racist?" The tendency to put feelings in the object rather than in themselves ("The Japanese are dangerous" instead of "I feel fear when I think about the Japanese") makes it almost impossible for people like Grant to realize that they are being racist. They don't have the kind of sequential experience that they think racism entails. They think they would know if they were being racist because they would be aware of the interjection of hostile feelings. Thus, what is a racist attitude—such as rejecting Boas's argument because he's Jewish—doesn't *feel* racist because there was no moment they thought to themselves, "I like this argument, but Boas is Jewish and so now I dislike it."

What, then, was the impact of Grant? And what is a way to describe his current impact on racists? The equivocation of Grant's argument, whether deliberate or not, enabled a variety of readers to imagine themselves part of a group whose political domination is the telos of world history. Such readers, especially if already committed to a political agenda of ethnic domination and threatened by the burgeoning political power of groups they wanted to see as other, found Grant's book politically useful, in that it seemed to legitimate their political agenda as grounded in the ontic. Whether they could follow the details of his argument (and I can't imagine they could) wouldn't matter. What would matter is that Grant's conclusions confirmed a story that justified the current situation, and justified the policies they wanted to enact.

"Race" spent the nineteenth century as a concept scrounging around in various disciplines in search of support. And, while it kept finding supporting evidence— in new methods of scriptural interpretation, anthropology, ethnology, zoology, linguistics—at some point, each of those methods collapsed, and advocates of "race"-based public policies went in search of another legitimating basis. That people kept having to prop up the concept with new arguments didn't change that it was itself the legitimating foundation for cultural and political arrangements, ranging from colonialism to exclusionary immigration policies. Race was a political concept, but pretending that it was an ontological category perceived by an epistemological elite meant that it could serve as the basis, rather than the object, of policy debate; demagoguery of the elite is one way to depoliticize political concepts, and to keep them from public deliberation.

Grant takes two postures in the book. One is the oracular posture common to philosophy (he is passing along an insight only someone like him can have) and the other is the data-heavy empiricist posture of the New Science (he is presenting data that any reasonable person would interpret as he does). The moments of grand pronouncement exemplify the former and the apparently carefully hedged specifics exemplify the latter. These two postures are, of course, potentially contradictory (as they are in his book). Given that his data is neither self-explanatory, nor presented in such a way that it can be scrutinized, it is a posture that might make nonexperts *feel* that the data would support the claims, if only they understood the situation better. Readers of Grant can neither scrutinize nor dispute the data, but can only accept or reject it. That the precise nature of the evidence was just shy of clarity was irrelevant; readers' assent to Grant's conclusions meant they performed the same demonstration of allegiance that Grant performed in his argumentation. Grant's argument is about the inherent and inevitable (if simultaneously victimizing and tragic) domination of inferiors by the right kind of man; being moved by his argument shows that one is just that kind of man.

Thus, readers' claims that they were moved, persuaded, or changed by reading Grant do not function as statements about how the text worked, about the process through which a reader goes, or, least of all, about the quality of the data or argumentation. Rather, these statements function as a claim to membership in the club of the epistemologically elect. It is performance of group identity. By making assertions as he does—ones that are not subject to scrutiny by a skeptical reader—Grant doesn't declare allegiance to a set of other scientists, but to his own insight, and sympathetic readers declare allegiance to him. The book, and especially his posturing of himself as the ideal Nordic demonstrating the astute perception of Nordics by perceiving a pattern in the mass of data, confirmed racism by the appearance of a kind of insight that is shared with the reader only at the level of conclusion and not of data. It is not an invitation to deliberate, or even argue, but to submit to his judgment. Submitting to his judgment marks one as sharing the best qualities of a Nordic, and resisting his judgment means that one belongs to an inferior race, with inferior judgment. Praising Grant, then, is not a statement about the quality of his argument, but a performance of loyalty to, and claiming of membership in, his elect.

5

Anti-intellectualism and the Appeal to Expert Opinion

Here, then, is a program for racial advance and national unity. It adds up to the sum of the rights, privileges and responsibilities of full American citizenship. This is all that the Negro asks. He will not willingly accept less. As long as America offers less, she will be that much less a democracy. The whole way is the American way.
—Mary McLeod Bethune, qtd. in Bilbo, *Take Your Choice*

Richard Hofstadter's famous work defines anti-intellectualism as "a resentment and suspicion of the life of the mind and of those who are considered to represent it; and a disposition constantly to minimize the value of that life" (7). As was indicated in the chapter on Grant, however, demagoguery can look very much like intellectualism, and, as will be shown in this chapter, it is common for demagoguery to claim to represent and rely on expert discourse. Yet there is something intuitively right about Hofstadter's argument, in that demagoguery does often appeal to something that looks very much like *ressentiment* about eggheads. It has long struck me that rhetors engaged in demagoguery often react with rage to the claim that "it's more complicated than that." And yet they are not uncommonly advocating a tremendously complicated conspiracy theory, citing as support an argument as intellectually challenging as Grant's, or presenting charts and data that are very difficult to understand. While the end claim is often very simple—the in-group is *essentially* good and the out-group is *essentially* bad—that claim can be supported with very complicated arguments.

There is a difference between complexity and ambiguity, however, and the academic's classic "it's more complicated than that" is an acknowledgment of an ambiguity inherent in the human condition, and *ambiguity* is what enrages some people. Scholarly discourse, at its best, is not just complicated, but an attempt to be clear about a situation the scholar is acknowledging has only been partially captured. "It's more complicated than that" also means "It's more complicated than this." Such scholarly discourse doesn't prevent cognitive closure, but is always understood as contingently conclusive, part of an argument in which every answer is partial. Not all scholarly discourse is like that, of course, and that is what distinguishes the kind of complexity with which demagoguery is comfortable from the kind that is prohibited: the former closes the argument, and the latter acknowledges the contingency of any closure.

In addition, scholarly deliberation, like political deliberation, depends upon and continually wanders into arguments about metacognition. In deliberation, every participation, no matter how definitive the posture or conclusions, is understood as a contingent closure. The question will be reopened at some point when it becomes clear that we were wrong. When that happens, and it will always happen, we may have to not only come to different conclusions, but to rethink how we came to prior ones. Deliberation requires that we think about how we think: metacognition. Demagoguery, on the contrary, promises certainty about our conclusions and our processes. Even in those circumstances when a rhetor engaged in demagoguery is forced to admit that the in-group has been in error, that will not be part of an admission that the cognitive processes were flawed. In fact, the most likely explanation will either be that muddled relativism discussed earlier, or an assertion that processes were tainted by the participation of the out-group. For fans of demagoguery, toggling between naïve realism and muddled relativism precludes the need to rethink cognitive processes: if everyone is equally biased, then the cognitive process that was used is just as good as any other; if the truth is obvious, then we should keep from having our vision distorted by the nefarious out-group's smokescreens.

The dichotomy of "expert" versus "populist" is not helpful for identifying this rhetorical posture and its effectiveness. Hofstadter identified a question not of intellectual versus populist, but a way of thinking about knowledge and its role in persuasion. Saurette's "epistemological populism" coupled with Kruglanski's "epistemic authority" points critics of public deliberation in a more useful direction than "anti-intellectualism" or "populism."

In the previous chapter I argued that Grant legitimated various racist policies by presenting an almost impenetrable argument that seemed to associate his grand narrative with an overwhelming amount of logically disconnected data; his argument relies on the authority that comes purely from the persona he creates in the text. And, as with other rhetors in this book, a large part of his authority comes from his confirming the views of his in-group—that confirmation signifies his in-group membership, just as readers' acknowledging his authority signifies their membership. In-group membership is epistemic authority.

Even if they can't understand (or, as in the case of many of his positive reviewers, don't agree with) Grant's conclusions, they can take his premise ("race is everything"), and confirm it through observation—they can look around and see race. Of course, they could also look around and see disconfirming data, as well as note the problems in his argument, but that isn't what we tend to do. We tend, as Arlie Kruglanski has argued, to reason syllogistically, using instances as minor premises that confirm our major premises: "The individual departs from a premise that links, in an 'if-then' form, a given category of evidence with a given hypothesis and proceeds to infer the hypothesis on affirming the evidence" ("Knowledge" 114). Scholars of rhetoric will recognize this as enthymematic reasoning, in which we don't necessarily make the major premise explicit: "Chester barks at the mail carrier because he's a dog." As Kruglanski says, "In validating or 'proving' a given idea we thus transmit our subjective confidence from our premises to our conclusions" (*Lay* 23). Thus, the same datum can be used to confirm different (perhaps even incompatible) premises—that dogs inevitably bark at mail carriers, that mail carriers are dangerous, that dogs bark at everyone who approaches the door, that Great Danes are easily frightened, and so on.

The extent to which we will use a single datum to confirm a premise depends upon various factors, especially what Kruglanski calls the "need for closure." A person with a high need for epistemic closure will, he argues, "freeze" on the first piece of confirming data. A person with a low need for closure, or even an aversion to closure, might keep looking for more information. If we're tired, cognitively exhausted, frightened, or even simply personally averse to ambiguity, we're more likely to make a quick decision on the basis of a small amount of evidence (think of a person in front of a vending machine at the end of a long day). Kruglanski, summarizing a variety of research, points out that the "self" is high in epistemic authority (meaning we tend to trust our own beliefs and perceptions) and that our willingness to close a thinking process is influenced by our personality type (whether we are dispositionally drawn or averse to closure), the availability (and relative cost) of cognitive resources, our motivation (such as the relative costs of being mistaken versus admitting one's mistake), and the situation (such as whether it is one in which we believe we have high epistemic authority). Demagoguery offers "epistemics" on the issue of the relative goodness of the in-group and the in-group's treatment of out-groups. Demagoguery justifies that closure on the grounds that people with high epistemic authority have pronounced that we do not need to gather any more information, and that our method of thinking about the issue is perfect. Demagoguery says the unambiguous situation requires no more thinking or deliberation—we only need to believe, and to act.

This chapter considers three nonscientists who claimed their arguments were supported by "science," with varying levels of odd relationships to scientific discourse: E. S. Cox, Theodore Bilbo, and William Tam. I have found that demagoguery often involves appeals to authorities rejected by the audience, or that do not actually support the argument being made. This invocation of authority and apparent demonstration of allegiance is often done with a citation method that looks as though it is expert discourse when, in fact, an expert audience would likely recognize that the argument does not engage the relevant sources, does not use sources responsibly, does not represent positions fairly, or use appropriate evidence reasonably. If the function of citation is performing allegiance, what does it mean to perform allegiance to a group one is treating irresponsibly? What does it mean to display an allegiance or invoke reverence for a community or orientation with which one is actually at odds?

Cox, Bilbo, and Epistemological Populism

Paul Lombardo's description of the rhetorical role of eugenics in the passage of Virginia's laws on "antimiscegenation" and sterilization is one explanation for how authority worked in prosegregation rhetoric (which was primarily, and fundamentally, about "mixed" marriage).

> The pseudo-science of eugenics was a convenient facade used by men whose personal prejudices on social issues preceded any "scientific theory." Stated more bluntly, the true motive behind the Racial Integrity Act of 1924 was the maintenance of white supremacy and black economic and social inferiority—racism, pure and simple. It was an accident of history that eugenic theory reached its peak of acceptability in 1924 so as to be available as a respectable veneer with which to cover ancient prejudice. For Powell, Plecker, and their ilk, eugenical ideology was not a *sine qua non* for legislation, but merely a coincidental set of arguments that provided intellectual fuel to the racist fires. (425)

John P. Jackson puts it elegantly. "Science provides racist ideology with important rhetorical tools that allow the perpetuation of racist claims that would otherwise not be tolerated in public discourse" (*Science* 5). Jackson's terminology is usefully precise: racialist science didn't provide the ideology with support, but with tools that enable rhetors to create a nice front. It's important that we not use the term "support," as there often was no real *support* provided to claims by the evidence— the evidence could collapse and leave the reader still believing the conclusions.

After all, as shown in the previous chapter, even positive reviews noted the lack of evidence to support Grant's claims, but they didn't really care, and that's interesting. This is another example of the phenomenon that Jackson notes: that racism can exist even when "there was no coherent concept of a race to support it" (7). The argument for racialist science and segregationist social policies was muddled, incoherent, internally inconsistent, but rhetorically powerful, and the important question is why.

Compared to many of the rhetors discussed in this book, E. S. Cox and Theodore Bilbo better fit conventional views of demagogues. Bilbo's name, according to Chester Morgan, "has become almost symbolic of the image of the southern demagogue" and "no southerner has been more universally accorded the designation by either the academic community or the public at large" (234). Though Cox is less famous and was never an elected official, he is given much of the credit for antimiscegenation legislation in the early twentieth century. He experienced considerable success with his self-published anti-integration pamphlet, and remains popular among white supremacists.[1] Bilbo's and Cox's rhetorical strategies are also much closer to popular notions of demagoguery, especially their purple passages of Scriptural cadence and hyperbolic predictions of catastrophe. Bilbo, for instance, says he "would rather see his race and his civilization blotted out with the atomic bomb than to see it slowly but surely destroyed in the maelstrom of miscegenation, interbreeding, intermarriage and mongrelization" (2). Yet, even their writings have many of the characteristics that surprised me when I started looking at demagoguery—the patina of reasonableness, a profusion of data, an emphasis on facts, a rhetoric of realism, heavy use of rationality markers, and the performance of scholarly authority. To say that their citation of authority is fallacious is an understatement. But the more interesting question, and the one to which I will return throughout this chapter is: why cite at all? Their citation methods will not impress a scholarly audience, and are unnecessary to persuade people who already agree with them (whose agreement is likely on cultural or religious grounds and impervious to scientific verification or falsification). So, why bother?

This move is surprising because argument from authority functions both rhetorically and logically only to the extent that the audience reveres the authority being cited. As Ken Hyland says, "By acknowledging a debt of precedent, a writer is also able to display an allegiance to a particular community or orientation, create a rhetorical gap for his or her research, and establish a credible writer ethos" ("Academic Attribution" 342). The concept of "allegiance" is important—the rhetor performs membership in a group considered authoritative by the readers whom the rhetor is trying to persuade: "The only environment in which a reference can be persuasive is in a community whose members share the opinion of the author about the persuasive reputation of a cited scientist" (Allen et al., 281). Walton paraphrases John Locke's point on the appeal to authority, "This type of argument is effective or successful because it exploits the attitude of reverence (*verecundia*) of the party who is on the receiving end of the appeal to the authoritative source" (*Appeal* 88).

Cox and Bilbo present their claims as unmediated descriptions of taxonomies of identity written into the ontic logos and, equally, as obvious to readers with similar clarity of vision. Thus, ultimately, the argument about "miscegenation" is not about race, but about the ontological basis of social order, and whether our cultural hierarchies will remain grounded in the ontic. This posture is not particular to issues of race; in the last part of the chapter, I'll argue that a similar perception shapes current arguments about the true identity of homosexuals. That is, although the terms of the argument have shifted, the basic notion of identities divinely written into the ontic logos and instantly interpreted by a person with good judgment continues to trouble our policy discourse.

Earnest Sevier Cox's *White America,* published in 1922, advocates segregation, antimiscegenation legislation, and exclusion (even forced emigration) of "nonwhites." Cox cites Grant's book (and Stoddard's) as supporting his argument ("the reader is referred to these publications for data bearing upon our immigration problem and the world-wide color problem" (9) and uses a long passage from Grant before the chapter "Amalgamation or Separation," in which he advocates "repatriation" of African Americans. Although claiming Grant as an authority in support of his argument, Grant's own argument (let alone evidence) supports neither Grant's own conclusions, nor Cox's. As argued in the previous chapter, Grant's narrative of the rise of civilizations implicitly promotes hybridity, and the kind of "race-mixing" that he was concerned was primarily about intra"white" races, a point Cox grants and then ignores. And, like all racialist science, the book never defines "race" and doesn't even use the term consistently.

Cox summarizes the "propositions" that "scientific research has done much toward establishing" (23):

1. The white race has founded all civilizations.
2. The white race remaining white has not lost civilization.
3. The white race come hybrid has not retained civilization.

Cox says he agrees with Grant that there are three white races: "We know that the 'white race' in reality includes three races" (23), a claim that undermines his entire argument because, if that claim is true, then either 3 is false, or his propositions are all false, since they refer to something ("the white race") that he grants on the same page does not actually exist. If "race-mixing" is disastrous for a race, then "hybridity" among the white races is just as harmful as mixing between whites and nonwhites, and is just as pressing a problem to be solved. Thus, Cox's comfort with the hybridity of "whiteness" highlights the inconsistency of his terror at other kinds of hybridity.

Like Grant, Ripley, Stoddard, and Bilbo, Cox's use of the word "race" is unintelligible, even though, like them, he performs the gesture of advancing a definition.

> Race, the descendants of a common ancestor. There is wide latitude in the use of this term. Ethnologically it implies well marked spiritual and physical attributes which are transmissible by the laws governing heredity, and which serve to set apart, visibly, from the rest of mankind the group to which it is applied. We speak of the human race, the Caucasian race, the English race, etc. There is no flawless classification of the races of mankind. Such classifications as exist need revision, but for the purposes of this book the popular classifications are satisfactory. The "Caucasian race" is in reality constituted of three well-marked divisions of mankind. (42–43)

The passage undercuts itself at multiple places. If "race" is the descendants of a common ancestor, then either Cox has to posit polygenism or we are all one race. And, if he is going to accept evolution (or science based on evolution) then all beings have common ancestors. Polygenism puts him at odds with Grant, and rejecting evolution puts him at odds with other authorities he cites. His comment about the "wide latitude" and admission that there is no "flawless classification" complicate his assertion that the popular notions (which he hasn't defined) are adequate. "Popular" conceptions of race were actually wildly in conflict with one another, with significant disagreement about whether various groups were white (leading to numerous judicial cases)[2]. Even "expert" taxonomies of race were in disarray, even among the older sources that Cox was trying to use. Peggy Pascoe says,

> For much of the nineteenth century, ethnologists and physical anthropologists had stood as the authoritative experts on scientific race classification, but despite their supposed expertise, they disagreed—often sharply—over the number and variety of races. Rather than give up the project of racial classification entirely, though, ethnologists solved their disagreements (and retained their professional authority) by either adding more categories or rearranging the ones at hand into major and minor groups. (117)

Thus, as with Grant, Cox's argument falls just short of actually making sense, but a highly sympathetic reader might *feel* confirmed by the text.

Cox's definition of race makes race both an epistemic and ontological category—something both in the observer and in the person being observed (characteristics that serve to set someone apart visibly are in the perception of the observer, and physical attributes controlled by heredity are in the person being observed). This is not only naïve realism (that a person can simply look and see characteristics), but also demonstrates what is called "entity theory." Social psychologists often distinguish between two ways of imagining the cause and status of personal attributes such as intelligence, musical talent, and so on. "Entity theorists" attribute those qualities to the very identity of the person, describing them as fixed in place before birth: "Entity theorists view human attributes as stable across times and contexts" (Kruglanski, "Thinkers' Personalities" 476). Racialist science is premised in entity theory—the whole project is about determining what characteristics different "races" have that are stable across time and context.

Entity theory enables cognitive shortcutting: to understand why someone did something, one can simply appeal to their membership in some group (as opposed to more cognitively complicated issues about the context). It enables, as Kruglanski argues, a quick closure to internal deliberation—you don't have to spend much time trying to figure out someone's motives, beliefs, behavior, values, and so on, because you can infer all that from their group membership. Relying on entity theorizing doesn't preclude all policy deliberation, in that one can deliberate about which policies will work best given the identities of various groups, but it does inhibit deliberating with out-group members. After all, they are already a known entity, with motives and not reasons, and relying on entity theories does make policies of exclusion, disenfranchisement, and so on appear to be practical solutions, since "they" are incapable of reason.[3] "Incremental theorists," on the other hand, "view human traits as malleable and capable of changing as a function of learning" (Kruglanski, "Lay," 476). Boas's attitude toward race exemplifies an incremental theory, and Grant and Cox are both (generally) entity theorists. Cox defines race as an entity in persons that other persons can perceive in an unmediated and reliable way.

Like Grant, Cox was an autodidact, and, like Grant's *Passing of the Great Race*, Cox's *White America* presents plenty of data—in the form of claims about various civilizations, conditions in different countries, the nature of Africans and African Americans—but much of it is explicitly speculation (see, for instance, Cox's statistics on the percentage of Egyptians with "negroid" blood, 99–101), and very little of it is cited in such a way that one can tell if he is repeating information from a source (and, if so, which one) or making his own assertions (as in his definition of "race" cited above). As with Grant's *Passing*, there is no process in *White America* of working through claims or data; there is an oracular quality to Cox's rhetoric, and informed, skeptical (let alone opposition) readers would not be moved to a new understanding. Like Grant, Cox probably would not *move* racist readers either, but might provide them with a basis for believing the things they already believe.

Also, like Grant, Cox does not engage with or rely on recent scholarship about race, heredity, and anthropology; although he cites books and gives information, his authority does not come from presenting himself as a credentialed scholar involved in current scholarly debate; he is not an academic expert. He does cite sources for direct quotes (approximately fifty), but, like Grant's direct quotes, Cox's sources fall into the category of what Jackson calls "nineteenth-century gentleman naturalist[s]" (25). Cox's *White America* was published in 1922. The most recent book referenced in it is Grant's *Passing* (1916). The preponderance of books cited by Cox were probably published between 1909 and 1915, with a fair number having been published in the nineteenth century.[4]

Take, for instance, how Cox establishes the authority of Dr. R. W. Shufeldt on whom he relies for generalizations about "the negro."[5] Cox's encomium for Shufeldt doesn't claim scholarly expertise or academic training for him, but first-hand experience.

> Dr. Shufeldt is a Northern man, a former member of the medical corps of the United States army and a naturalist of profound learning. His experience with the negro has extended to all the Southern States and to the West Indies. During the fifty years of his scientific observation of the negro, he has accumulated a knowledge of that race second to no other. (320).

Shufeldt has first-hand experience that gave him direct knowledge; his legitimate authority (as a naturalist and doctor in the army) give him authority on "unrelated issues" (race and genealogy), and Cox's indications of the strengths of *his* feelings about Shufeldt ("second to no other") serve as endorsements of Shufeldt's reliability. Cox does not present Shufeldt as having relevant academic or professional credentials, as having published in appropriate scholarly venues, or as a member of pertinent professional organizations; Shufeldt's expertise is not from having relevant training or being engaged with a scholarly community.

What, exactly, makes Shufeldt's observations "scientific"? There are two ways to understand Cox's insistence on Shufeldt's observations as scientific: first, as a (conscious? unconscious?) assertion of what the rhetor knows (at some level) to be untrue (that is, strategic misnaming); or, Cox has an older view of "scientific."

Strategic misnaming means simply adopting the name of the opposite kind of behavior from that in which one is engaged, and thereby attempting to refute criticism. Kenneth Burke noted this move on the part of Hitler, when Hitler routinely characterized his posture toward Jews as one of "love" and "peace"—a strategy that Orwell called "blackwhite." While it may be that Cox is engaged in that kind of move, it's also possible that his use of the word "scientific" was an idiom of the nineteenth century that remains in use today—especially on the part of homophobic, creationist, and new age invocations of "science." Used in this way, "science" refers to a kind of posture, a direct and unmediated access to the truth on the part of a certain kind of person.

That is, "science" is the activity of a certain kind of person; the activity is derived from the identity of the person, and that identity is inferred from the rhetorical posture—a chain of syllogisms related to how I'm arguing that people infer the "rationality" of an argument (as a deduction from the posture of the arguer). Jackson, drawing on David Hollinger, refers to the "knower persona" in which the rhetor is self-presented "as the discoverer of a truth that existed in nature rather than a truth created by artistic endeavor" (*Science* 8). It is this older sense of the scientific persona on which Cox is drawing: Shufeldt's claims are "scientific" because Shufeldt is a knower with direct experience of the ontologically grounded taxonomy of identity. And, of course, Shufeldt's whiteness is a crucial part of his (and Cox's) ability to claim the knower persona: "The belief in objectivity, coupled with positioning white people as outside of culture (and thus the norm for humanity), allows whites to view themselves as universal humans who can represent all of human experience" (DiAngelo 59).

Cox's performance of expertise is a good example of what has been called "epistemological populism." Paul Saurette and Shane Gunster say that epistemological populism "borrows heavily from the rhetorical patterns of political discourses of populism to valorize the knowledge of 'the common people,' which they possess by virtue of their proximity to everyday life" (5). Epistemological populism is a claim for a certain kind of credibility, an expertise of the everyday, and it is, as Saurette and Gunster argue, a rhetorical performance.

> Epistemological populism is established through a variety of rhetorical techniques and assumptions: the assertion that individual opinions based upon first-hand experience are much more reliable as a form of knowledge than those generated by theories and academic studies; the valorization of specific types of experience as particularly reliable sources of legitimate knowledge and the extension of this knowledge authority to unrelated issues; the privileging of emotional intensity as an indicator

of the reliability of opinions; the use of populist-inflected discourse to dismiss other types of knowledge as elitist and therefore illegitimate; and finally, the appeal to "common sense" as a discussion-ending trump card. (5)

Saurette and Gunster say that epistemological populism "does not seem to promote real political debate" (by "real political debate" they seem to mean what I am calling "arguing policy qua policy"). Instead, it "serves to naturalize certain political and policy conclusions" (17) putting them beyond debate by making them seem to be the "natural" state. The consequence of making certain positions "natural" is that their contingency and very particular constructedness gets hidden.

So, for instance, Cox's placement of race in the person obscures that the "race" of any individual depends upon cultural context—that "whiteness" was continually up for debate, and in Cox's own home state, was so vexed that it had to be determined by a governmental commission. As will be discussed later in this chapter, oppositions to "gay marriage" posit it as a change to "marriage" itself, as though "marriage" does not have a tradition of change and reconstitution. Like Cleon's attempt to make an entirely new and radical policy the "nomos" (or traditional), epistemological populism functions to make a possibly very new policy seem to be the pre-existing (and, really, irresistible) norm. It hides, not only the constructedness and contingent nature of various taxonomies, but also the contingent nature of interpretation ("You aren't arguing with me; you're arguing with God").

Because it positions certain stances as opposed to what is obviously the "natural" one, epistemological populism undermines inclusive deliberation in that it functions to "dismiss others as worthy of ridicule" (17). Instead of genuinely engaging the arguments of the other, epistemological populism relies on simply making fun of anyone stupid enough to disagree. Policy discourse in this world consists of one obviously good and sensible option proposed and defended by obviously good and sensible people, and anything else—a policy, policies, or candidates advocated by stupid people—is ascribed to bad people with bad motives. This method of presenting argument is entertaining, and hence we have "argutainment," something that

> teaches us that we can judge the validity of a particular comment not merely by the ad/pro hominem shorthand offered by epistemological populisms (such as the subject position and experience of the speaker) but by an even more immediate shorthand of the passion and brevity of a speaker's communication style for our emotional reaction to it. (16)

The veracity of a claim and our emotional reaction to it are identical; as with Cox's definition of race (in the ontic *and* in our perception), race is in someone and in our feelings about him or her; reality and our feelings about reality are one and the same. We say Muslims, Mytileneans, the Arab world, Japanese "are threatening" rather than, "I am afraid of them" because the latter is adequate proof of the former.

Of course, not everyone's feelings function as proof of what is in the ontic. The feelings of "negrophiles," according to Cox, come from their not having direct contact with "the negro" (see especially 25–26); such inexperience means they are misled by "tenderness" (26); "the sentimentalist will ignore the facts" (310, see also 311). Cox's position is shared by all those with "direct contact" with the negro (see especially 25–27). At various points (perhaps a suspicious number of times) Cox emphasizes the importance of direct experience. He begins his "General Introduction" with a quote from Patrick Henry, "There is no lamp by which my feet may be guided but the lamp of experience" and goes on to say, "Experience is knowledge" (11). Earlier, I mentioned that Cox's sources are primarily from the early teens. In the preface, Cox explains that the book was finished just as the United States entered WWI, and thus publication was delayed. So, there is nothing nefarious in his sources being dated, but it is interesting that his explanation about the publication delay is not in service of explaining the older sources. On the contrary, he almost seems to apologize for using as many sources as he does: "The opinions of others have been sought even when the research of the writer may have placed him in more favorable position for the acquirement of the data than the authority cited" (9–10).

Privilege and rhetorical authority are always closely connected for Cox, with a strong sense that whites have more authority than nonwhites on issues of race (because "we aren't angry about race," as a white student patiently explained to me once). So much of Cox's rhetorical authority comes from being a white Southerner. But he also represents his claims as coming from unmediated experience and the clarity of his vision. These three assumptions (whites have more epistemological authority, Southerners know more, and his vision is universal and unmediated) are all tied together, even if they're contradictory—Cox's race means that he can have clearer vision than nonwhites, so that his knowledge is both in him and in the world. Just as race is an ontological and epistemological category, so his vision is particular to people like him and universally grounded in the world.

Part of this rhetorical posture is Cox's continual insistence on the facticity of his beliefs—his claims come from "indisputable evidence" (244); his contempt for Africans and African Americans is not "sentimental arrogation of the white man" but the consequence of his having chosen to "seek the fact of race history from which to induce generalizations" (310); he relies on "a cold fact that is verifiable" (296).[6] That nonwhites have never started a civilization "*is the most solemn fact of human history, the only fact that bodes ill for the future*" (299, his emphasis). The repetition of "fact" for something already disputed in Cox's era is an example of that interesting move—vehemence as substitution for evidence, and an example of what Saurette and Gunster described as "the privileging of emotional intensity as an indicator of the reliability of opinions" (5). While Cox's view is grounded in "fact," his opposition is motivated by feminine traits of sentimentality. This is not logic versus emotion, but manly emotions (certainty and pride) versus traditionally feminine ones (sentimentality).

Earlier, I noted that Cox's definition of race makes race something that is simultaneously in the observer and the observed; there is perfect correspondence between the perception of someone like him and the (possibly hidden) essence of reality. Cox cites authorities not because their agreement shows that he is correct in his judgment—a reason that would suggest that his position would be threatened by the (larger) amount of expert disagreement with his claims—but simply to show that his insight is shared. Whether it is shared by current or past scholars is irrelevant for the kind of authority he is performing: it is epistemic authority that comes from saying things with which the in-group already agrees.

This kind of authority does not come from the logical connections between data and claims, but from two other sources: the authority being right, and the authority being a good person (which, usually, means a member of one's in-group). The validity of the argument, then, is determined by the identity and the person making it. This sense of authority may explain why some people cannot even understand or imagine a realm of public disagreement focused on issues of policy. To them, that feels like an unnecessarily complicated set of topoi that are entirely unrelated to what really demonstrates credibility and authority. In-group membership for them is all the authority a rhetor needs. The paradox is that this authority comes from agreement, so the role of authority is both logically and rhetorically circular. The conclusion is true because it was asserted by a person with authority. The person has authority because his or her conclusions confirm what we already believe to be true. So, what does this kind of rhetoric do? And why is there so much of it?

Of the many very strange texts that I have read for this project (and for the course I teach on demagoguery), Theodore Bilbo's *Take Your Choice: Amalgamation or Separation* remains the strangest. Jackson calls it "probably the last statement of Radical southern racial ideology published by a major political figure in the United States" (41). Bilbo himself is enraging, and was even in his life. He was once famously described as a pert little monster, glib and shameless, with the sort of cunning common to criminals which passes for intelligence. The people loved him. They loved him not because they were deceived by him, but because they understood him thoroughly, they said of him proudly, "He's a slick little bastard." (Percy)

Pat Gehrke describes Bilbo as "overly aggressive, excessively competitive, and verbally abusive, he cared more for winning the arguments than for what he had to do in order to win" and "as blustery and as nasty a politician as any of his day" (96). David Brinkley remembers him.

> He seemed to hate everyone: communists, Jews, union leaders, union members, anyone who could, by any definition, be called a foreigner, and above all, of course, blacks. And Bilbo never hesitated to make his hatreds known. When he ran for the Senate in 1934, he denounced an opponent as "a cross between a hyena and a mongrel . . . begotten in the nigger graveyard at midnight, suckled by a sow, and educated by a fool." When he received a hostile letter from a woman named Josephine Piccolo in New York City, he wrote back and addressed her: "Dear Dago." (77)

Jackson calls him "an extreme racist even by the standards of the time" (*Science* 34). Personally corrupt, Bilbo presented himself as an anticorruption candidate. His lack of fiscal and moral integrity and even incompetence were well documented, but he was continually re-elected. Thus, if any American were to embody the demagogue-as-magician, it would be Bilbo. Or, as Reinhard Luthin says in his chapter on Bilbo, "For decades Mississippi voters were bewitched and beguiled by Theodore Gilmore Bilbo" (44). That conception of demagoguery presents the demagogue as essentially the master rhetorician: an autonomous individual who assesses the situation cunningly, identifying what Aristotle called "the available means of persuasion," and using them to control the audience, getting them to do or believe what he wants. Motivated by a desire for power, demagogues say whatever is necessary to gain the compliance of any given audience, throwing principle under the bus whenever necessary.

Yet, it's also possible that isn't how demagoguery works; it's possible that Bilbo's demagoguery was not a deliberate set of moves he adopted in order to get votes, but an accurate representation of his sincerely held views. He may have been successful simply because voters sincerely liked those views. After all, had Bilbo's demagoguery been strategic, he would have, like other Southern politicians, altered it when he reached a national audience (something that would have benefited his career).

Instead of shifting to dog whistles, modifying his policies, or otherwise accommodating a new rhetorical situation, Bilbo pursued his scheme "with the single-minded doggedness of a dedicated zealot" (Hendrix 165). Since his commitment to the "back to Africa" policy became a standing joke in the Senate, and his tendency toward race-baiting quotes (such as the infamous one advocating violence to silence African American voters) became an embarrassment to Southerners, it seems to me reasonable to infer that they were not cunning—it would have been more cunning to have muted them. The most plausible explanation is that he was perfectly sincere.

The question of the deliberateness of his rhetorical strategies gets even more entangled when one considers *Take Your Choice*. It is not entirely clear what Bilbo was hoping to do with the book, and it is thus difficult to tell whether the book is a rhetorical masterpiece or a complete failure. It is hard to imagine that it is not one or the other. Self-published in 1947, the book had no discernible impact. While some sources say it was tremendously popular within the state, others say it had poor sales. Biographies of Bilbo generally emphasize his political activities and speeches, and have little or nothing to say about the book. It was published shortly before his death, and was probably composed while he knew he was dying. It had almost nothing new in it, and is mostly a rehashing of Cox's *White America*. The only new part—that is, the only part not simply restating what others had said—is the distinctly odd chapter responding to Rayford Logan's 1944 collection *What the Negro Wants*.

The purpose of questioning Bilbo's motives in writing and publishing *Take Your Choice* is not to determine whether Bilbo was personally racist—an issue irrelevant to whether he engaged in demagoguery (a question that is part of, as I've been arguing, precisely the model of demagoguery that contributes to its effectiveness). Bilbo's motives in writing the book are necessary for determining whether the book was persuasive, a point which can't be pursued without a plausible hypothesis as to what the effect and audience were intended to be, and it is very difficult to infer either intention or audience.

At the sentence level, *Take Your Choice* is easier to follow than *Passing*, but is logically an even worse train wreck than either *Passing* or *White America*. Appealing to any evolutionary explanation of racial origins or character *and* "purity" of races is inherently contradictory, but to appeal to evolution *and* "Noah's curse" as the origin of races (113) is simply unintelligible. If Grant's explanation of the origin of races is right, then Genesis 9 is false; if the latter is an authoritative narrative, then Grant is wrong. That many of the texts cited by Cox would be discredited by their association with Nazism is not something Cox could know in 1922; it was something Bilbo did know in 1947, and yet he used many of the same sources. Bilbo's book has far more sources than Cox's, with some of them having been written in the 1940s, but, as with Cox, those that support his point are not scholarly sources; in fact, the scholarly sources he cites all contradict him. At the time that Cox and Grant were writing, the gentleman naturalist and the Romantic strain in science (in which an insightful person intuited the types never empirically present) were recent traditions. By 1947, there was a stronger cultural understanding of science as a discipline requiring specialized training.

It's unlikely that Bilbo was trying to be taken seriously as an expert (in the way that Grant clearly was), or was even trying to have what he said to be taken at face value, given his tendency toward hyperbole. One of the more entertaining moments of hyperbole is in his billingsgate about Franz Boas, when he says, "As Professor and Dean of Anthropology and Ethnology at Columbia University, this immigrant from Germany—totally un-American to the last—literally prized open Pandora's box" (164)—since, of course, Bilbo doesn't literally mean the word "literally." Similarly, his claim about what he has read on the subject isn't meant to be taken literally: "For nine years I have read, studied and analyzed practically all the records and everything written throughout the entire world on the subject of race relations, covering a period of close on to thirty thousand years." Bilbo makes no pretense of reading any other language, and the bibliography, although longer than Cox's, is obviously a very partial number of the books on the subject. So, when he says "practically all of the records," he doesn't mean that; he means, simply, he has read some books.[7]

Bilbo's book is highly figured, with scriptural cadence and a kind of rolling eloquence, relying heavily on emphatics that make clear he is someone who sees things in terms of all or nothing. His first chapter ends:

> Separation of the races is the only way to solve properly, adequately, and permanently the race problem and safeguard the future of this Republic. No obstacles are insurmountable when the life's blood is at stake. The blood, culture, and civilization of the white race are our heritage. Shall our generation possess the vision, foresight, and courage to solve forever the race problem so that ours will be the heritage of all the generations of Americans yet unborn? Or shall we pass the problem on and on to grow in magnitude with the passing years until our posterity sinks into the mire of mongrelism? God forbid that we choose the latter! (10)

Bilbo's emphatics position him as someone passionate about the topic, looking at a situation that appears to him perfectly clear, unambiguous, and pointing toward a single course of action.

Yet the book has many of the qualities noted in other instances of demagoguery: facticity, realism, and insistence on unemotional clarity of purpose. He uses the word "fact" (or "facts," "factual") over one hundred times, the "truth" he speaks is "incontrovertible" (1, 3) and "indisputable" (4); to condemn and ostracize any one "who by word or deed endorse or encourage the mongrelization of the Nation . . . is not bias, bigotry, un-American or undemocratic" (146; on the contrary, the NAACP is the one he accuses of "bigotry and intolerance" 111). He spends an entire chapter showing "that both history and science defy the theory of the equality of the Caucasian and Negro races" (69).

But, again, what Bilbo means by "science" is not experimental science, nor even recent expert discourse. He cites as authorities Gobineau, William Smith (*The Color Line,* 1905), Madison Grant, Lothrop Stoddard (1921), the Bible, Shufeldt, Pickett, John Irwin (*Let's Keep the United States White*), and E. S. Cox's *White America.* Of those, not cited by Cox were John Irwin (author of the only recent book—it was published in 1945—to support his arguments), and William Smith. Stoddard is the only author with professional credentials as a scientist, and, by 1947, his attitudes on race had been somewhat discredited by his early and open admiration of Nazi treatment of Jews. In order to "refute" the arguments made in *The Races of Mankind,* written by Columbia anthropology professors Ruth Benedict and Gene Weltfish, Bilbo cites Cox as though Cox were an authority on scientific method. Bilbo also says:

> Although those who are advocating complete equality for the whites and blacks in the United States claim that "a modern science" supports their demands, neither this argument nor their shouts against what they call "racial prejudice" can refute facts and logic. The chief points which are characteristic of the Negro race may be listed as follows. (73)

He goes on to give a list from William Smith's 1905 *Color Line.* Smith got the list from A. H. Keane's 1896 book *Ethnology.* It is the standard list of characteristics (brain size, hair) used frequently in the nineteenth century and out of favor even among racialist scientists by the 1930s. Smith, a professor of mathematics at Tulane, was primarily known for his writings on Scripture; Keane's reliance on linguistics to make ethnological distinctions was considered dated in his lifetime (and, not coincidentally, made his racial taxonomy incompatible with Grant's). Thus, Bilbo, who has read "practically everything" about race relies on an old book by a nonexpert that itself relies on an even older book with yet older information, and which is incompatible with Bilbo's argument. Bilbo's reliance on old sources is odd in that Bilbo was perfectly willing to use discredited, amateur, and flawed science. He could have found more recent texts to support him—work by Charles Davenport, Henry Laughlin, and Charles Coon. Many biology or genetics textbooks from the 1930s would have had chapters that would have better supported his claims about race than the works he cited. In short, one of the many things that makes the book so strange is that it manages to be an even less competent argument for racism than books written thirty years earlier. It isn't just an inaccurate argument, it's an incompetent one.[8]

Bilbo's assertions contradict each other and his sources, but his book isn't about logical consistency or even logical relations. He uses a strategy that is often noted in polemical writings—Mark Jordan describes the technique in regard to Paul Cameron's homophobic polemics: "What remains constant across the sources is the technique of proof-texting: quotations taken out of context and identified only by brief citation are expected to produce conviction in the reader" (175). I would quibble with Jordan's use of the phrase "produce conviction"—the conviction already exists, and this cherry-picking draws attention to that shared conviction. Bilbo was certainly making one last effort to get the values he shared with his readers—about white supremacy, for example—connected to his pet project of expulsion of African Americans. But, why cherry pick *science*. It's hardly as though his audience would have been less persuaded by his book had he failed to cite any scientific authorities—old or new.

Unlike Cox or Grant, Bilbo does discuss opposition points of view, such as recent experts who refute the very sources on which he builds his argument. In addition to discussing the Benedict and Weltfish pamphlet, he quotes from Gunnar Myrdal's *An American Dilemma* (1944), Frank Hankins's essays in *The Progressive,* and Giuseppe Antonio Borgese's article in *Negro Digest.*[9] With each of these authors, he quotes from or summarizes an argument they make against segregation and white supremacy; he then quotes at length from someone else who condemns that author or condemns the author himself, usually through an attack on "amalgamation" (which the author may or may not have mentioned). There is, then, a strange disjuncture in his argument—his own citation method makes it clear that current scholars, professors, and trained scientists all advocate racial equality and intermarriage; yet Bilbo claims that "science" supports his position.

In his chapter on Rayford Logan's collection *What the Negro Wants*[10] Bilbo accurately quotes long passages from various African American intellectuals and academics who had contributed. Bilbo reminds his readers of the academic credentials of each author, and that the author is African American —putting "(colored)" after the name. Having accurately quoted them, he attributes to every author, whether it's mentioned or not, a desire for "social equality"—which was the code for black men marrying white women.

For instance, Bilbo quotes "Mary McLeod Bethune (colored), President of the National Council of Negro Women" and her argument for full rights.

Here, then, is a program for racial advance and national unity. It adds up to the sum of the rights, privileges and responsibilities of full American citizenship. This is all that the Negro asks. He will not willingly accept less. As long as America offers less, she will be that much less a democracy. The whole way is the American way. (Mary McLeod Bethune, qtd. in Bilbo 71)

After pointing out that Bethune is Eleanor Roosevelt's "special friend, associate, and co-worker," Bilbo explains that she is really demanding

> total social equality between the two races. Surely, any one would know that this would in the end mean miscegenation, bastardization, amalgamation, and intermarriage of the races. Regardless of what Mrs. Roosevelt and her associate, Mary McLeod Bethune, have actually said or may say about social equality of whites and Negroes and the complete intermingling of the two races, their preachments and practices will eventually lead to the amalgamation, mongrelization, and destruction of both the white and black races. (72)

This obvious conflict between what the texts say and how Bilbo uses them is perplexing; it may be that Bilbo sincerely believes that the only reason African Americans want the vote is so that African American men can sleep with white women, or it may be that Bilbo thinks his readers can be counted on to make that inference. It's also possible that the main rhetorical force of the chapter is simply to inhabit and enhance a kind of anti-intellectual and racist *ressentiment,* to raise ire on the part of his intended audience at African American scholars who are better educated than they. Given the fear that African American intellectualism has long raised among racists, it may be nothing more complicated than tapping that anxiety.

It isn't just African American intellectuals about whom Bilbo raises fears; he attacks a professor with an Italian last name (another group about whom he was notoriously racist). Having discussed Borgese's advocacy of interracial mixing, he says:

> If the President of the University of Chicago and the members of the Board of Trustees are informed of such damnable and un-American teachings which are being disseminated by Professor Borgese and refuse to take prompt action by discharging him from the faculty, then they are thereby condoning, endorsing, and sponsoring a philosophy which will mongrelize white America. If they refuse to remove such a cancerous sore from their great educational Institution, every white American

who believes in the integrity of his blood and race will be forced to say that the University of Chicago needs a complete and thorough house cleaning. (145)

Bilbo was famous for his micromanagement of the university system in Mississippi resulting in disaccreditation and or censuring of state universities by such organizations as the American Medical Association, the American Association of University Professors, and the Association of Colleges and Secondary Schools of the South. While he has some defenders,[11] at the time he bragged of his "house-cleaning" and appears to have enjoyed the posture of opposing the eggheads.[12] And, certainly, neither intellectuals nor universities come off very well in Bilbo's book. At another point he accuses the "modern intellectual" of "relativistic dogmas," and asks rhetorically

> if [the intellectual] can quote "authorities," if something that calls itself "science" supports his views, if the assertion of opposed views is not intellectually respectable, what of it? What kind of "science" is it that has to support itself in this manner? (67)

This passage, and the book generally, complicates the easy accusation of "anti-intellectual" for rhetors like Bilbo. The scare quotes on "science" suggest the possibility of an apparent versus real science—a science of head size, and nose shape, and skin color, in which race is something you cannot define but you just know: a "science" of common sense and popular consensus, and in clear opposition to the relativism of professors and intellectuals. Bilbo was "anti-intellectual" only when intellectuals disagreed with him. That's an important point, which we miss if we expect that demagoguery always appeals to anti-intellectualism; it doesn't. It can, as in the case of Grant, be intellectual. It is only nasty about intellectuals who disagree.

Luthin and Gustainis both make a point of the anti-intellectualism of demagogues, but the accusation is complicated. As Aaron Lecklider has shown, the long history of popular culture and intellectuals is not one of clear and consistent antagonism, with other factors (such as anti-elitism, anticommunism, and anxiety about liberal intellectuals' stances on race issues). One possible reading is that he is appealing to a different sense of the word "science": it is not a skilled practice of establishing and testing falsifiable hypotheses, requiring considerable training and expert knowledge; it is something else—it is something done better by amateurs like him and Cox, and by experts in the late nineteenth century. This is, in essence, a very old view of what science and authority are. Peter Bowler and Iwan Morus describe the philosophy of science central to the Scientific Revolution:

"Protagonists agreed what was special about their approach to knowledge was that it was based on the interrogation of experience rather than authority" (51). As described earlier, Romantic notions of science rely on the sense that there are types in nature that astute individuals can see, and it is a convention in the history of Western philosophy that direct experience is supposed to be more reliable (have more "epistemic authority") than argument from authority. Even if unintelligible in their details, the assertions made by "experts" like Madison Grant confirm the perceptions of Bilbo's ideal audience. Rhetors like Boas, Benedict, or Weltfish are asking readers to reject what those readers would *know* to be true: that some races (such as theirs) are better than others, that the fear and anger segregationists feel at the idea of abandoning segregation is an ontologically justified foundation for political action.

"Science" like Gobineau's confirms or explains common perception, but with the advent of the twentieth century, "science" seemed more and more to disconfirm common sense. Lecklider has argued that part of what made Einstein's theory of relativity so troubling to many people, and that hence triggered a surprising amount of media interest, was that

> the theory created a fissure between ordinary and intelligent Americans at the same time as it revealed the simple wrongness of ordinary people's knowledge. It was not simply a matter of inequality, then; the brainpower of the intellectual class was suddenly revealed to be objectively better, more honest, and totally inaccessible to all but the most elite dozen. (51)

Lecklider describes the hostile reaction to much of this devaluing of ordinary knowledge, and it seems probable that many of Bilbo's intended audience would have had direct experience with such devaluing. Matt Wray describes the long history of elite intervention in the lives of the "not quite white," an intervention that seemed to say that everything poor people knew about farming, animal husbandry, child-raising, health, and other topics was entirely wrong. And, of course, it's likely that quite a few of those experts themselves were entirely wrong. While experts did make great strides in regard to reducing hookworm, for instance, there were also projects like eugenics that were openly hostile to common people. As Wray says:

> The symbolic boundaries eugenicists used to elevate themselves above the liminal whites they studied became widely shared scientific perceptions, which would soon become social boundaries with profoundly discriminatory effects. For poor whites, some of the most pernicious,

invidious, and damaging distinctions imposed by eugenicists were those that focused on intelligence and cognitive skills. (83)

Bilbo was tapping an often-legitimate frustration with expertise. He was not dismissing all expertise, but dismissing the kind that contradicted the beliefs and experiences of his audience—the kind of situation that Lecklider identifies as a moment of anti-intellectualism.

Mark Noll has argued that one of the mistakes in the history of American evangelical Christianity was a shift to church life that was "activist, immediatistic, and individualistic" (64). While Noll grants many of the benefits of it, he also argues that it contributed to a troubling anti-intellectualism, particularly due to "its scorn for tradition, its concentration on individual competence, its distrust of mediated knowledge" (64). Noll argues that evangelicals have a tendency to rely on what he calls "naïve Baconianism" and this epistemology/hermeneutics means that

> under the illusion of fostering a Baconian approach to Scripture, creationists seek to convince their audience that they are merely contemplating simple conclusions from the Bible, when they are really contemplating conclusions from the Bible shaped by their preunderstandings of how the Bible should be read. (198)

I'm suggesting that this sense of reality, and how it is not interpreted, but simply read, is precisely what explains the simultaneous appeal to authority/anti-intellectualism of Bilbo's argumentation. The Bible can only be read as prohibiting interracial marriage if one takes a fairly complicated narrative to it (thoroughly discussed in Haynes's *Noah's Curse*); yet, if one has heard that Genesis 9 is the origin of races for one's entire life, it's hard to recognize that that narrative is not *in* the Bible at all. Just as one could look at various people and "see" race, one can look at the Bible and "see" a defense of segregation.

Saurette and Gunster's notion of "epistemological populism" is more precise and therefore probably more useful than "anti-intellectualism," but potentially damaging if it is assumed that there is some kind of binary between populist and elite knowledge, with the latter being necessarily more reliable. Grant, a member of the elite, also appealed to epistemological populism, although he was an elite writing to an elite. Noll's description of a flawed way of thinking about expertise in the evangelical tradition nicely captures the complexity.

> This overwhelming trust in the capacities of an objective, disinterested, unbiased, and neutral science perhaps was excusable in the early nineteenth century, but in the early twentieth century it was indefensible.

Fundamentalist naivete concerning science was matched by several other nineteenth-century traits that also undercut the possibility of a responsible intellectual life. These included a weakness for treating the verses of the Bible as pieces in a jigsaw puzzle that needed only to be sorted and then fit together to possess a finished picture of divine truth; an overwhelming tendency to "essentialism," of the conviction that a specific formula could capture for all times and places the essence of biblical truth for any specific issue concerning God, the human condition, or the fate of the world; a corresponding neglect of forces in history that shape perceptions and help define the issues that loom as most important to any particular age; and a self-confidence, bordering on hubris, manifested by an extreme antitraditionalism that casually discounted the possibility of wisdom from earlier generations. (127)

The rhetorical power of authors like Grant, Bilbo, or Cox comes from confirming the audience's beliefs about the ontological grounding of the current social hierarchy and racial taxonomy, and legitimizing it through an argument that cannot quite be followed but the conclusions of which are attested to by proof texting.

Yet even their conclusions are oddly entangled. As Spiro points out, both Grant and his protégé Stoddard came from families that had been among the elite for hundreds of years. By the doctrine of signs, then, Grant's family was a member of the elect, entitled by God's will to their political, cultural, and economic dominance. Or, in Grant's terms, the "native American aristocracy . . . has, up to this time, supplied the leaders of thought and the control of capital, of education, and of the religious ideals and altruistic bias of the community" (5). But, Grant says, "In America, we have nearly succeeded in destroying the privilege of birth; that is, the intellectual and moral advantage a man of good stock brings into the world with him" (6). Instead of continuing to choose leaders like him, voters are choosing average men, and other ethnicities are succeeding economically.

Bilbo was one of a set of Southern politicians who mobilized poor whites to overturn the traditional political machines, run by old families who felt entitled to their positions by virtue of their heritage. Those old families, called the "Bourbons" or "planters" (not entirely ironically), were the Southern equivalent of the New England families to which Grant and Stoddard belonged. Grant is fairly nasty about the current crop of politicians from the South:

> The change in the type of men who are now sent by the Southern States to represent them in the Federal Government from their predecessors in ante-bellum times is partly due to these causes, but in a greater degree it is to be attributed to the fact that a very large portion of the best racial

strains in the South were killed during the Civil War. In addition the war shattered the aristocratic traditions which formerly secured the selection of the best men as rulers. The new democratic ideals with universal suffrage among the whites result in the choice of representatives who lack the distinction and ability of the leaders of the Old South. (38–39)

Bilbo was precisely the kind of *nouveau blanc* against whom much of *The Passing of the Great Race* was directed. By Grant's narrative, his great race was passing because of people like Bilbo.

Grant's book, in short, was read in two logically incompatible ways at once. It could be read as a jeremiad about the need to return to a time when Nordics (not just "whites") were in political and economic dominance. It was, for Grant at least, a condemnation of the political hierarchy shifting to people like Bilbo. People like Stoddard and Bilbo, however, read it as a performance of Nordic whiteness that enabled newly empowered "whites" (of any race) to legitimate their recent ascension as predestined. For Grant, it was nostalgia for an irrecoverable past; for Bilbo, it invoked nostalgia for what might become the immediate past. In short, while the book functioned to reinforce the just-world hypothesis for both Grant and Bilbo, theirs were opposite worlds. Or, to be more blunt, both Grant and Bilbo saw the dominance of their in-group as predestined and just; they just didn't agree on the membership of that group.[13]

"It's in the Internet"

Despite the perception of demagoguery as the most powerful rhetoric (it may be), no single instance of demagoguery has impressive agency. When demagoguery tells people what they want to hear, it works; but it's difficult to say when and why it gets people to move into new beliefs. Demagogic texts work because (and to the extent that) they reinforce the same taxonomies of identity, narratives, and policies as the world of demagoguery in which the audience lives. Demagoguery, then, depends on consensus; it may be that it is less manageable in a world of agonism (a variation of the argument made by scholars ranging from John Stuart Mill to Chantal Mouffe). And that is probably a major reason that a recurrent theme in demagoguery is that one should not listen to any other viewpoint, and that figures whose power comes from demagoguery, such as Bilbo, so often try to shut down sites of alternate points of view. In the era of newsprint, shutting down opposition media was relatively straightforward, and given the media conditions through most of the twentieth century, getting to different points of view would be difficult for many (most? all?) citizens. In 1942, California media gave far more coverage to rumors of Japanese sabotage than to refutations of those rumors. Citizens would have had to depend on summaries of the Roberts report, many of which were misleading. Although Knox sent a telegram to Tolan clearly stating that there had been no sabotage, no statement of his along those lines received any media attention, and reporters could easily have asked him. People in California would have had trouble finding sources of information to contradict the fear-mongering.

This is all different, as people are fond of saying, in the age of the internet. Primary sources are easily available; arguments, counterarguments, and counter-counterarguments abound. Scholarship on counterpublics has often been evangelical, spreading the good news of admirable groups who enact social change and resist oppression. Manuel Castells summarizes that hopeful view.

> By constructing a free community in a symbolic place, social movements create a public space, a space for deliberation, which ultimately becomes a political space, a space for sovereign assemblies to meet and to recover their rights of representation (11).

As Castells points out, there later emerged a more corrective approach. Some scholars have argued that digital media increased factionalism and polarization, fostering enclaves and echo chambers rather than diverse communities of deliberation.[14] In such enclaves, a problematic text that is positioned as "expert" discourse can be preserved from the kind of examination that would expose its problems. Thus, as I will argue in the last part of this chapter, the internet can increase the normalization of demagoguery so that it is not recognized as such.

In May of 2008, the California Supreme Court ruled that limiting marriage to heterosexual couples violated the California Constitution, and, hence, "gay" marriage was legal. Almost immediately, various organizations acted to put a proposition on the November 2008 ballot that would alter the state constitution, restricting marriage to heterosexuals. One of those organizations was the Traditional Family Coalition, of which Hak-Shing William Tam was executive director, and another was the America Return to God Prayer Movement, of which Tam was secretary. Proposition 8 passed (by approximately 52 percent to 48 percent), and was promptly subject to various lawsuits. One of those lawsuits concerned the denial of marriage licenses to two couples—Kristen Perry and Sandra Steir, and Paul Katami and Jeffrey Zarrillo—and became the case generally known as *Perry v. Schwarzenneger.* Tam was asked to testify in this trial because of his work in the organizations listed above, and for the website with which he was involved, 1man1woman.net. Briefly, the point of issue was whether the revocation of a right (homosexuals had the right to marry between the time of the *In re Marriage Cases* and the passage of Proposition 8) had been grounded in what Walker, in his decision, called "private moral or religious beliefs without an accompanying secular purpose" (10; see also Becker 68). An issue that brings to the fore what kinds of arguments were made for Proposition 8—not just *could* it be justified on secular grounds of public welfare, but *had* it been argued on those grounds. And, hence, Tam's rhetoric was part of the trial.

Tam is an interesting figure for this issue, and especially for thinking about demagoguery. Since he was almost certainly sincere in his expressions, he was not particularly hateful in affect, and there was no benefit to him of his political activism. He didn't invent any of the arguments he promoted, and he could point to sites and sources that seemed to him to be reliable and credible expert testimony. Promulgator of assertions that were misleading, inaccurate, fallacious, damaging, and sometimes fraudulent, Tam was certainly sincere, and he was able to cite sources for his claims. Tam's rhetoric was demagoguery, and it was damaging, and it is a kind far more common than the kind we associate with famous rhetors pounding on a podium. One cannot watch Tam and find him anything other than a mildly befuddled person whose opposition to gay marriage comes from sincerely held concerns about his children and his faith, concerns fueled by organizations he considers authoritative, like NARTH (National Association for the Research and Therapy of Homosexuality, which he cites). His affect is calm, cautious, attentive to the questions, and perfectly sincere. On the whole, he seems to be rather a nice person, except, of course, for the hate-mongering. His sincere, well-meaning, and *nice* reliance on demagoguery shows how important it is not to think of demagoguery in terms of what some bad group of people does. It is a way of arguing and not a kind of arguer.

Tam's organization had relied on unfortunately typical arguments against homosexuals, not just against gay marriage. An entire page of 1man1woman.net has links about homosexuality and pedophilia (including the notorious claim that homosexuals are twelve times more likely to commit pedophilia, discussed later in this chapter), claims that legalizing homosexual marriage is the first step in a slippery slope that quickly leads to legalizing bestiality and polygamy, that homosexual parents are worse parents, and "if everyone in the world practices same-sex marriage, the human race would soon become extinct."[15] Some arguments, however, are not just false, but have been repeatedly demonstrated to be false, and constitute sheer hatemongering, such as claiming a link between pedophilia and gay men.

It is this kind of rhetoric that earned various homophobic organizations the designation "hate groups" by the Southern Poverty Law Center (SPLC), which called them purveyors of "demonizing propaganda aimed at homosexuals and other sexual minorities" and propagators of "known falsehoods—claims about

LGBT people that have been thoroughly discredited by scientific authorities" (Schlatter). Claiming that homosexuality is sinful is one (deeply flawed) way of reading Scripture; claiming that homosexuals are child molesters is hate speech. Our common image of hatemongering is a demagogue like Hitler pounding the table, segregationist crowds screaming epithets at school children, or hooded bigots burning crosses. We generally assume that people engaged in hate speech have a hateful affect. That isn't the case, however, with much demagoguery; in fact, Tam typifies what is actually the far more common posture of someone advocating the restriction of rights of some out-group (or even their expulsion or extermination) out of a reasonable set of concerns grounded in reliable evidence. That is, however, just a posture, a way the rhetor looks, and not a way the argumentation functions.

The same claims to facticity, realism, common sense, and even science described throughout this book run throughout what is a profoundly religious argument on the part of various homophobic groups. For instance, 1man1woman.net promises to provide "a rational and logical reasoning" on the issue of gay marriage. The Family Research Council (note the significance of having "research" in its name) states its goals.

> Since 1983, Family Research Council (FRC) has advanced faith, family and freedom in public policy and public opinion. FRC's *team of seasoned experts* promotes these core values through policy research, public education on Capitol Hill and in the media, and grassroots mobilization. (emphasis added, "About FRC")

The Family Research Institute (with "research" and "institute" in the name) describes its mission: "The Family Research Institute was founded in 1982 with one overriding mission: *to generate empirical research* on issues that threaten the traditional family" (*Family Research Institute,* emphasis added). This kind of claim to represent expert consensus is not restricted to antigay rhetors, nor is it even new. The "white separatist" David Duke (and member of the KKK) has an autobiography with over one thousand footnotes (something that impresses the reviewers on Amazon.com and no doubt contributes to its overwhelmingly positive ranking). Theodore Bilbo's 1948 *Separation or Amalgamation* has dozens of citations. Madison Grant's 1911 *Passing of the Great Race* (influential in the eugenics movement), looked learned, with its discussions of head shapes and race migrations, and the lower court decisions upholding antimiscegenation laws claimed that science was on their side.

The citations for all these rhetors are, of course, deeply troubled, but not generally in ways that are obviously and immediately apparent, especially to the nonexpert. And much of the rhetoric depends on the tendency to conflate the difference between "accurate" and "precise" (for more on this see especially Gross 97). But, as is narrated so effectively by Mark Jordan in *Recruiting Young Love,* Christian opposition to homosexuality has a complicated relationship to scientific "expertise" throughout the twentieth and twenty-first centuries. Until the 1970s, relevant sciences (such as psychology) had narrations of corruption and fall for the roots of homosexuality, especially in regard to failures of patriarchal family relations (albeit with, as Jordan shows, very complicated trends and histories). In the 1970s, however, the major expert organizations moved away from narratives of homosexuality as a diseased and failed heterosexuality, and fundagelical heteronormative Christians found themselves at odds with "science."

As mentioned regarding Workman, Bilbo, and Cox, segregationists had found themselves similarly isolated from mainstream science. John P. Jackson narrates what happened when the political agenda that was, at one point, at the center of a disciplinary consensus (racial mixing leads to the collapse of civilization, nonwhites are racially inferior) gets moved to the fringes: people committed to that political ideology form their own journals and organizations. Those journals are entirely politically motivated; that is, they only publish research that supports their political agenda. Yet, the articles in those journals continually accuse the other journals of being politically motivated, of lacking objectivity, and, to be clear, doing exactly what they are doing to a far greater degree—a clear instance of cunning projection. Organizations that read the apostle Paul as condemning homosexuality (but, oddly enough, not sexuality in general) found themselves at odds with secular experts in the mid-1970s, and so founded organizations such as FRC, FRI, or NARTH that, while they will only publish materials that support their policy agenda (preventing gay marriage, keeping homosexuals from being able to adopt, "therapy" for homosexuals) condemn other organizations and journals for being politically motivated, biased, and methodologically flawed. In short, they engage in cunning projection. Yet, there is no reason to doubt the sincerity of the people involved in these groups, nor to assume that they have personally benefited as much from this activity as they would have from other ventures. They probably mean well, at least by their own lights.

Hak-Shing William Tam was asked to testify because his arguments were seen by opponents of Proposition 8 as typifying the rhetoric; hence, there were two important points in his testimony: what arguments had he (and his organizations) made, and what was the authority used for those claims. And the issue of authority was deeply troubling. Several times, when he is asked for support for his claims, he gives some version of the answer: "It's on the internet." As my middle school son said while watching the YouTube video of the deposition, "'On the internet'? You can find talking cats on the internet—that doesn't make it true." Yet, Tam seems to expect that his having accepted information from "the internet" is a reasonable explanation. For instance, when asked what the phrase "gay agenda" means, Tam answers, "If you google those two terms, you'll find out. It's in the internet" (at approximately 9:51.46); when pressed further on the issue, he says that "there are several different websites describing the gay agenda" (9:5220). When asked where Tam got the idea that the Netherlands legalized incest and polygamy shortly after legalizing gay marriage, Tam answers, "It's in the internet." The attorney pushes Tam and there is the following exchange:

> Q. Somewhere out in the internet it says that the Netherlands legalized incest and polygamy in 2005?
> A. Frankly, I did not write this, all right? Polygamy was legalized in 2005. Another person in the organization found it and he showed me that.
> Q. And you just put it out there to convince voters to vote for Proposition 8?
> A. Well, I—I look at the document and I think that was true.
> Q. Did you ever look up what the law was in the Netherlands or ask anybody to do that?
> A. Yes. There is—there are different documents out there that shows that was true.

From this exchange, it seems that Tam believes that simply being published "on the internet" is proof that an assertion is true. Yet, that can't be entirely accurate—surely Tam was aware that there are also pages on the internet making opposite claims. So, there is something odd going on in Tam's use of "the internet" as an authoritative source: some claims are ipso facto proven by appeal to authority but others are not, and he seems to think that he can tell good from bad appeals to authority simply by looking at them (someone "showed me that").

When pressed on the notion that homosexuals can change their orientation, Tam says he got that information from the NARTH website. The plaintiffs' attorney points out that NARTH is at odds with major organizations like the American Psychological Association, and then asks, "You thought it was better to get your scientific information about this issue from the NARTH website as opposed to the American Psychological Association. Is that your testimony?" Tam answers, "Uhm, yeah, I believe in what NARTH says." That's an important moment in a discussion of expertise: Tam defends NARTH not on the grounds of who they are, their methodology, their expertise, but *his* belief: "I believe in what NARTH says." Expertise is determined by his belief.

This determination of authority is particularly significant in regard to a specific claim: Tam's organization claimed that homosexuals are twelve times more likely to molest children. When pressed on his source for that point, his answer is, "Apparently, academic papers." He is referring to the popular, and fascinatingly muddled, claim by Paul Cameron. It's a popular meme, showing up frequently in antigay arguments, often without any clear citation (as it does in the "Are Pedophiles Criminals or Victims?" article linked to at the 1man1woman.net site). As far as I can tell, it appears to trace back to Cameron's 1985 article, "Homosexual Molestation of Children/Sexual Interaction of Teacher and Pupil" in the impressively titled journal *Psychological Reports*.

The twelve-times-more-likely claim is first mentioned on page 1231 of the 1985 article. In order to ensure that I'm being fair, I'll reproduce the crucial part of the argument in full:

> Were we to assume that every heterosexual molestation was committed by a heterosexual, the 96% of the populace which is heterosexual appears to commit no more than between 60% (median of all studies in Table 1 regarding sexual act of offender) and 67% (median of all studies in Table 1 regarding gender of victim [assuming that all molestations of boys were by homosexuals and all molestations of girls were by heterosexuals]) of all molestations of children. However, we know that a substantial number of heterosexual molestations are perpetrated by those who have molested both sexes. Bisexuals accounted for at least 18% of the molesters in the Fitch (1969) series; at least 9% in the Nedoma, Mellan, and Pondelickova (1971) study; and in the Groth and Birnbaum (1978) work, at least 26% of the 125 molestations of girls and 39% of the 82 molestations of boys were performed by bisexuals—54% of all the molestations in this study were performed by bisexual or homosexual practitioners. Taking this fact into account, it would appear reasonable to assume that at least 10% of all the molestations of girls were committed by bisexuals. If we adjust the proportion of molestations of girls committed by heterosexuals so that we subtract the 10% committed by bisexuals (i.e., a bi-sexual correction), then our estimates would change to heterosexuals committing between 54% to 60% of the molestations of youth, and the 4% of the population which is bisexual or homosexual accounts for between 40% to 46% of the sexual molestations.

If the molestation ratios in Table 1 bear a reasonably close approximation to empirical reality, then it appears that those who are bi- to homosexual are proportionately much more apt to molest youth. If we assume that every heterosexual molestation was committed by a heterosexual, then those who are bi- to homosexual are at least twelve times more apt to incorporate legal minors into their sexual practices than are heterosexuals. If we include the correction factor which assumes that bisexuals account for 10% of the heteorsexual [*sic*] molestations, then bi- to homosexuals are at least sixteen times more apt to molest children than their heterosexual peers. (1230–31, the comment in brackets is Cameron's)

There are several points to note about this argument. First, even assuming it's a valid method of calculating the relative likelihood of heterosexual versus homosexual molesting (it isn't), it does not actually support the claim that homosexuals are twelve times more likely to molest children—that was the number Cameron got by including "bi-sexuals." Thus, the twelve times more likely statistic is only even plausibly valid if one takes the definition of "homosexual" to be "a person who has ever had any sexual activity with a member of the same sex"—a definition that antigay groups intermittently use and reject.

Were Cameron to use that definition consistently (or, indeed, if any antigay group used that definition consistently) then he would determine the percentage of "homosexuals" in the overall population by the percentage who have ever had any same sex experience. Yet, that isn't what he does. Thus, for purposes of determining the number of "homosexuals" who are pedophiles, Cameron uses an extraordinarily broad definition of homosexuality, but for purposes of determining the percentage in the population as a whole, he uses a very narrow one (an equivocation still found in material put out by groups like Family Research Council, American Family Association, and Family Research Institute).

Second, although there appears to be a tremendous amount of data, and Cameron's metadiscourse suggests the data and his interpretation of the data are logically connected, the passage actually works through a kind of intimidation. One can't, in fact, look at the data and see any clear connection to his interpretations or conclusions, and this is a problem throughout the article. At another point, using a slightly different method, Cameron infers that "a pupil appears about 90% more likely to be sexually assaulted by a homosexual practitioner" (1232); it's unclear to me how that statistic maps onto the twelve to eighteen times more likely claim. In fact, despite his narration, it's actually impossible to tell from this data (even with the accompanying chart) how Cameron got those numbers. Cameron's Table 1 sometimes gives the sample size of the various studies and sometimes other information (e.g., "51 cases of child molestation in follow-up" versus "6 child sex rings"); "bisexuals" are not listed. Thus, the obvious question—when

Cameron recalculated the percentage, did he add up all the instances of molesta-tion and then take the percentage of that total, or did he average the percentages from each study? This can't be answered without going back to every study he mentions and recalculating.

Third, I didn't go to that trouble, because his numbers can't be valid, given other problems with this study. Cameron has pulled together data collected with different methods, from different eras, in different places, by different people, and for different purposes and treats them the same—data from Wisconsin in 1964, Toronto in the late fifties, Bristol in the early fifties, and California in the late forties.[16] His data, in other words, is virtually worthless. And he manipulates this data on the basis of deeply problematic assumptions. Among those problematic assumptions are: the number of molestations that happened and the number reported are the same (or, at least, have the same statistical relations), that all molestations of boys were by "homosexuals" (using a definition that presumes precisely what is at stake), that the ratio of molestations reported is the same as the ratio actually occurring (so that there is not a different rate for different kinds of molestations), that 4 percent of the population is homosexual or bisexual, and so on. Those are simply assumptions, and the most favorable ones possible for his argument. Assuming a higher rate of homosexuals would significantly change the number. Assuming that the rate of reporting is not the same as the rate of occurrence would make the entire study invalid.

Fourth, even were his data valid, Cameron's math is problematic in a way not necessarily immediately apparent. The logic behind his math is something like this. Imagine that there is a sample of one hundred people and ten dogs. In a set period of time, those populations bite a total of twelve people—ten of those people were bitten by a human, and two of those people were bitten by a dog. What is the relative likelihood of being bitten by a dog versus a human? There are two very different ways of calculating the likelihood, with dramatically different results, depending upon whether one knows (or assumes) that the dog-bites-hu-man cases were evenly distributed among the dogs.

Two bites from the "dog" category is a very different statistic from "two dogs bit people." In the first case, the two bites might have been by the same dog, so only one-tenth of the dogs are biters. If all the people biting people was done by different people, then, in fact, dogs are no more likely to be biters than humans are. In the second case, however, it is specified that there were two dogs doing the biting. In that case, dogs are twice as likely as people to be biters. Cameron assumes the second case in regard to "homosexual" molestations, with no partic-ularly good reason to do so.[17] In other words, even assuming his data was valuable (it isn't), his conclusion is unmerited.

According to the SPLC, Cameron's research permeates the antigay groups such as Americans for Truth About Homosexuality, Concerned Women for America, Coral Ridge Ministries, and the Illinois Family Institute. Cameron was the founder of the Family Research Institute, whose work continues to be cited. A large number of those articles were published in *Psychological Reports*. *Psychological Reports* is not as good a journal as one might infer from its name (or webpage, which emphasizes that it engages in peer review). As Gregory Herek says about Cameron and his coauthors, this has important implications for thinking about the credibility of their research.

> Thus, the Cameron group has published all of its survey reports in academic journals with low prestige and, at least in the case of *Psychological Reports,* with a low rejection rate and a publication fee required from authors. Given the multiple, serious methodological flaws detailed in the first section of this chapter, it is reasonable to conclude that the Cameron group's papers would have been rejected by more prestigious scientific journals. (245)

With an extremely low rejection rate, an equally low citation rate, and a charge per page to publish, *Psychological Reports* is not a scholarly source. Tam's comment "apparently, academic papers" is an apt description, with emphasis on the "apparently."

Cameron is a fairly extreme case, having been dropped from membership in the American Psychological Association for violating the ethical principles of the organization, the subject of a successful motion by the council of the American Sociological Association, which stated that the "American Sociological Association officially and publicly states that Paul Cameron is not a sociologist and condemns his consistent misrepresentation of sociological research" ("Report of the Committee", see also "Council Acts"). The "expertise" of a cited expert is not often so unequivocally rejected by experts in the discipline; yet, despite such clear rejection, Cameron's "research" was still being cited thirty years later. FRI, FRC, NARTH, 1man1woman, like Grant, Cox, and Bilbo, position themselves as engaged in expert discourse in sociology, psychology, and anthropology when they are not, in fact, engaging in the discursive practices appropriate to those discourses. They are posturing themselves as engaged in one community's discourse, when they are really in another. FRI, FRC, NARTH, and 1man1woman are thoroughly grounded in patriarchal fundagelical conversations. Grant was supported by the fledgling field of eugenics. Cox and Bilbo were in a prosegregation conversation.

Arguments from authority have long been a part of deliberative rhetoric. In early rhetorical theory, there seems to have been the hope that every rhetor, if not actually every listener, could know enough about enough different things to be an expert on every important public decision. In Book I of *Rhetoric*, Aristotle has an ambitious list of the things a deliberative rhetor should know—such as the economic, military, and cultural weaknesses and strengths of his country and other countries. Cicero's advocacy of general training in *De Oratore* is similarly hard to achieve. We are continually asked to make decisions about things on which we lack the technical expertise but not because we lack information. If anything, the problem is too much information, and the difficulty of deciding which information to believe. Brian Hilligoss and Soo Young Rieh begin their article on credibility assessment: "Every day people encounter more information than they can possibly use. . . . But all information is not necessarily of equal value. The challenge that most people then face is to judge which information is more credible." (1467)

Douglas Walton's discussion of the issue in *Appeal to Expert Opinion* emphasizes the inappropriate deference that people can have to information that presents itself as scientific, or to authorities who claim to be scientists.

> Many of the things we accept are, inevitably, accepted on the basis of authority. If I get a diagnosis of my illness from a physician, I may get a second opinion, but even that opinion has been put forward by a certified expert. I may look up accounts of my illness in a medical library, but these too are written by experts. (1)

Walton argues that the effectiveness of fallacious appeals to authority tends to come from one of two main sources—the halo effect, and obedience to authority. "With appeals to scientific expert opinion, in particular, there is a powerful institutional halo effect that seems to exclude critical questioning by a nonscientist, and make the claim seem to be unchallengeable by reasoned argumentation" (260). That is hardly the situation one sees in the texts discussed here—there is simultaneously an invocation and rejection of scientific authority to persuade an audience whose beliefs are probably not falsifiable through any kind of scientific debate.

None of the people discussed in this chapter (nor in the book) "exclude critical questioning by a nonscientist"; they are nonscientists representing themselves as fully qualified to participate in a scientific debate with people who have credentials, expertise, and scholarly practices that Bilbo, Cox, and Tam don't have. Their lack of expertise and credentials is not what puzzles me. It isn't clear why demagoguery relies at all on appeals to science. The claims about "science" undermine the possibility of persuading an informed and intelligent expert audience. Their claims about "science" are simply false, but why make them at all? With Bilbo,

I've suggested that part of the rhetorical goal might be to polarize expert from non-expert knowledge, or, more accurately, to privilege one kind of "expertise" (that of direct experience and instant judgment) over scholarly training, contingent judgment, and experimental practices. As such, it shifts the stasis from claims about the world to the identity of the speakers.

Yet, the question remains: why use "science" to do this kind of work? Certainly not because the beliefs of Bilbo, Cox, and Tam were significantly affected by the "science." Lombardo explains the beliefs of the people most important in getting "racial purity" principles enacted in Virginia: "The zealous racism that is reflected in their private papers and their public propaganda has little to do with a rigorous application of the principles of genetics, even as they were imperfectly understood in 1924" (451). When "eugenics" supported their views, they cited it, and when it didn't, they didn't. Why appeal to some mythical univocal construct, particularly by the time that scientific disciplines and journals no longer supported the claims trying to gain their authority from invoking "science"? I'm suggesting that arguments about race and racism, like the use of the word "science" by Bilbo, Cox, and Tam, depend upon the notion of an eternal and immutable taxonomy of identity written into the ontic logos, which good people can perceive. Some people might perceive it, and some people might not, but it must always have been there to perceive. Given the tendency for this cultural epistemology (truth is eternal, and intermittently perceived by people of good judgment) to coexist with a particular strain of evangelical Protestant, it's interesting to speculate whether there is a significant connection. Briefly, American Protestantism has long promoted the notion of nature as "God's Other Book," a variation on the concept of the "ontic logos" (that is, God's word written into ontology). As Samuel Morse puts it in his *Foreign Conspiracy,*

> Zealous according to the strength of his belief in the dogmas of his sect, the Protestant calls to his aid the treasures of science. He believes that the divine Author of truth in the Bible is also the author of truth in nature. He knows that as truth is one, He that created all that forms the vast field of scientific research cannot contradict truth in Scripture by truth in nature. (133)

Morse makes this argument in service of the claim that Protestants allow religious toleration and Catholics don't (in, not without irony, a text arguing that Catholics are in a massive conspiracy against democracy, an argument with distinctly *in*tolerant policy implications). This idea of scriptural truth being revealed in nature was (and still is) an argument for religious support of scientific research. When the "truths" of Scripture that are confirmed by science are relatively abstract, there is no particular harm in this view (e.g., Polkinghorne's argument that Christian theology is confirmed by quantum physics). But someone like Polkinghorne assumes that both fields of knowledge—interpretation of Scripture and interpretation of the world—are in flux. For people who believe that the meaning of a foundational text is stable and known, the "other" text has to be interpreted in light of that stable meaning. For someone like Tam, the stable meaning is that homosexuality is an abomination, for Bilbo it's that God wills white supremacy. Expert opinion is expert only insofar as it supports the truths that are already known. Thus, as with Grant, these forms of epistemological populism don't just reinforce specific notions about policy agenda (homosexuals should not be allowed to marry, segregation should be maintained) but reinforce a perception about the world itself: that it is unchanging. Demagoguery says that this unchanging truth is easily perceived by good people, and is continually under attack by bad people. Probably the single most damaging aspect of demagoguery is its worldview of a beleaguered in-group fighting for survival against a nefarious out-group, whose expulsion, suppression, or extermination is justified as necessary self-defense.

This worldview seems persuasive for a variety of reasons, and under a variety of conditions, and one of the reasons is that it provides a sense of clarity in the midst of anxious uncertainty. The complicated situation, demagoguery says, is actually very simple. But the simple solution, I have argued throughout this book, doesn't necessarily mean that demagoguery always has simple texts—the data can be tremendously complicated, even unintelligibly so. The solution is simple, and the overall claims are as well—there is an in-group, and it is good, and there are out-groups, and they range from potentially good (if they can be assimilated) through neutral (if they are willing to remain submissive) to evil (if they resist). But the data necessary to defend this simple solution can be so complicated that it's clear it is not intended to *persuade* or even "support" the claims—it acts as an empty promise that the claim could be supported, and an assertion of the identity of the rhetor as a knower. Audience members can be persuaded that the policy is justified, but only if they already accept most of the claims. The data acts to confirm the perception that the advocate is the sort of person to be trusted.

The data can be simple, and there can be a simple, logical relation between it and certain claims ("The Japanese intend to harm aircraft manufacturing because they have bought land near aircraft manufacturers"), but it can also be incomprehensible (such as Grant's data about various groups). Even when there are logical relations between specific claims and data, the overall argumentation is internally contradictory in that various specific claims and data appeal to premises that contradict other premises. For Workman, segregation is good because African Americans like it, and segregation is necessary because African Americans resist it; there is race mixing yet the South is generally pure, and race mixing, once started, cannot be stopped. The Japanese are evil because they buy land near aircraft manufacturers; such buying of land is nefarious because the Japanese are evil.

One might argue that there is a kind of logic that operates with demagoguery—identity as logic. Demagoguery plays on the premise that in-group identity is sufficient for political deliberation—that all one needs to know about any policy debate is the group identification of the various rhetors. Rhetors who are good people (that is, loyal to the in-group) must be advocating good policies. One can deduce everything one needs to know about a rhetor's argument from his or her group identity. That a policy might be impractical is, by this logic, not necessarily bad. First, advocating an impractical policy—refusing to worry about whether something can work—demonstrates more loyalty to the in-group, since it shows that the rhetor believes the in-group can do anything with sufficient will. Arguing that a policy is good but impractical suggests that the in-group's powers are limited, and that "good" might be out of our reach—a clear lack of faith in the in-group. Second, if one believes that God is on the side of the in-group, then issues of practicality don't matter—settling on a policy that can only work if there is a miracle is itself a statement of faith that God is on our side. To worry about the practicalities suggests that one thinks God might fail us; it is a betrayal.

In-group politics can thereby lead to a kind of impractical one-upmanship. in which various rhetors compete in their demonstration of in-group loyalty by advocating increasingly impractical policies, which then, through repetition come to be stances rhetors are required to take. Communities forget, if they ever knew, that the policies were presented as extreme (as I have argued happened in regard to what was initially a posturing threat about secession over slavery, and what seemed to happen in the 2012 GOP primaries regarding going to war with Iran, or the "War Council" in Flint).

The topic I have been unable to pursue in this book is how that notion of agency and self (the in-group can do anything with sufficient will, and raising concerns about practicality demonstrates a lack of faith) is connected to a muddled version of imputed righteousness. Building on Mark Noll's argument about evangelical wrong turns and Kate Bowler's discussion of the prosperity gospel, I would like to suggest that the notion of someone with sufficient will being able to do anything is strengthened by the assumption that people of true faith are ontologically changed into new and good people. Such an assumption means that examining the past for failed *policies* is a waste of time—the failure of a policy is not a procedural or policy issue, but one of identity, that the advocates or enactors of the policy were not truly good people. When all of that is entangled with the sort of sloppy Calvinism that is once again popular, the prospects for thorough policy deliberation are grim.

Our culture's weak grasp of logic doesn't help either. For many people, an argument is logical if it's true, and one determines whether it's true by simply asking oneself: belief is assumed to be evidence. Further, an argument is logical if the person making it is rational, and that is determined by the unemotional and controlled posture he or she takes. We have, then, a tight circle: an assertion is true if it is said by someone we believe to be truthful, which we determine by whether we believe the person's assertions.[18] With such a process of testing assertions, we are unlikely to move beyond existing group consenses, except to new and more extreme policies that, paradoxically, cannot be argued qua policies.[19]

The most important logical failure is the failure to apply major premises across groups. Take the relatively straightforward enthymeme: "The Japanese are evil because they buy land near aircraft factories." The major premise (buying land near aircraft factories shows a group is evil) was not a premise on which Warren relied consistently—he didn't look to see whether members of other ethnicities at war with the United States (Germans, Italians, French) had bought land near factories. The argument for displacing Saddam Hussein was, among other things, "He is a bad person because he engages in torture." The way that various supporters of the invasion have defended US torture shows that argument to be in bad faith—they don't accept their own major premise.

There are several ways one might describe the practice of putting forward an argument the logic of which one doesn't actually accept: claiming that the argument is illogical, that the rhetor is irrational, that this is not good faith argumentation, that the rhetor is being unreasonable. For a long time, I was persuaded by the notion that "unreasonable" was a useful middle term between rational and irrational (and didn't invoke the cultural misunderstandings about the rational/irrational split) but delving deep into demaguery has persuaded me that that term is probably not helpful. Whatever term we use should help people see when we are relying on premises our own arguments violate, and "reasonable" instead suggests that we either rely on the ethos of the rhetor (does she *seem* reasonable) or whether we can think of reasons to support our position. And, as Kruglanski's work makes clear, we can always find reasons. Tam could find supposedly expert sources to say that homosexuals are child molesters, and Cox could find published authors to say Africans are inferior. David Duke has over a thousand footnotes.

I find the phrase "good faith" argumentation compelling, especially for characterizing someone who is not engaged in argumentation oriented toward greater understanding of the issue. I'll admit that I understand others' discomfort with the term: it seems to suggest to people that those not engaged in good faith argumentation (that is, they're willing to change their minds, to abide by various rules) are bad. Although it is supposed to be used to describe how someone is behaving in an argument, it can be heard as a statement about whether they are good people, and now we're back to arguing identity.

It is conventional to distinguish between a logical argument and a rational stance, with the latter being a characteristic of the person engaged in argument, and the former an assessment about much more specific claims. I find that focus on the person less than helpful, and instead find the notion of a "rational-critical" argument helpful—how one acts discursively in the course of argumentation. Within that frame, one might have logical arguments in the midst of irrational argumentation, as when a participant draws a valid inference from a premise—but a premise that has already been refuted. For instance, Cox, Bilbo, and Tam all drew conclusions that logically followed from premises, but premises that had (years before) been shown to be false, ranging from the distribution and importance of head shape to bad statistics about child molestation.[20]

But this raises the issue that has to be discussed: whether any distinction between rational and irrational is useful. When people argue against making a distinction, I have found, there is a tendency to appeal to a fixed model of the mind: to use scholarship showing that people are not perfectly rational in order to argue that people are entirely irrational. To me, that seems like showing that most people have bad math skills in order to show that math doesn't exist. Carol Dweck uses the term "fixed mindset" for people who imagine that the capacity for intelligence is fixed at birth, and all that happens in our lives is that we expose how much of that fixed quantity we were given. There is, it seems to me, a similar assumption about logic. It may be that most people don't reason logically most of the time, but most people are also bad at statistics. Being better at statistics would help us, as a community, argue better about policies. We don't always need to engage in rational-critical argumentation, and we don't always need statistics, and neither of them represents a perfect foundation for perfect decision making. They provide information, just as thinking about how people feel provides information. Rational-critical argumentation, statistics, policy argumentation, opinion polls, and questions of identity are all things we should include in our public discourse, but no single one is sufficient.

Jonathan Haidt, in *The Righteous Mind,* uses the metaphor of a rider on an elephant, with the elephant representing intuitive methods of thinking, and the rider representing what we conventionally call intellect. Haidt argues that the rider often rationalizes decisions made by the elephant, but not always—the rider can, at times, direct the elephant (or, as Kahneman puts it, we spend most of our time in System 1 thinking, but we do also use System 2 thinking). The appeal to authorities in which demagoguery engages is consistently the kind that legitimates the rhetor's (and intended audience's) intuitions; it legitimates closure and enables the demonization of deliberation. Demagoguery is not, then, anti-intellectual, as much as antideliberative; it says that the truth is easily attained, easily expressed, and easily enforced.

Conclusion: Snakes, Vehemence, Snark, and Argumentation

It's a strange lot that insists that pythons, rattlers, constrictors, vipers and other reptile species make good pets.
—Jennifer O'Connor, "Federal Snake Ban Lacks Bite"

This book project is motivated by the notion that definitions of demagoguery matter. Underlying the book is a model of policy argumentation—a particular definition of a need (or problem or ill) implies a policy response. If we define the ill of demagoguery as coming from certain individuals, then we purify our community of those people. If we define demagoguery as an ill inherent to democracy, then we abandon democracy. As Robert Ivie has said: "Democracy too often is troped as a disease" (*Democracy* 30) in which "demagoguery is the source and symptom of democratic distemper" (*Democracy* 34). This demophobia can grease the wheels for oppressive political actions. "Political power is displaced from the public to a ruling elite by portraying the masses in the image of a primitive Other subject to the delirium of demagoguery, not unlike the barbarian beyond the walls of the polity" (*Democracy* 50). If, as I'm suggesting, we define demagoguery as a damaging way to argue when the stakes are high, then it becomes a pedagogical issue, in that we try to identify ways to teach people (in and out of classrooms) to be suspect when demagoguery is inviting us to play.

As with Madison Grant—an elite writing to other members of the elite—some of the most appalling cases of bad public decisions are not usefully described as an ignorant public overwhelming a resistant (and right-thinking) elite. For instance, Dr. Harry Laughlin, whose highly quantitative report (over fifty-seven pages of charts) was important for legitimating the 1924 Immigration Act (which severely restricted the immigration of "non-Nordic races" and had horrifying consequences in the Holocaust) had sterling credentials: with a PhD from Princeton, he was superintendent of the Eugenics Record Office at Cold Spring Harbor. His bleak view of the innate tendency toward criminality and feeblemindedness of eastern European immigrants was shared with other scientific experts who testified during the hearings; the expert who most objected did so in ways that at least one scholar characterizes as fairly technical (for more on this point, see Kevles). Laughlin was not cunningly manipulating uneducated masses; he was expressing the consensus of eugenics experts to political elites.[1] This was not populist rhetoric. But neither was it an elitist imposition on an unwilling populace. Any description of this situation that assumes an expert versus populist dichotomy will fail.

The problem with the anti-immigration rhetoric of the 1924 act was not that it was populist, nor that it was elitist, but that it was demagoguery. Scholars in the discipline of rhetoric waver as to how prescriptive our scholarship should be, and whether we are simply describing what works, or advocating better means of public argument. Sometimes, it seems to me, scholarship in rhetoric has been helpfully normative—describing what the ideal public deliberation would resemble—with little discussion as to how to get there: what do we do about bad ways of arguing? How do we identify those bad ways?

In this book, I've argued for this definition of demagoguery:

> *Demagoguery is a polarizing discourse that promises stability, certainty, and escape from the responsibilities of rhetoric through framing public policy in terms of the degree to which and means by which (not whether) the out-group should be punished/scapegoated for the current problems of the in-group. Public debate largely concerns three stases: group identity (who is in the in-group, what signifies out-group membership, and how loyal rhetors are to the in-group); need (usually framed in terms of how evil the out-group is); what level of punishment to enact against the out-group (restriction of rights to extermination).*

I've argued that, to be demagoguery, a text (or culture) must have:

- in-group/out-group(s);
- scapegoating of an out-group;
- emphasis on identity (which is group membership);
- motivism;
- the insistence that the in-group is victimized;
- a call for purifying the community of the out-group(s).

And I've argued it generally has:

- binary paired terms
- categories that are grounded in the ontic logos
- naïve realism
- projection
    mote/beam projection
    cunning projection
- strategic misnaming
- apocalyptic metanarrative
- strict father model
- metaphors of control, purity, masculinity, rigidity, strength for in-group, and vermin; hybridity, contamination, femininity, infection, demonic for out-group
- authoritarianism
- arguments from personal certainty
- deductive reasoning
- aversion to rational argumentation (internally consistent logic, application of same discourse rules across in-groups/out-groups; openness to other positions; fair representation of other points of view)

And notice that I have *not* argued that it is generally populist, distinguished by emotionalism, restricted to major political figures, specific to democracy, or even specific to politics. Nor have I argued that it is magically effective or necessarily evil.

In my teaching I sometimes use an article from People for the Ethical Treatment of Animals (PETA) about the 2012 federal ban on the international and interstate trade in various types of constricting snakes (O'Connor) as an instance of demagoguery. According to the PETA article, Ken Salazar, secretary of the interior, reduced the number of constricting snakes banned from interstate and international commerce from nine to four (with the four including the species that are the major problem in the Florida Everglades). Whether an interstate and international ban on commerce is effective is an interesting question, since bans only work to reduce trade that is both legally conducted and international or interstate, and even if both of those conditions are met, only if there is money for the ban to be enforced. If the majority of snakes released to the Everglades are intrastate or smuggled, the ban fails the stock issue of solvency and is, at best, performative. It may have unintended consequences, such as taking money away from programs that might be more effective, increasing smuggling (which the PETA article says is generally cruel and harmful to snakes), or encouraging people who are moving to dump snakes rather than taking them when they move. It's possible, then, that PETA's plan would worsen the problem of nonnative snakes in the wild. It might not, of course, and that's why a good discussion of the issue would involve deliberating the plan, not just characterizing snake owners as creeps.

The PETA article never argues the stock issues of solvency, feasibility, or unintended consequences of their plan or any other. Instead, a large part of the article concerns the identity of snake owners. They are, according to the article, "a strange lot" who have bad motives for owning snakes, don't really understand what snakes want, often fail to care for them adequately, and fail to give them pleasure, which snakes would derive by "exploring lush jungles and swamps and experiencing all the pleasures that they are so keenly attuned to." The thesis of the piece appears to be: this ban (on constricting snakes) is inadequate because people who own snakes (including kinds never considered in the original ban) are strange, incompetent, and mean. Even were the article right, and everyone who owns any kind of snake were a creepy, strange, and mean person who doesn't care for snakes properly, that wouldn't make an interstate and international ban of nine very specific species of snake a reasonable, effective, feasible, or fiscally responsible policy. I doubt the PETA article on snakes had much effect, other than serving as a useful example of demagoguery for students in my classes.

Our shared world is not neatly divided into good and bad people. It is false to hope that policy issues can be usefully reduced to the easily comprehended binary of us (good) them (bad). Snake owners may or may not be creepy people—the few I've known didn't seem especially creepy, but I'm more or less phobic about snakes, so I don't know a lot of snake owners. As a vegetarian and animal lover, I'm more sympathetic to the avowed PETA agenda (which is supposed to be promoting animal rights) than to people who want to keep rattlesnakes as pets, but I don't see the issue of a ban on interstate commerce as one that is usefully framed by "vegetarian animal lovers versus rattlesnake owners." That might make an interesting grudge match for World Wrestling Entertainment—although it would probably end quickly if the snake owners brought their rattlesnakes—but it isn't a useful way to argue about a policy issue. Again, that isn't to say that PETA should be banned from public discourse, or even shamed into saying nice things about snake owners.

Nor is it to say that the problem is that the author of the PETA article is emotional on the issue. The problem isn't that the author of the post feels icky things about snake owners—the argument is illogical because those feelings have nothing to do with whether a broader ban on interstate commerce in snakes would make any difference to the ills the article identifies (banning interstate commerce in constricting snakes has nothing to do with the creepiness of a person who owns, buys, or sells nonconstricting snakes). And yet there are some feelings that are logically related to the issue. For instance, part of the argument is that the situation in the Everglades is bad—just as much a *feeling* as the feeling that snake owners are creepy. That feeling, however, is logically related to the issue of the ban, since two of the snakes banned were the ones wreaking havoc in the Everglades. The feeling about snake owners isn't logically related to the argument in the PETA article, but the feeling about the Everglades is, and so it is logical to arouse horror about the damage that released pythons are doing in the Everglades—as argumentation theorists like Walton and Van Eemeren have argued, appeals to feelings are fallacious when the appeal is irrelevant, not any time they are made. That isn't to say that raising the fear about the Everglades frees a rhetor from the responsibility of making the case about the plan—if a ban causes snake owners to release more snakes into the Everglades, then it would be harmful—but it's at least connected. The feeling is logically connected, but not sufficient; it simply establishes a need to do something about the Everglades, and not the need for *this* ban.

My argument about demagoguery can be summarized in six points. First, past scholarly projects on demagoguery have run aground because they described demagoguery as speech by demagogues, and tried to distinguish demagogues from normal politicians on the grounds of the former being more populist, more emotional, and motivated by selfish ambition rather than a desire to help the state or community. Thus, those projects were inherently demophobic, elitist, and rationalist. Because people who are oppressed are likely to be angry about it, and claiming the posture of calm control is easier for those who wish to maintain the status quo, those approaches were also implicitly against social justice movements.

Second, acknowledging the problems with some definitions of demagoguery doesn't necessitate abandoning the goal of coming up with a useful definition and set of criteria for demagoguery. People use the term, so instead of coming up with a new one, we should find a more useful way to define and use it.

Third, I'm proposing a three-part way to look at demagoguery: a definition, a list of criteria, and a set of characteristics that correlate strongly to demagoguery. This is a proposal, intended to contribute to a conversation about the advantages and disadvantages of various definitions; I'm not certain I've hit exactly the right one—I'm trying to contribute to an argument, not end it.

Fourth, demagoguery is not a discrete category of discourse; a text exists somewhere on a continuum depending on how many of the constituent characteristics it has, and to what extent it has them. Being high on the continuum of demagoguery doesn't necessarily mean that a text is extremely harmful. The harm of demagoguery has two other relevant axes: how widespread is the scapegoating of that out-group, and how widespread or powerful are the media or individuals who are promoting the demagoguery. Even low-grade demagoguery can be very harmful if there's cultural consensus that *that group* is evil, and the demagoguery is being promoted by powerful media and/or individuals (such as the extraordinarily widespread scapegoating of black men that, at least in much mainstream public discourse, remains at the level of dog whistles and abstractions, but directly contributes to tragic policies). Rhetoric that is highly demagogic, but about a group rarely scapegoated, and promoted by a not-very-powerful group, such as PETA demagoguery about snake owners, isn't likely to have much impact, let alone harm.

Fifth, demagoguery is, fundamentally, the reduction of all policy arguments to questions of in-group/out-group identity and loyalty. It operates on the assumption that good people do good things, and so we don't need to argue policy; we just need to figure out who is good and put them into power. And, since we're good, people like us are good; therefore, all we need to do is figure out who most embodies in-group identity and we're done. Just as good people do good things, so bad people do bad things; thus, most (perhaps all) of our problems are the consequence of the out-group(s)—perhaps their actions, perhaps simply their presence. Demagoguery scapegoats one or more out-groups for all of the community's problems. That reduction and scapegoating can happen with appeals to expert opinion, a calm affect, in elitist language, and on the part of someone who means well, so emotionalism, populism, and motivism aren't useful criteria.

Sixth, demagoguery appeals to the assumption that the truth is absolutely and immediately clear to good people (us), and so it toggles between naïve realism (the truth is absolutely and immediately clear to everyone) and a sloppy relativism (all beliefs are arbitrary, but our beliefs are simultaneously arbitrary and true).

There have been topics I've been unable to pursue in this book, simply because of time and space, but I think it's important to mention them, especially issues of gender (particularly masculinity), the interplay of popular religious beliefs and demagoguery (especially the just-world model and narratives of conversion), charismatic leadership, the role of reification, the universality of demagoguery, and whether demagoguery is only harmful if the out-group is an essentialized identity (as opposed to a political or ideological agenda that can be changed).

Demagoguery is generally closely connected to specific constructions of masculinity (the ideal male thinks in black-and-white terms, makes decisions quickly, controls himself and others, and doesn't allow insubordination). It often appeals to rigid notions of gender, and to accusations of some kind of queerness on the part of out-groups. But there have been famous and powerful women rhetors engaged in demagoguery (Anne Coulter, Aimee Semple McPherson, Bernardine

Dohrn), and many profoundly demagogic projects have been rhetorically aided by women's groups, so it would be interesting to dig more into the various ways that constructions of gender interact with demagoguery.

At least in the United States, there seems to be a strong overlap between demagoguery and the prosperity gospel, both of which appeal to a sense that when people are saved they are ontologically changed. They are therefore free of all previous actions (so that it's almost tacky to point out that a person who is claiming to be, for instance, Christian has a long and recent history of behavior that belies the supposed values, or that a person who claims to be great at business doesn't have a great record). It may be that this line of thought is attractive in the United States because American evangelicalism has long had a strain of antinomianism, or, as I've often suspected, because American Protestantism has been slipping back into imparted (rather than imputed) justification—another project it would be interesting to pursue. But it's also possible that it's simpler, and that it's all just a manifestation of the just-world model, a belief that the world is just, and that people get what they deserve.

Possibly related to the role of evangelical Christianity in American culture is the desire for consumers of confirming demagoguery to claim they were converted. I've argued that it's common for people to insist that they were persuaded and moved by demagoguery (even when it is not at all clear how their views were actually changed) because a narrative of change allows people to claim membership in the epistemological elect. What I haven't been able to pursue is how that narrative might be connected to the role that conversion has in Western notions of a true identity. It might be that insisting that one was converted serves to legitimate what a person might deeply suspect is sheer prejudice. As various scholars have argued, we privilege the experience of someone who is converted, as though that insistence on a changed perception is necessarily a more enlightened one. Were David Duke, for instance, to admit that he wasn't converted to anti-Semitism, but was raised that way, it would make his beliefs seem like sheer prejudice, rather than what he wants to pretend they are: a new ideology to which he was converted against his will. It would be valuable to look at the overlap between demagoguery and conversion narratives.

Most scholarship has focused on demagogues rather than demagoguery because of the complicated connection between demagoguery and charismatic leadership. The two are connected, but not in the sense that charismatic leadership leads to demagoguery, nor is it a necessary correlation. Not every charismatic leaders is engaged in demagoguery, and not everyone engaged in demagoguery is a charismatic leader. When the two work together, however, the leader is effectively beyond criticism. One of the more disturbing moments in Dimitra Stratigakos's book on how Hitler's image was carefully manipulated through his control of space is a quote from his long-time interior decorator (and less famous architect) Gerdy Troost in which she "flatly refused to believe that Hitler had known about the atrocities carried out in his name" (140).

The charismatic leader is not just different from the leader who gets authority from law or tradition, but is also different from one whose authority is grounded in expertise (the kind described by Hannah Arendt in "What is Authority"). The legitimate leader is one who is given authority by the followers because she has demonstrated context-specific knowledge. Charismatic leadership, on the contrary, presumes a personality trait that enables universally valid and instantaneous decision-making abilities. Charismatic leadership is a relationship that requires complete acquiescence and submission on the part of the follower. The charismatic leader is threatened by others taking leadership roles, pointing out her errors, or having expertise to which she should submit because it assumes that power is limited (the more power that others have, the less there is for the leader to have). It is a relationship of pure hierarchy. It is simultaneously a robust and fragile relationship because it can withstand an extraordinary amount of disconfirming evidence (that the leader is not actually all that good, does not have the requisite traits, is out of her depth, is making bad decisions) by simply rejecting them; it is fragile, however, insofar as the admission of a serious flaw on the part of the leader destroys the relationship entirely. The power of the leader is reduced by giving power.

As Arendt argued, the leader whose power comes from legitimacy (she uses the term authority, but that's a vexed term) benefits from discursively egalitarian systems. Her authority is strengthened by the expertise, contributions, and criticism of others. Management theory, by setting out the charismatic leader as the ideal leader, has precluded leadership grounded in legitimacy. And management theory is nearly univocal that good business leaders should rely on charismatic leadership, and it is nearly a given in wide swaths of lay political theory that businessmen (rarely businesswomen) make good political leaders. The consequence is an uncritical admiration of what is actually a very dangerous model of political leadership. According to the 2007 *Encyclopedia of Industrial and Organizational Psychology,* "Charismatic leadership is a relatively new and distinct paradigm," putting its origin in "the 1970s" (Bullock 70). The entry, like much other work in management and organizational theory, emphasizes the "positive effects" of charismatic leadership, while granting one sentence to some drawback (charismatic leaders can "create divisions within the groups they lead, display an authoritarian management style, and focus on trivial matters" 70). Since research on charismatic leadership began at least with Weber's 1919 lecture "Politics as a Vocation," and since historians typically characterize such figures as Adolf Hitler, Pol Pot, and Josef Stalin as charismatic leaders, claiming that the paradigm is recent and reducing the potential negatives of that model of leadership to one sentence might strike readers familiar with that scholarship as surprising, if not shocking.

But that history (and idealizing) of charismatic leadership is typical in current management doctrine. Bruce Avolio and Francis Yammarino, in their introduction to *Transformational and Charismatic Leadership*, describe charismatic leaders as ones who "foster performance beyond expected standards by developing an emotional attachment with followers and other leaders, which is tied to a common cause, which contributes to the 'greater good' or larger collective," an approach they define as "representing the moral high road of leadership" (xvii), a claim that might be called something even stronger than shocking, such as appalling.

Management theory has had inadequate discussion of the dangers of charismatic leadership, although some work (e.g., Steyrer) points out the connections between charisma and narcissistic traits. By far, the dominant way of talking about leadership is to privilege charisma over Weber's other sources of authority, and to present it as nearly ideal (as in Bullock), with some mild criticisms). We are, in short, in an era of nearly unqualified infatuation with a model of leader and follower/employee that is actually a very dangerous one, and profoundly antidemocratic, even authoritarian.

Since we are also in an era in which, despite market meltdowns and other troubling signs, the business leader is idealized as the ideal kind of leader (with universally valid judgment), we are in an era when the charismatic leader—that is, the antidemocratic and authoritarian type—is imagined as the only and best model. That's dangerous.

Demagoguery seems to be associated with reification. It's surprising how many current demagogues advocate a return to the gold standard and talk about gold as having a *reality* to its worth not shared by, for instance, money. But, of course, gold has no inherent value—its value is just as much determined by the market as the value of rubies, leaves, or ivory (the mistake made in Hitchcock's demagogic *End of Money*). Like the topos "they're going to take our women" (another oddly common one), the goldbug theme, may or may not be significant.

I've remained unclear as to whether demagoguery is a universal, American, or Western European ideology, because I don't know. Brief forays into the rhetoric surrounding genocides of other cultures show strong overlap (for instance, the 1990 "Hutu Ten Commandments" look very much like the 1366 Statutes of Kilkenny, and a student once wrote a fascinating paper arguing that Ho Chi Minh's use of Confucianism was much like what Burke said Hitler did with Western Christianity), but that may simply be the consequence of Western rhetorics finding their way into other discourses. Mao Tse Tung's pro-Cultural Revolution rhetoric does not clearly fit many of the characteristics I've been describing in this book. But it was certainly harmful.

The issue of harm, for me, raises the question of whether the discourse is demagoguery if rhetors are scapegoating concepts, schools of thought, or belief systems. G. K. Chesterton is not uncommonly racist, but rarely demagogic regarding races or ethnicities. He does, however, scapegoat belief in evolution; in "The Shadow of the Shark" he says belief in it is necessarily connected to contempt for human life. The way in which he does so remains a theme in current anti-evolution rhetoric: that atheism and immorality necessarily go hand in hand, and that belief in evolution is necessarily connected to genocide (thereby scapegoating evolutionary science for the Holocaust). While I don't think there is a plausible case that can be made that this scapegoating causes or enables violence against evolutionary biologists or advocates of teaching evolution, it may contribute to some people's tendency to fear that fascism is being imposed upon us, and that Christians are in danger of being rounded up in camps. It might be connected to the nontrivial amount of "Christian" terrorism in the United States, the panic that some people feel at the notion of paying for someone else's birth control, the rage that the failure to say "Merry Christmas" inspires in some, or the urgency with which some "Christians" oppose the extension of civil rights to homosexuals. It would be interesting to engage in empirical testing about the consequences of depersonalized demagoguery.

And, while demagoguery does seem to favor rhetoric that can be framed as some kind of return, it isn't restricted to one political agenda. The Weathermen certainly engaged in demagoguery, and much of their political action was explicitly about performance of identity rather than policy argumentation. Bernardine Dohrn explained the motives behind the "Days of Rage" (a several-day period of damaging property, attacking police, and deliberately provoking retaliatory violence): "We were determined to carry out an action that would reveal how passionately we felt and that we were on the other side" (Bernardine Dohrn, qtd. in Jacobs 66). It was a performance of group identity. It was, of course, supposed to have material consequences—it was supposed to draw thousands of students, instigate revolution, to "destroy the motherfucker from the inside" (qtd. in Burrough), but it would do so not by showing that their organization had the most effective and sensible political agenda: it would do so by the revolutionaries performing an identity that others would find compelling. The irrationality of the action, the self-destructiveness, was part of the rhetorical force, in that it was supposed that people were that committed to the ideology. Within the organization, at least according to various members, a premium was put on loyalty to the group and willingness to act irrationally; the very irrationality of the actions demonstrated the depth of commitment. Jim Mellen described the argument about whether to go underground: "The argument, as usual, was in personal terms. I didn't have the character to be a revolutionary. I lacked audacity. I couldn't do it" (qtd. in Burrough 81).

Weather Underground was criticized in its own time for the tendency to assume binaries of identity, such as their univocal condemnation of members of the military, a simplistic condemnation that ignored the economic, race, and class issues that made it impossible for some people to avoid the draft. Being outraged at various aspects of the US domestic and foreign policies in 1968 was, it seems to me, reasonable. But however much outrage one might feel doesn't necessarily mean that the Weathermen had plausible plans for making things better. Being angry with Saddam Hussein for his policies seems to me logical, but that doesn't mean that invasion was the right policy. Americans were frightened and angry about Japanese success in the Pacific War, and those feelings contributed to support for mass imprisonment. But the people who argued against imprisonment weren't arguing from a position free of feelings; they argued from premises of compassion, fairness, and, sometimes, personal affection. It isn't about feelings versus reason; the feelings *are* reasons, and they can be good reasons, but we have to argue about them. Martha Nussbaum has argued eloquently for the importance of political emotions, "For a public culture based upon love extended sympathy, which can support the goals of a just society and ensure the stability of its commitments" (58). That we love our country, the environment, animals, our children, is a fact that can enhance our political deliberations, and all of those emotions figure into our policies whether we acknowledge them or not. In a way, that aspect of my argument is simple: a public sphere of deliberation should involve the kind of disagreement that helps us think critically about the bases of our arguments; since our arguments are often based on our feelings, we should argue about our feelings.

The question of the efficacy of a ban on constricting snakes is complicated; figuring out what exactly the proposed ban is, what has happened with similar bans, where the snakes in the Everglades really come from, and, generally, whether the ban would be effective—all those things are cognitively difficult, lead one into ambiguous territory, and take time. Similarly, considering the feasibility of an invasion means thinking critically about American troops, something no American wants to do, and looking carefully at the outcomes of previous attempts at regime change. All of that is hard. Screaming for Saddam Hussein's blood or hating creepy snake owners are both way more fun.

Part of the pleasure of hating Saddam Hussein or creepy snake owners is that one gets to feel part of a group, and that pleasure—the sensation of being a loyal member of a community of people who are also loyal to the group—arises at least partially out of our sense that other group members will be loyal to us. There is nothing populist about that; it operates in elite as well as populist groups. People new to academia often express surprise at the clubbiness of much behavior at academic conferences. A certain kind of citation signals that one is a member of a particular group—a theoretical orientation, scholarly approach, school of thought. Sometimes that group membership is signaled by stylistic choices (e.g., the backslash in my field at one point in time), topic, term (when I started graduate school it was "dialectic," which quickly gave way to "hegemonic"), or even clothing style. Being in a particular school of thought (much like a school of fish) provides protection, companionship, familiarity; there's nothing inherently wrong with it. When membership prohibits internal disagreement, or when membership is defined in a disjunctive binary (so that any praise of the out-group or criticism of the in-group is treated as disloyalty), then it's damaging. But not all groups function that way. In other words, the mere existence of in-groups and out-groups doesn't necessarily lead to injustice or demagoguery. Demagoguery, as I've argued it should be defined, does, however, depend on the in-group/out-group distinction being perceived as an ontologically grounded distinction of safe/dangerous.

Carl Schmitt described the extraordinary power of the friend/enemy distinction, and its role in motivating political action. It may be that identifying an "us" without at least some kind of "not us" is impossible. But, as others have argued, that "not us" doesn't have to be an enemy. Certainly, some people seem incapable of distinguishing between "not us" and enemy, and all of us are prone to perceive disagreement as disloyalty under some circumstances. I am not saying that such people are bad people, nor that we are bad people for thinking in terms of friends and enemies at times. I am arguing that the "us"/"not us" distinction, as pleasurable as it may be, should not be the basis for political deliberation. It may or may not be part of the deliberation. I can imagine situations in which it might be helpful, but it isn't the basis (either in the sense of being the solid ground on which the deliberation takes places, or in the sense of being the only foundation from which we argue—that is neither *the* basis, nor the *basis*).

If the audience is in (or, more importantly, feels itself to be in) a state of existential threat—if it feels that its identity or existence is being challenged, then in-group entitativity becomes stronger and more desirable (for more on this, see Hogg et al.). Much scholarship, and common sense, connects demagoguery to what Staub calls "difficult life situations" (he is discussing the process by which communities can be moved to adopt genocidal policies). It doesn't matter, I've come to think, whether conditions *are* difficult, as much as whether people can be persuaded that they are. Demagoguery regarding race in the US South did not correlate with economic conditions—if it had, then it would have been worse during the Depression than it was after World War II, but it was worse after the war.[2] It might have been a response to the re-energizing of the postwar civil rights movement, but it's quite possible that race baiting and red-baiting, initially simply a strategy for mobilizing poor whites, became so necessary that avoiding them amounted to political suicide (as has been argued happened with abolitionist baiting in the 1830s).

James Waller persuasively describes the factors that contribute to ordinary people participating in genocide and mass killing, and he argues that the three major factors are: a culture that values authoritarianism and social dominance; a psychological tendency toward us-them thinking and victim blaming; and social arrangements and rhetorics that manage the cognitive dissonances created by extraordinary cruelty (see especially the chart on 138). Waller, drawing on the research of Staub and others, argues that

> the major cause of violence is high self-esteem combined with an ego threat. . . . Committing evil against a perceived ego threat achieves a symbolic dominance over that threat and affirms one's esteem to the extent of being superior to the victim. (257)

If a group with considerable privilege begins to lose its entitlements, they can frame that change as an improvement toward a more just and fair world, as a transcending of previous prejudices and an improved social order. Or, they can frame it as an existential threat, the end of the world, and a destruction of all order. Those are always the options available to us, and demagoguery invites us to do the latter. And it sometimes does that by strategically distracting us from what is actually causing the loss in privileges.

For instance, it's plausible to argue that working class men have been losing privileges and entitlements since the late seventies. As unions and social safety nets have been weakened, pension funds robbed, the tax burden shifted downward, public schools deliberately underfunded, jobs lost to automation, and entire lines of work (such as small-engine repair) decimated, a class of people have watched what looked like predictable and reasonably secure work and achievement (including home ownership, good schools, health benefits, secure retirement) become fragile, insecure, and mercurial. It may be that young white men of that socioeconomic class are drawn to demagoguery against nonwhites because it presents a much more straightforward solution to their plight than acknowledging that their political parties have served them ill (particularly if they have supported parties that engaged in union busting, outsourcing jobs, or undermining health benefits). There are always difficult life conditions; they don't always result in a culture of demagoguery, but demagoguery is the cause and consequence of some group being scapegoated for them.

At the beginning of this book, I mentioned demagoguery's tendency toward strategic misnaming and cunning projection, both of which might be characterized as deliberately misleading. For instance, policies intended to prevent members of minority religions from being able to practice their religion (e.g., religions that want to solemnize same-sex marriage) or intended to force dominant religious practices onto others (e.g., prayer in school) are instances of religious repression. These policies are intended to restrict freedom of religion. But they're called protection of religious freedom—strategic misnaming. And trying to characterize resisting such repression as itself repressing religion (or a war on Christianity) is projection. There are two interesting issues this strategic misnaming raises.

The first is the role of claims as performances of group identity. As much research has shown, there are certain political issues that appear to be impervious to persuasion, and which are strong predictors of political affiliation (e.g., denying global warming). While it may seem that people are Republican because they deny global warming, the cause and effect probably goes the other way. As Sandra Marquart-Pyatt et al. say, "Current political polarization on climate change appears to have led to a situation in which political orientation eclipses actual climatic conditions, and this does not augur well for mobilizing public support for effective policy-making." Insisting on certain claims isn't really an epistemic move, as much as a performance of identity—those claims take on the status of dicta in a statement of creed. They constitute group identity and signal group loyalty. The more absurd they are, the more rigidly one holds them regardless of disconfirming evidence, the more loyal you are to the group, and the more cohesive the group.

The second interesting issue raised by strategic misnaming is what it means for the tendency to perceive people engaged in demagoguery as "authentic." As discussed earlier, demagoguery often relies on claims that are clearly hyperbolic, if not actively dishonest, yet demagogues are generally described as "authentic" and the out-group is always condemned for dishonesty. Thus, given the centrality to demagoguery of claims that simply and obviously aren't true, why do people perceive rhetors engaged in demagoguery as honest and authentic?

That question has puzzled me since I began working on proslavery rhetoric, which often relied on obviously false claims (such as that slaveholders were outraged at mixed-race relationships, or that slaves thrived in swampy areas) coupled with representations of themselves as passionate about the truth and condemnations of abolitionists as liars. At the time, I thought that it was a phenomenon that George Orwell noted—you demonstrate in-group loyalty more powerfully by insisting on the truth of things you do and don't know to be untrue ("blackwhite"). But, the more I read about demagogues, the more I came to believe that many people sincerely believe them to be honest. Antony Beevor describes soldiers encircled by Soviet troops, clearly abandoned by Hitler, insisting that Hitler would save them. "'I believe in Hitler. What he said he'll do, he'll stick to'" (277). More recently, Donald Trump, having led audiences in cheers about jailing Hillary Clinton, and insisting she has to be locked up, announced he wouldn't try to prosecute her after all, and his fans continued to describe him as honest, straight-shooting, and trustworthy. No matter how often he changed positions, or said things that were clearly untrue, many perceived him as authentic and honest. This point seems important to me, because it has implications for what we try to do about demagoguery, and how we talk about accuracy and public deliberation.

What people perceive as authentic is the lack of filter, an apparent absence of forethought. The apparent lack of calculation is, for many people, reassuring. They believe that they are seeing the *real* person, and believe that authenticity matters more than accuracy. If a rhetor says what she really thinks, regardless of consequences, then she is being truthful to her own views, and people believe that is true. That expression of inner truth is, for many people, a more valuable quality than being truthful about our shared world. I think it has to do with the sense that the audience can then believe that a person is truly a member of the in-group, so the authenticity comes from believing the person is incapable of being dishonest, and *really* is one of us. Paradoxically, this privileging of a supposed true identity over an external world means that people who claim to be realists, and who claim to reject relativism, are ultimately endorsing a highly relativist notion of truth.

This true self is performed by saying outrageous things, and, in a culture in which demagoguery is rewarded (by winning elections, getting more viewers, being able to charge more for speeches), there is necessarily a demagogic one-upmanship that happens. The previously outrageous becomes normal, and so a person has to make an even more demagogic claim, or advocate an even more extreme policy against the out-group.

What one can see in times of rising demagoguery is a kind of concatenation (not necessarily conspiracy) of factors: a large section of the public anxious and frightened, a large number of rhetors engaged in demagoguery, a large number of political figures who propose policies that reinforce and enact demagoguery, a situation in which media and political figures are engaged in in-group loyalty one-upmanship, a public that doesn't expect to participate in policy argumentation, a large number of media outlets engaged in demagoguery either directly (through the programs they show) or indirectly (by giving more voice to rhetors who engage in demagoguery).

I took on this project because, for several years, it has seemed to me that our current situation has created considerable incentives for demagoguery. Herbert Simons has famously argued that we are now in an economy of attention. As many media critics have noted, in an economy of attention, a headline that conveys a "simple answer that will make you feel better about yourself" has more capital than an article that suggests it will be a "complicated, nuanced, and highly contingent argument in which you and people like you might be implicated and which you can only assess by considering other arguments." Pundits who reinforce in-group entitativity with unambiguous certainty are more popular than ones who speak with nuance and complexity, regardless of whether they are actually more accurate (for more on complexity being more important than accuracy, see especially Tetlock, *Expert*).

People who trust those who speak with certainty more than they trust those who speak with nuance do so for various reasons, including a model of the mind that suggests that we are good judges of our own level of certainty, and that judgment is itself reliable. We want to believe that a person who is more certain is more likely to be accurate. It is comforting to think that accuracy and certainty are the same thing, and that we are the best judges of our own perception. Were that model accurate, then not only would it be relatively easy to know but it would be very straightforward to know whether we know. In contrast to that world, the world of nuanced and uncertain expertise is a very uncomfortable one.

And arguing about identity is more fun than arguing about policies. John Hibbing and Elizabeth Theiss-Morse argue that most Americans don't want to argue about policies. Ever. They say, "Participation in politics is low because people do not like politics even in the best of circumstances; in other words, they simply do not like the process of openly arriving at a decision in the face of diverse opinions" (3). In fact, most people think such a process is unnecessary because most people believe "that any specific plan for achieving a desired goal is about as good as any other plan" (224) *and* that everyone agrees on the big goals: "they believe a properly functioning government would just select the best way of bringing about these end goals without wasting time and needlessly exposing the people to politics" (133). People believe that any legitimate policy needs are obvious to all reasonable people, and it would be easy for a sensible person to find a solution to them. In that case, how do they explain that there are policy disagreements? Special interests. Hibbing and Theiss-Morse argue that decades of research show that people believe that our interests are universal, but any other interests are "special." In other words, disagreement arises because of bad motives on the part of those who disagree with us. There is no such thing as genuine, well-intentioned, and reasonable disagreement.

> Analysts often suggest that people use the term "special interests" to refer to anybody adopting a position with which they disagree. This may be true, but we are suggesting an important addition: People use the term "special interests" to refer to anybody discussing an issue about which they do not care. (222)

Demagoguery appeals to those premises about disagreement—it says that all issues can be decided in terms of identity. And it may be that appeal that means that, eventually, a demagogue arises—someone who will claim to be above special interests, who will take the obvious course of action we desperately need.

In the long run, the best response to demagoguery is to make people comfortable with uncertainty and skilled at metacognition. It seems to me that the main attraction of demagoguery, the main pleasure it provides, is that it grants us permission to stop thinking about something (or never start). It says that "this is simple" and "you are a good sort of person because those people are awful." The same pleasure is gained by reading snarky advice columnists, hate threads in social media, and comedy shows about how awful other people are. That pleasure is easy. Demagoguery invites us to take the elevator instead of walking six flights; what's more, it tells us we are good and smart people for taking the elevator. The more unpleasant the stairs, the less often we walk stairs, the harder it is to take them. And, so, what we can do is acknowledge that the elevator is an option we sometimes take, but we take the stairs often enough to be able to do it.

There is another way to take the elevator, which isn't necessarily demagoguery, but which does help it thrive, and that is to flatten all discourse into "approve" or "disapprove," with any kind of criticism falling into the latter category, and itself condemned as demagoguery. Condemning other people, even vehemently, is not necessarily demagoguery. Even calling people nasty and ugly names is not demagoguery. Stalinist attacks on others as "Trotskyite" was demagoguery under Stalin, since that was a group identified as so dangerous that it had to be killed; to be called a Trotskyite under other circumstances might be praise, an insult, an inside joke, or simply odd. Unless that name has been connected with something of which the body politic needs to be purified, identifying a person as a member of a group is not necessarily demagoguery. Calling someone a liar, saying he or she has done something bad, holding him or her responsible for things—none of those are *necessarily* demagoguery.

Determining whether a particular name, accusation of blame, or condemnation is demagoguery means looking into the situation and trying to figure out whether the blame is scapegoating (meaning the person or group is being held responsible for something they didn't do, or for which they should not be held responsible), whether someone or some group is being rightly condemned, whether they have done the thing for which they are accused and whether it was bad. It means looking at an argument fairly carefully, and in context. It takes work, and, just as it is easier to accept one version of whom to blame without looking into it and managing the uncertainty, so it is easier to say "both groups are at fault."

Some people don't want the work of critiquing argument, especially in-group argument, because it makes them anxious. One of many striking characteristics of proslavery rhetoric was the presence of barely repressed fear. Social psychologists describe the anxiety that lack of closure brings some people (see especially Kruglanski). Gordon Allport noted in the late 1940s that racism correlated to trouble handling ambiguity. Much demagoguery seems to evince a terror of hybridity, and bizarre logical contortions to avoid acknowledging its inherency in our world—lines used to be clear, things used to be stable, there used to be purity, and *now,* this group is threatening all that with a hybridity. Hybridity reminds us that boundaries are fluid, and many of them are social constructs, and therefore might change; if they have not existed since the beginning of time, then perhaps they are not right, or perhaps change is not wrong. We cannot reject all change qua change, but have to work through the uncertain processes of deciding which changes we want to prevent.

And, of course, if things are not certain, regardless of whether we are, then we cannot simply rely on our own feelings of certainty to determine if we are right or wrong. If we are wrong about whether we are right, we might be wrong about anything. For dualists, there is certainty (which means you have a foundation for your judgments) and there is everything else (a realm in which you have no foundation for your judgments). Because of that binary, dualists hear criticisms of certainty as advocating what they call "relativism" (or postmodernism), something they understand as saying all viewpoints are equally valid. Left out of the discussion is the wide range of kinds of skepticism. There is an almost existential leap that people have to make to participate in argumentation—into the realm of reasoned but contingent judgment—but that means jumping into what they think is relativism, to find that there is something else.

But that other realm, the one that ranges from kinds of realism through postmodernism, is a place of argumentation, of commonality, of contingent judgment that provides a kind of foundation. What seems to me important is not whether people have a foundation for their judgments, but whether they are willing to argue about those foundations. This means that we need to be willing to argue about what we believe, but also why we believe it, and how we feel about it. Argumentation always means we will discover we are wrong, sometimes very wrong, sometimes a little wrong, but we're always wrong. Walton describes one of the central obligations in argumentation.

> If an inconsistency of commitment is challenged by the other party, the party who has been challenged needs to resolve the issue one way or the other. A participant may need to retract commitments. It is taken to be an indicator of rational argumentation in a persuasion dialogue if a participant makes a decision to retract one of a pair of inconsistent propositions she had previously been committed to, once the inconsistency of commitments has been pointed out by the other party. (Witness 167)

If the conflicting commitments are foundational ones, then we will have to argue about our foundations, and arguing about those foundations means acknowledging what they are, and being able to think about the ground on which we stand; it means metacognition. Demagoguery isn't always bad, but when it is, it's not because of *their* demagogues; it's because *we* choose too much of it.

How we define demagoguery implies what we will do about it. If we define it as a disease of the body politic that comes from the emotionalism of the masses, then we are headed toward profoundly antidemocratic policies, and yet our objection to demagoguery is supposedly that it threatens democracy. Our cure is worse than the disease. It's the same problem if we say that demagoguery is the consequence of bad identities in the public sphere—we're now purifying our community, and that's demagoguery. If we define it as the evasion of policy argumentation through reducing all questions to issues of in-group/out-group identity, and we say that it comes from fear of uncertainty and aversion of metacognition, then the solution is to teach people to be comfortable with policy argumentation, uncertainty, and metacognition. That seems like a good plan to me. And no one is banned, and no one dies.

NOTES
WORKS CITED
INDEX

Notes

Introduction: Demagogues and Demagoguery

1. Definitions in general (versus specialized) dictionaries emphasize the emotional appeals of the demagogue, while scholarly definitions (such as Luthin's or Signer's) emphasize the identity and motives of the demagogue. The problem with these definitions is that they are either demophobic—since appeals to emotions are necessary in democratic discourse—or circular. Luthin, for instance, says, the demagogue

> is a politician skilled in oratory, flattery, and invective; evasive in discussing vital issues; promising everything to everybody; appeals to the passions rather than the reason of the public; and arousing racial, religious, and class prejudices—a man whose lust for power without recourse to principle leads him to seek to become a master of the masses. (3)

Most of the characteristics Luthin identifies apply to almost all political figures, especially in a democracy. J. Justin Gustainis's 1990 summary of the research shows the extent to which definitions emphasize the person of the demagogue, thereby implying that it is such persons who should be silenced or excluded. As I will argue, this emphasis on individuals is both inaccurate and unhelpful. For more on common definitions of demagoguery, see my essay "Democracy, Demagoguery, and Critical Rhetoric."

2. One of my hopes in positing this definition of demagoguery is that I think it opens the possibility of empirical research on various cultures and the relationship between demagogic rhetoric and eliminationist policies. On the whole, the United States was more demagogic on all three axes than the UK, and less demagogic than Weimar Germany, and, similarly, had policies more eliminationist than the UK, but less than Germany.

3. Because the term "demagoguery" is so vexed, it seemed sensible at one point to adopt Neiwert's term "eliminationist," but that too is problematic in

that admirers of that sort of rhetoric are generally unwilling to admit that it is eliminationist. That he also uses the term "hate talk" implies the error I'm trying to avoid, of connecting the rhetoric to the affect. Another influential book I eventually decided not to follow too closely is Berlet and Lyons's *Right-Wing Populism* because my research didn't confirm any necessary connection to populism. Madison Grant was an elite speaking to other elites, for instance.

4. Again, the important term here is *dominated*. Demagoguery is harmful when it's the norm.

5. Mann's narrative is much more complicated than this; he mentions, for instance, the possibility that a politically and rhetorically powerful group might perceive its repression of another group as necessary to survival (or a foundational right), and he also discusses the place of resistance (*Dark Side*, see especially the chart on page 477 and his summary 502–6).

6. As is clear in early classical texts, "demagogue" was initially a neutral political term—even for someone like Thucydides or Aristophanes—meaning someone who led the *demes*. Plato's use is mixed, Aristotle describes demagoguery within elites, but in Plutarch and thereafter it is a dyslogistic term used exclusively for populist politicians. For more on this, see Lane.

7. Speculating about the motives of an interlocutor is not entirely inappropriate; it is something to consider when trying to determine whether people involved in an argument are open to persuasion. Motivism is a problem when it's the only stasis. We are so confused on this issue, however, that it's commonplace for people to characterize criticism of an argument as *ad hominem*. For someone who believes that disagreements are always, necessarily, and inherently contests of the relative goodness of various groups, then any criticism is a personal attack. Thus, the perception of argument as identity-based ensures a misunderstanding of *ad hominem*.

8. I'm rarely clear why the "both sides do it" argument arises in the first place. It's relevant if the stasis is "which side is made up of better humans?," but why would that be the stasis?

9. The persistence of this submission/domination binary initially made me think that I was simply seeing instances of the kind of authoritarianism identified by Adorno et al., but I have since come to be persuaded by criticisms of Adorno's criteria (as essentially non-falsifiable, in complicated ways); it seems to me that Lakoff's strict father model points to the same phenomenon, but somewhat more precisely.

10. Naïve realism is just one kind of realism, and there are various kinds that involve considerable skepticism, such as critical realism or fallibilism. The unfortunate tendency in rhetorical scholarship to assume a binary between "realism" and some version of poststructuralism has become part of our creed, and one way we show in-group loyalty. It has truncated what could be

interesting and rich discussion about the potential role of empirical research in our field, the falsifiability of our own ideologies, and how big a tent our discipline could and should have.

11. This is fascinating to me, perhaps because it is a perfect confirmation of what Wayne Booth long ago observed in a vexed, dated, but still interesting book, *Modern Dogma and the Rhetoric of Assent*. Those two positions—there are facts, and people should simply submit to them, and people hold beliefs for profoundly irrational causes—are the two dogmas that Booth identified.

12. The "both sides do it" topos is useful for keeping bystanders from intervening in repression, and helps bystanders rationalize their own inactivity; for more on this point, see Roberts-Miller, *Fanatical Schemes*.

13. I'll admit that this is a pet peeve of mine in both student papers and much scholarship: the tendency to use "believes" as a synonym for "argues" or "says." As I will argue later, demagoguery often involves a conflict between what rhetors claim their beliefs are and the logical premises of their arguments.

14. Some kinds of demagoguery don't involve the patriarchal quality Lakoff identifies in the strict father model, such as demagoguery that purports to be in favor of gender equality (some Soviet demagoguery), some radical feminist demagoguery (e.g., Andrea Dworkin, Trans Exclusive Radical Feminism, the SCUM Manifesto), some environmentalist demagoguery, *Prairie Fire*, or Madison Grant's *Passing of the Great Race*.

15. A thread I have not been able to follow is the role of hybridity in demagoguery. Since demagoguery puts so much emphasis on purity and purification, it makes sense that hybridity would be an inherent evil. Hybridity creates a kind of panic that is managed through laws that try to preserve the order that is supposed to be inherent (see Bhabha, especially 266–82).

16. The one way to criticize in-group members is to accuse them of not really being in-group members—this move enables the dismissal of disconfirming examples.

17. This piece exemplifies how complicated the place of the strict father model can be in demagoguery. While condemning Sanders (and his base) for sexism, exclusion, and deafness to gender/sexuality issues, the insults in it appeal to traditional gender/sexuality norms.

18. Recent scholarship often refers to this move as "constitutive rhetoric," perhaps because there is some potentially complicated theoretical baggage with the term "interpellation." I'll use the term "interpellation" because I'm not sure it's important to engage arguments about that baggage for these purposes—the point is simply that one method of "persuasion" is to deny that persuasion is taking place. While this fits with the thread in demagoguery that denies its rhetoricality, it's in tension with the narrative that people often have about demagogic texts—that they were deeply moved and changed by the argument.

19. See, for instance, Neil Gregor's *How to Read Hitler* (especially 38–40) Joseph Bendersky's *A History of Nazi Germany, 1919–1945* (especially 21–25), and Ian Kershaw's *Hitler: 1889–1936, Hubris* (especially 124).

20. Garver 1109–18; for more on this point, see also 1111; see also Zolberg, *A Nation by Design*, 249.

1. Invasion of Iraq and Evasion of Policy Deliberation

1. Those are three of the four mindsets that Richard Solomon and Nigel Quinney argue that American negotiators shift among: the moralistic missionary whose obviously good intentions will compel acquiescence; the "wheeler dealer'" who desires to get the best business deal; the superpower that wants to dictate terms; and the legalistic mind (the only one not obvious among these texts; 5, see also 19–46).

2. That isn't to say that they claim to be accurate, or, if they do, it's a somewhat troubled meaning of "accurate." People with a high need for closure prefer expressions of certainty over accuracy and nuance in experts (Tetlock), pundits, and leaders (Kruglanski and Orehek 12).

3. This was the basic point of Erich Fromm's *Escape from Freedom*, but more recent research on authoritarianism—even among those who significantly modify the concept (such as Altemeyer, or Pratto et al.)—emphasizes the personal, institutional, and societal security provided by these ideologies.

4. Ivie is here paraphrasing the arguments made by John Murphy, Denise Bostdorff, and David Noon, all of whom pointed to the importance of a Machiavellian worldview in Bush's prowar rhetoric; this phenomenon was even more stark in talk radio, the blogosphere, and various evangelical calls for war that were less circumspect in comparing this (favorably) to the Crusades. For an excellent discussion of this point, see also Herbert Simons "From 9/11."

5. For a smart discussion of the Iraq public discourse as melodrama, see Herbert Simons, "From Post-9/11."

6. The reframing as psychodrama was depressingly common, with articles like "Can Dubya Do Iraq like Dad?" (*Winnipeg Free Press*, August 25, 2002) and "Bush Seeks to Avoid His Father's Mistakes" (AP, *Tulsa World*, August 25, 2002).

7. With the earlier model, that relies on competition to ensure good products, the role of government is to maintain the open access and fairness necessary for competition. Good products survive the competition. This efficiency model seems to be more vague as to why consumers are getting good products, and it seems to me it's defended by appealing to the kind of prosperity gospel that Bowler discusses (*Blessed*).

8. There is good reason to believe that the Bush administration made arguments for war different from what their real motives were, since that is

what many members of the administration have said they did. Either they were misleading the public then, or they are misleading it now. Michael Klare's highly critical narrative of Bush administration justifications for war points out the flopping around that was done to explain a decision (129).

9. While prayer is important in my life, and certainly a part of major decisions, even I will grant that it is naïve to think that I am likely to get counterarguments, disconfirming data, or an argument that will challenge my premises.

10. By "this war," Bacevich means, World War IV—that is, continued conflict in the Middle East—and not simply the invasion of Iraq, which is, he argues, simply one part of that war.

11. For the high estimate, see Roger Stern, "United States Cost of Military Force Projection in the Persian Gulf, 1976–2007," *Energy Policy* 38 (2010) 2816–25.

12. One might argue that there was also risk aversion, in that much of the argument regarding US "unfinished business" in Iraq was that we would lose the ground we had gained in the Persian Gulf War.

2. Punishment/Reward and Binary Paired Terms

1. Thucydides's account of public discourse is here much more nuanced and useful than Plato's: Pericles flatters *and* chastises his audience, and is clearly a rhetorical hero for Thucydides; Archidamus, also a model, chastises. Nikias chastises, and is a rhetorical blunderer; Alcibiades flatters, and is a rhetorical adept, but has no wisdom, and so misleads his audience. For Thucydides, the tendency toward flattery is not particularly significant; of more importance is whether the rhetorical skill is coupled with wisdom (*sophrosone* or *phronesis* in Thucydides, and not *episteme*, as in Plato).

2. Not simply because I disapprove of genocide, although I do, but because, as Thucydides tells the story, Athens's willingness to shift to increasingly brutal relations with its allied city-states is part of what contributes to its downfall. You cannot, Thucydides suggests, be oppressive abroad and democratic at home.

3. See also Pericles's speech (2.43), the unnamed Athenians in the Spartan assembly (I.75), the Mytileneans also at Sparta (3.11.3).

4. For more on this point, see especially Henderson, "Demos, Demagogue" in Morgan, *Popular Tyranny*; see also Ober, *Dissent* 101. Not everyone agrees that Athens is forced into being a tyranny: "We know that no friendship between man and man, no league between city and city, can ever be permanent unless the friends or allies have a good opinion of each other's honesty, and are similar in general character" (Thucydides 3.10.1).

5. He also argues in the alternative, rejecting the issue of right and wrong, saying, if the Athenians are "resolved to maintain [their empire], then you must punish these people in defiance of equity as your interests require" (40).

6. One might wonder, since that policy of punishment through example did not work this time, why it would work in the future. But, Cleon's argument is slightly different from that rephrasing: he is not claiming that punishment keeps city-states in subjection, but that failure to punish leads to revolt. And it doesn't really matter whether the policy has worked, but that it should.

7. This point about Cleon's rhetoric of realism is crucial—it is common for people to claim Thucydides as an advocate of a "realist" foreign policy; on the contrary, the villains in his narrative are the realists (as the term is currently used).

8. In the course of coming to personify them, his position embodies tradition. At various moments, Cleon opposes the out-group's fascination with newness to the in-group's deference to what is generally translated as "the law." But, it is not "the law" (at least, not in the sense in which we use the term); the word Cleon uses is some variation of *nomos*, which is more accurately translated as "custom" or "tradition." It isn't so much that Cleon uses the word incorrectly, as that he is engaged in a subtle sort of equivocation in regard to the word *nomos*, appealing to different senses of its usage.

9. It is interesting that John Cotton offered to dissenters the option of becoming part of the body of Christ, or setting themselves in open rebellion. As various proslavery rhetors said, a slave is either submissive, and thereby part of the property of the master, or in open rebellion.

10. Ernesto Laclau uses the term "equivalential chain" for the same concept, pointing out that such chains use empty signifiers to constitute an identity; the chain manages to be overdetermined and empty of positive content, an "undifferentiated fullness" (see especially 94–97). I am using Perelman and Olbrechts-Tyteca's terminology because it is both more familiar among rhetoric scholars and seems more intuitive for readers to understand. In addition, while Laclau's argument concerning the excess and absence of signification often applies, I'm not certain that it always does.

11. Wohl says, "The language of hardness and softness recurs throughout Thucydides' discussion of Athenian imperialism; in the speeches of Athenians and Peloponnesians alike it is recognized as the idiom of empire" (174). This reliance on a manly/unmanly binary recurs throughout demagoguery; it is not simply that alternate policies are characterized as inaction, but as a kind of impaired masculinity—sometimes as womanly, but more often as men behaving like women.

12. By the time this manuscript went into production, I had changed my mind about the claim that the manly/unmanly binary recurs throughout demagoguery. It is certainly common, especially in the kind of demagoguery that Paul Johnson calls "masculine victimhood," a strategy for reasserting control in response to precarity ("The Art of Masculine Victimhood: Donald

Trump's Demagoguery," *Women's Studies in Communication*, vol. 40, no. 3, 2017, pp. 229–50). But not all demagoguery.

13. Demagoguery, as I've said, relies on binaries, which means that we are invited to see the world in terms of us and them, never and always, order and chaos. People engaged in demagoguery often put their oppositions' arguments in similarly binary (and extreme) terms, putting in "never" and "always," or, in this case, "necessarily" when that wasn't the original argument. While this move—the rhetorical fallacy of "straw man"—makes the opposition argument easier to disprove, I'm not sure that rhetors realize they are doing it; it's as though they have trouble understanding the significant difference between the two claims "this tends to do that" and "this necessarily does that."

14. His scapegoating of abolitionists for the postwar lynching of African Americans was a common topos that relies on making one group responsible for the feelings of another. The argument (which shows up in such varied places as Wilbur Cash's 1941 *Mind of the South* and the 1961 South Carolina Supreme Court decision *Edwards v. South Carolina*) is that criticism of slavery or segregation is so enraging to whites that they cannot help but engage in retaliatory violence; therefore, the critics are responsible for the violence. This is also the argument made at moments in the Tolan hearing, and in *Hirabayashi v. United States:* people who engage in violence are not responsible for their inability to control themselves; the responsibility lies in the potential victims of that violence.

15. For an explanation of peculiarly American attempts to ensure various kinds of cultural stability as a result of the contradictions of emergent capitalism in the nineteenth-century United States, see Herring.

16. There are obviously connections to certain paradoxical constructions of masculinity, in which the ideal male is simultaneously in control and yet not responsible.

17. Lieutenant General John L. DeWitt, in command of the Western Defense Command, was a major and influential advocate of mass imprisonment, whose insistence on military necessity was not only implausible but probably insincere. For more on his role, see especially Kashima 129–39.

18. The federal court decision to reverse Korematsu's conviction politely notes some of the problems with the report by General DeWitt on which the Supreme Court relied for both *Korematsu v. United States* and *Hirabayashi v. United States*.

The Final Report of General DeWitt (which is dated June 5, 1943, but which was not made public until January 1944) is relied on in this brief for statistics and other details concerning the actual evacuation and the events that took place subsequent thereto. The recital of the circumstances justifying the evacuation as a matter of military necessity, however, is in several respects, particularly with reference to the use of illegal radio transmitters and to shore-to-ship signaling by persons of Japanese ancestry, in conflict with information in the possession of the Department of Justice.

Korematsu v. U.S., 584 F. Supp. 1406, 16 Fed. R. Evid. Serv. 1231 (N.D.Cal. Apr. 19, 1984). That decision also notes that Korematsu's petition for reversal of the decision contains documents in which "several Department of Justice officials pointed out to their superiors and others the 'willful historical inaccuracies and intentional falsehoods' contained in the DeWitt Report."

19. Rutledge read the decision as deciding "that there is no action a person in the position of General De Witt here may take ... which will call judicial power into play." This is the only point of the decision with which Rutledge disagreed, insisting that, while the situation creates "wide latitude" for [De Witt's] power, "it does not follow there may not be bounds beyond which he cannot go."

20. For a discussion of US court decisions regarding whiteness and Asians, see Coulson.

3. Scapegoating and Rationality Markers

1. There might have been a particularly pressing need to explain the effectiveness given the kind of braggadocio common to prewar military talk, the kind that Warren describes.

It was commonly held that our naval forces could knock out the Japanese Navy by lunchtime on any given day, that the Japanese were not innovative, that they would only copy our methods, that they were far behind us in every military field, and that because of bad eyesight they could not man the essential weapons of successful warfare. (147)

2. It should be noted that this agitation was often on the part of groups and individuals who had argued for mass expulsion of Japanese long before the war; for more on this point, see Roger Daniels, *Politics of Prejudice*. For more on the debates within the Roosevelt administration regarding which policies to pursue, see Robinson, *Tragedy*.

3. Robert Shaffer says the hearings had been organized by "liberals such as Carey McWilliams ... in an attempt to forestall drastic anti-Japanese American actions" (88). Shaffer has a careful list of all the people who spoke in opposition to race-based evacuation (88–91), showing that there was substantial dissent to the policy.

4. This chapter will consider the first three sets of hearings: the February hearings in San Francisco, the Portland hearings, and the Seattle hearings. By

the time of the last hearings, in March of 1942, the hyperbolic and paranoid appendix to the US Congress House Report on Un-American Propaganda Activities (also known as the Dies Committee's "Report on Japanese Activities" and sometimes "Dies Yellow Paper") had come out (for more on this, see Tanner), and seriously troubled any possibility of considered deliberation.

5. For more on the prewar anti-Japanese fear-mongering, see especially Robinson, *Tragedy*, chapter 1; Daniels, *Politics of Prejudice.*

6. I still run across this argument in various places—negative reviews of scholarly books about the mass imprisonment, for instance, web pages and blog posts defending DeWitt's policies, and so on. The authors assume that all Japanese are the same, a racist assumption, and so the fact that the Japanese government attacked us means, for them, that anyone of Japanese ethnicity was at war with us. It's the standard move—treating all members of an out-group as identical, the same move that can be seen in arguments that Muslims "really are" at war with us.

7. This isn't to say that Pearl Harbor immediately provoked outrage against all "Japanese." Tolan's "Preliminary Report" on the hearings (March 19, 1942) points out "For at least a month thereafter, however, the temper of the American people remained relatively calm" (2). Robinson concurs: "In the weeks that followed the outbreak of war, there was no public outcry for government action to control Japanese Americans" (Robinson, *By Order* 75; see also Okihiro and Sly). It wasn't until January that there was something that might be characterized as a popular movement for extreme measures, and even that movement might have been, if not manufactured, then at least strongly encouraged by publishers and groups long hostile to Japanese Americans. This possibility was raised by various witnesses at the Tolan Committee hearings, who bemoaned the "hysteria" being whipped up by interested parties (see, for instance, Sakamoto 11464; Boyd 11584; Goldblatt 11181; Fisher 11198; Omura 11230–1).

8. Tolan said an attack on the Pacific Coast "is not only possible but it is probable" (11104) and "we all agree that the Pacific Coast is the most vulnerable part of the United States" (Tolan 11397; see also 11053); the American legion resolution refers to the belief "that the Pacific coast area of the United States, with its many vital industries, is ever in danger of attack" (11434; see also Ward testimony 11262). The statement of the Committee for Church and Community Cooperation says, "At any moment, Japanese military forces may attempt, at least, a token attack on the Pacific shores of the United States" (11624). The Astoria Chamber of Commerce letter to Secretary of the Navy Knox (entered into the record for the Migration Hearings) says "According to statements just made by the President of the United States, even cities as far inland as Detroit may be justified in expecting bombings" (11318). This is a

reference to something Roosevelt had said during a press conference; see W. H. Lawrence, "President Warns Foe Could Shell or Bomb New York," *New York Times* (1923-Current file); Feb 18, 1942; ProQuest Historical Newspapers: *New York Times* (1851–2008) p. 1.

9. The following analysis concerns his approximately seven-thousand-word oral testimony; all numbers that follow are approximate.

10. There is some ambiguity about what he means in terms of which consensus. Two paragraphs earlier, he mentioned "the consensus of opinion among the law-enforcement officers of this State" (111014). If that is the consensus he means, it is not supported by the letters he submitted in support. Several of the letters don't mention the issue of nonaliens at all, and none made the claim that American-born Japanese are more dangerous. If he means some other kind of consensus, then it can't be disproven—he doesn't cite opinion polls, for instance—and it's irrelevant.

11. What is most interesting for me about this story is that Johnson didn't notice that his evidence disproved his own conclusion, nor did Tolan remark on the contradiction.

12. "Now, we can't go out overnight and say to the canning industry that we will get an acreage pledged by American farmers to take up the acreage that is vacated by the Japanese unless the tomato plants are available" (11089).

13. At best, the topos that people of Japanese ancestry are in danger is an argument for temporarily opening camps along the lines of the Farm Security Administration—places to which people who felt threatened could go should they choose, and part of the JACL plan.

14. This assertion that "everyone agrees" in the face of disagreement fascinates me. It shows that the rhetor means that only in-group members count.

15. Another person testifying at the Portland hearings says that agriculturalists will only hire Japanese if they are under armed guard (11360, 11362).

16. Travoli, of Tulare County, advocates putting "them" (it isn't clear to me whether he means citizens, noncitizens, or both) on an "Indian reservation" and not letting them stay in California, but "I wouldn't advise a camp" (1066–7). His description of families who have come from a restricted area, and whom his county throws out, and who then return because they have been thrown out of somewhere else, is heart-wrenching (11065). The police, he says, "[float] undesirable citizens out of one city on to the next city to take care of them" (11066), a remark that makes his statement, "I am not in favor of abusing any of them," (11068) somewhat puzzling. Apparently, he doesn't see floating families around the state as abusing them.

17. By handing over control to a proxy agent, these rhetors can avoid the responsibility that goes with agency; they can deny the ethical implications of what they are actually doing, by claiming they aren't doing it. This evasion of

responsibility puts in mind Erich Fromm's discussion of the desire to "escape from freedom" or Hannah Arendt's discussion of the agency-free participation in "the social."

18. The myth that fifth-column activities significantly contributed to the disaster at Pearl Harbor was invoked repeatedly (Rossi 10967, Brady 10991, Warren 11010, 11018; see also 11868; 11109; Clark 11173; the Portland City Council resolution, 11306; 11404; Resolution of the American Legion ["whereas bitter experience has taught us" is the phrase used in many of the chapters' adoption of this resolution] 11434, see the resolutions from 11434 through 11436; 11588, 11612), and was used to argue for the differential treatment of Japanese and Italians and Germans (Rossi 10967; Cutler 10971; Sparkman 11184).

19. Christian Deporte notes that the propaganda advocating the myth of the fifth column was a "shared myth"—"it can be found in the propaganda of all belligerents" (64).

20. It might have to do with ambiguity about the term "espionage"—in the middle of widespread promulgation of urban legends about sabotage, and after years of such legends being given publicity by anti-Japanese groups, Roberts's use of the term "espionage" might be read as including both spying and sabotage (after all, although Roberts never mentions sabotage, neither does the report explicitly deny it).

21. While the myth was almost certainly helped by the repetition of rumors and urban legends, there is also the possibility of ambiguous language seeming to confirm the specific narratives. There are three overlapping concepts invoked repeatedly in discussions of Pearl Harbor—treachery, espionage, and sabotage. Roosevelt (and many others) characterized the actions of Japan as treacherous because Japan engaged in an act of war before declaring war, and while negotiations were still ongoing. Whether this is a fair characterization of Japan's action is not relevant. What is relevant is that synonyms for treachery were frequently applied to "the Japanese." The Roberts report made a point of the effectiveness of Japanese espionage in determining the exact defenses of Pearl Harbor. To the extent that Knox was referring to such spying activities (almost exclusively conducted by the Japanese consulate), his describing of fifth- column activities at Hawaii is accurate. With these specific meanings, referring to Japanese "treachery" or "espionage" may be hyperbolic, but not necessarily out of the realm of standard political discourse; more important, either of those accusations is irrelevant in terms of Japanese Americans on the continent (the "treachery" referred to the actions of the Japanese government, not Americans of Japanese ancestry, and "espionage" is only a factor in the event of an invasion). Readers for whom "espionage" and "treachery" were synonymous with sabotage could read Knox's comments or the Roberts

report, and believe they had authoritative sources for their belief in significant Japanese sabotage. And some rhetors may have allowed the misunderstanding. It is striking that Knox, who did tell Tolan that there was no sabotage, did not appear to try to correct the general public impression that he had been talking about sabotage when he described the fifth-column activities in Hawaii.

22. Walter Lord, in a more recent history of Pearl Harbor, mentions the urban legend about a pilot with a University of Oregon class ring circulating during the attack itself, along with rumors that pilots had McKinley High School sweaters (193). He speculates on some of the reasons that such myths may have been plausible in the moment; they certainly should not have been taken seriously much later.

23. I have not found any such photographs, or even photographs that could be misinterpreted in this way. The story is absurd even on the face of it; Honolulu is not between the army and the harbor; Honolulu at the time had far more than one road; I'm not sure how one could get a photograph of hundreds of cars. This seems to be a garbled version of an urban legend, refuted as early as March 1942 by police and military in Honolulu at the time, that Carroll had in his December article about Japanese farmers using their trucks to block some road. It may be related to a phenomenon described by Stanley Weintraub, of "a chaos of cars" at the main gate to Pearl Harbor; the cars belonged to workers trying to get to the harbor (263). There is a different version of this legend that persists: someone reports someone else having seen Japanese deliberately blocking a road near the fish market.

24. As absurd as this argument is, it was also made by DeWitt, and more recently by apologists for internment, who argue that the lack of Japanese sabotage is proof that internment worked.

25. As intransigent as Tolan seems on this point during the hearings, it turns out he was moveable on the issue. After he received thorough and multiple reports from various authorities in Hawaii, and from Secretary of the Navy Knox, that stated unequivocally that there had been no sabotage, he retracted his claim that sabotage had occurred. Hearing reasonable arguments from witnesses during the hearing, including from an authority like Bellquist, as to just what was wrong with the narrative seemed to have no impact, and that is troubling for the hope of deliberative discourse.

26. See, for instance, Jennifer Whitson and Adam Galinsky's "Lacking Control Increases Illusory Pattern Perception," *Science* 3, vol. 322, no. 5898, October 2008, pp. 115–17.

27. There is an irony to dismissing the Roberts report in favor of a conspiracy theory about Japanese sabotage: the Roberts report notes that Short and Kimmel were exclusively concerned with sabotage; many historians argue

that Short's "sabotage psychosis" (Prange et al. *At Dawn* 402) significantly contributed to the disaster at Pearl Harbor, partially because Short's obsession with sabotage meant that this obsession (shared with Kimmel) made the navy facilities more vulnerable to air attack (such as by grouping the planes together) and also because Kimmel and Short failed to pay attention to other issues. Thus, to take from the attack on Pearl Harbor the moral that one should be obsessed with sabotage is to replicate precisely the mistake that contributed to the disaster.

28. Some scholars speculate (with good reason) that the initial success of Japan in late December 1941 and January 1942 would have increased anxiety (see, for instance, Robinson, *By Order*; Daniels, *Prisoners* 27); if so, the desire for scapegoating would have also increased. During the Tolan hearings, when a witness, Louis Goldblatt, argues that going after Japanese American citizens who have done nothing when there are open advocates of Mussolini on draft boards is "going after the little fry." Tolan says, "So you are not worried about Japan. They seem to be winning a good many battles over there" (11182). Tolan's logic is a little hard to follow, but it seems to assume an inherent connection between Japanese success and failure to control Japanese in California. The mild incoherence of Tolan's argument suggests that Robinson may be right.

29. As the Roberts Commission concluded, all of the spying activities that did assist the success of the Japanese in Pearl Harbor were conducted by members of the Japanese embassy. And, as high-ranking military officials knew, Japan tended to rely on either such officials or non-Japanese for intelligence. As various witnesses testified, anyone with any connection to suspicious Japanese organizations had been arrested already (and, as Louis Goldblatt testified, one could not say that about members of Italian or German fascist organizations), so why intern anyone else?

30. The perception of Japanese as un-Americanly clubby would remain through the sixties and early seventies. I remember people complaining that Japanese farmers and businesses engaged in unfair competition because their families all worked toward the family business in ways that American families would not. The same complaint was later made about the Vietnamese, and one now hears it about Koreans.

31. This notion of a people incapable of critical or independent thinking was crucial to the topos that Japanese citizens were inherently dangerous because they often spent some time in Japan. As Warren says, "And while they are over there they are indoctrinated with the idea of Japanese imperialism . . . and they come back here imbued with ideas and the policies of Imperial Japan" (11014). A short time in Japan indoctrinates them in a way that a lifetime in the United States does not.

32. One letter writer says that Japanese Americans can demonstrate their loyalty by submitting to the perception of them as inherently disloyal, "It of course stands to reason that if they should object to such treatment, they could not be looked upon as being true and loyal Americans" (McDonald 10999; see also 11072; 11092). Robert Fouke, of the California Joint Immigration Committee, formerly the Japanese Exclusion League, says that loyal "Japanese or Italians or Germans, as the case might be" can best show their loyalty by "acquiescing" in regard to military restrictions of their presence in combat zones, and "hence all those whose loyalty is not unquestioned should be removed from that area" (11072). Since, if I'm understanding Fouke, one shows one's loyalty by removing oneself from the area, then anyone who remains has questionable loyalty.

33. Something similar happened when US homophobic groups visited Uganda, with propaganda about homosexuals as child-molesting agents of Satan; those groups then disavowed any responsibility for Uganda's adopting the death penalty for homosexuals, although they never disavowed their alarmist and false rhetoric.

34. Tolan tries to get this witness (Tatsuno of the JACL) to say that there are definitely Japanese agents in California, and Tatsuno keeps saying he doesn't know. If he did, he'd report them to the FBI (11153–4)—another damned if you do and damned if you don't. If he says he knows enemy agents, then he confirms the premise that they are in contact with every Japanese person; if he says he doesn't, then he looks like he's hiding them.

35. The sabotage narrative was crucial for the policy of differentiating the Japanese from the Italians and Germans—it was supposed to signify that they were singularly dangerous. But, even if one accepted the sabotage narrative, that was not reason to imprison or evacuate the Japanese and only the Japanese. Louis Goldblatt pointed out that the reason that there were not large numbers of Italian and German saboteurs was that it was the Japanese attacking; were the Germans or Italians to attack, then those groups would be just as problematic (an argument made, it should be emphasized, in service of no mass evacuations of any group; 11185).

4. When the Choir Claims to Have Been Converted

1. Rhetoric scholars were, at one time, interested in "mystagoguery," but it slid into anti-intellectualism. I remain interested in the problem of distinguishing between texts that are initially mystifying because the terminology is specialized or the argument is complicated and texts in which language is used to seem to be saying something but isn't.

2. Ryback's title comes from an incident in which it was reported that Grant showed a letter from Hitler in which Hitler called Grant's book his "Bible" (114–115), despite Grant's claims that the Nordic race *originated*

in the Baltic region and quickly moved to Scandinavia, where it is most pure.

3. It isn't necessarily "white" men. The story of Solomon and his foreign wives, interpretations of the consequences of Antony's dallying with Cleopatra (in both Plutarch and Shakespeare), the anxiety about the English becoming weakened by intermarrying with the Irish made manifest in the Statutes of Kilkenny, even Odysseus and Circe—all are pre-Darwinian stories that exhibit anxiety that male strength is weakened by sexual contact with the Other. This myth is central to narratives of imperialism, as Anne McClintock has argued, in which "the augural scene of discovery becomes a scene of ambivalence, suspended between an imperial megalomania, with its fantasy of unstoppable rapine—and a contradictory fear of engulfment, with its fantasy of dismemberment and emasculation" (27). The narrative presumes and justifies the rape of women (and feminized resources) by utterly powerful men (the megalomania) who are paradoxically weakened and victimized by their lust for women (the fear of engulfment).

4. In fact, many of Grant's supposedly new arguments are present in that speech. In addition to claiming all great achievements for the Saxons (whom Lodge also calls Norse), he warns of the non-Saxon immigration and the consequences of interbreeding.

> If a lower race mixes with a higher in sufficient numbers, history teaches us that the lower race will prevail. The lower race will absorb the higher, not the higher the lower, when the two strains approach equality in numbers. . . . The lowering of a great race means not only its own decline but that of human civilization. (Lodge, March 16, 1896, 2820).

Lodge's argument on race is more coherent than Grant's, in that he argues that, until now, races developed slowly, and changed slowly. So, the problem is not that amalgamation is always bad, but that it has to be slow, and the current rate is too fast. He thereby avoids the contradiction into which Grant falls. For more on Lodge, see Petit, especially 15–16.

5. And, as shouldn't be surprising given his lack of definition, Grant doesn't use the term consistently, sometimes referring to a group, as in regard to Aryans, as a race (62) and saying that group is not a race (3, 132). The problems inherent in defining race have been described in some detail in Douglas Coulson's forthcoming *Race, Nation, and Refuge: The Rhetoric of Race in Asian American Citizenship Cases* (SUNY).

6. Boas had already shown the problem with the skull-shape argument, in that skull shapes changed in America, among European immigrants. Grant simply ignored Boas.

7. This argument is another instance of Grant's flickering determinism, in which something is inevitable yet subject to human agency.

8. Having worked through the "History of the European Races" chapter multiple times, and even drawn various charts, I still cannot figure out how the various identities he describes are related to one another—I cannot draw his taxonomy. He has three "sub-genera" of humans: Mongoloid, Negroid, and Caucasian (29). Yet, at one point he says "there is not now, and there never was either a Caucasion or an Indo-European race" (62) and he also says the Caucasian race is "mythical" (3). On that same page he says the European races are all races within the Caucasian, although the Alpine is Asiatic, and has the round skull of the Mongoloid. Yet, somehow, the Asiatic Alpine is not and never was Mongoloid—where did it come from, then?

9. Even in the fourth edition of Grant's book, in which he was supposed to add the missing citations, this relation of claim and evidence is entangled. Grant adds to this passage, "although there must have been some Alpine strains mixed in with the Nordic element" (154). He gives citations for this passage, one of which supports his claim concerning the Nordic element, and it was published in 1918, two years after the first edition came out. So, Grant is not giving a citation that enables the reader to come to his conclusion, nor does he give any data (that good qualities come from the Nordic is what his book is supposed to prove, so taking the presence of good qualities as proof of Nordic blood is assuming precisely what is at stake). A reader cannot get to Grant's conclusion from the evidence, reasoning, or citations he gives (or fails to give) unless the reader already agrees with him.

10. Jenifer Haard et al. call the use of meaningless but apparently impressive language "scientese" and show, unhappily, that people tend to find a claim more plausible when it uses scientese, even people who are well trained in science ("Scientese and Ambiguous Citation").

11. In this, my argument is slightly different from another set of critiques of Grant. John P. Jackson ("Whatever Happened") and Elazar Barkan have each looked carefully at the data regarding the "cephalic index" (essentially, head shape) and concluded that the data was inconclusive. Thus, both sides—those who wanted to use the data to argue for racist policies and those who didn't—were on opposite sides of the "argument from ignorance" move. My argument is the cephalic index issue is irrelevant for assessing the validity of his argument: Grant's errors are rhetorical; one didn't need the "cephalic index" data to come to mistrust Grant's argument—his narrative of racial migration is contradictory and incoherent.

12. At various moments—see especially his discussion of race mixing 15–19 and 56—Grant asserts that the mixing between the higher and lower

will tend toward the lower. This common misinterpretation of regression toward the mean (an unusually tall person and an unusually short person are likely to have a child in the middle) coupled with the tendency to give "higher" and "lower" values to characteristics was common.

13. Walton uses the phrase "objective evidence," a phrase I think is neither accurate nor helpful. Disagreements often rest on what counts as relevant evidence, and so there is little or no agreement as to what evidence is "objective," let alone what that word means. We don't have to resort some external standard of objective, but can rely on the evidence provided by the authority—does *that* evidence support *those* claims. And my point about Grant is that his "evidence," to the extent it can be identified (that is, to the extent that one can infer what he means) does not support his claims. And that is what undermines his authority on the issue.

14. He has to grant that other "races" try to improve, but asserts that the Nordic is the only race whose desire to improve is from within (85–86), an excellent example of "hermetic wording."

15. I argue with white supremacists over positive reviews and descriptions of Grant's argument, including on sites regularly used as sources for students.

16. While advertising for the book echoed that claim, it wasn't true; as noted before, Grant's entire "history" is lifted from the 1899 *Races of Europe*, sometimes verbatim, and the general approach ("race" not linguistics) was Ripley's. As Ripley says, "Let us at the outset avoid the error of confusing community of language with identity of race" (17), suggesting instead the study be focused on head shape (37).

17. This review is quoted later, since it is also critical of Grant's "misstatements" in regard to genetics; that the review is so close to the one written by Hyde for *Geography* makes me suspect that Hyde wrote this one as well, but Hyde was a classicist, and neither a geneticist nor anthropologist.

18. I infer that this move enabled prosegregationists to use the book to argue for a policy (white versus black) that was not the main thrust of Grant's argument—that, in fact, ignored the point of most of the book and almost all of his evidence. Thus, they were invoking his authority while ignoring most of his argument.

19. It's intriguing that Woods admits that Grant's evidence is weak; the argument is true, Woods says, because it is supported by statistical evidence (419)—a kind of evidence Grant doesn't use. That is, Grant's argument is true because Woods believes it for reasons Grant doesn't give.

20. This is the same point that Jackson makes about the "science" journals that were formed in order to promote segregation: "They refused to

recognize that *their* science was imbued with their values and ideology" (*Science* 9).

21. No reviewer who praised the book did so by discussing his arguments in any detail (although some simply reproduced long passages of it), and not even in light of what other experts had done with the same information. While Grant's argument was praised for using the "latest" anthropological theories, that claim was never supported with specific examples. I suspect that Spiro is right, and that readers who agreed with Grant's argument didn't recognize that it was nonsense, but did recognize that it used the markers of pedantry and authority, and inferred from the presence of logical metadiscourse that the logic was sound. Or, in short, his argument was taken as true because it felt true to people who already agreed with the implicit political agenda.

22. The same thing could be said of his contradictions. When the Nordics succeed, the success signifies their essential superiority; when they fail, it is due to environmental causes. When other races succeed, those successes were either due to a Nordic in their midst (such as Jesus being a Nordic rather than a Jew), to whatever small amount of Nordic blood they had (such as the people of ancient Athens), or to the environment (as when he says that other races don't really desire improvement). One has what many argumentation theorists call "hermetic" wording, but that is more colloquially (and accurately) known as the "no true Scotsman" fallacy. The claim looks like a specific claim about reality, but is nonfalsifiable, since any counterexample can be dismissed as not really representative.

23. Scholars of whiteness have noted this in regard to "whiteness," the definition of which continually shifted over the nineteenth and twentieth centuries, largely when granting whiteness to some previously nonwhite or marginally white group was politically rewarding. Sometimes the "whiteness" designation is contingent; Matthew Jacobson, David Roediger, Noel Ignatiev and others have shown how throughout the nineteenth century, in Jacobson's words, various groups "were becoming less and less white in debates over who should be allowed to disembark on American shores, and yet were becoming whiter and whiter in debates over who should be granted full rights of citizenship" (75). Less remarked is the same dynamic in regard to the term "Christian," which, like "whiteness," is defined in opposition to some Other (Anglicanism, Catholicism, Orthodox, Islam), and strategically narrowing and broadening (so that, in terms of election, someone like Bill Clinton was not a "true" Christian, but for purposes of arguing the "Christian" foundation of our country, Jefferson is).

24. For reasons unclear to me, there is a popular conception that the United States did not engage in imperialism until the late nineteenth century,

which means that the intra-continental imperialism of "westward expansion" is somehow not imperialism.

25. E. S. Cox explains the presence of the "mixbreed element" in America, despite whites' natural horror at race mixing, "The vaunted pride of the Southerner has more than once succumbed to the mulattress" (246).

26. Kenneth Greenberg pointed to what I think is the same phenomenon, but with different terminology, in regard to how the marks of whipping were interpreted by people with a slavery ideology. For them, the marks of having been whipped meant that a slaver had identified the slave as unreliable—insubordinate, unruly, and therefore having no word.

5. Anti-intellectualism and the Appeal to Expert Opinion

1. For more on Cox's political influence, see especially Ward 87; Lombardo 438; Spiro 253–4.

2. For more on this issue, see especially Malik, *The Meaning of Race*.

3. This isn't to say that the public sphere should be freed of entity theorists, or that we should ban entity theorizing. As the research of Kruglanski and various others shows, we are all entity theorists when the constraints, pressures, motives, and situations tip us in that direction.

4. I say "probably" because Cox often did not provide book publication dates, and sometimes misspelled authors' names, misattributed authorship, or gave incorrect titles; so I am not certain, in some instances, that I have correctly identified a given source. The errors are minor and are not an indication of ill will or even sloppiness, but likely indicate standard problems that authors faced in Cox's era and situation (such as the difficulty of typesetting). That Cox had errors in his citations is not a criticism of Cox, but does explain why my own claims about his work can't be precise.

5. According to an obituary in *Auk: A Quarterly Journal of Ornithology* (October 1935), Shufeldt was an army surgeon from 1876 to 1919, and a self-trained ornithologist, especially regarding the osteology and paleontology of birds—impressive accomplishments (with 160 articles on the osteology of birds) but hardly scholarly credentials for a polemical book about humans, *America's Greatest Problem: The Negro*.

6. In this case, the "cold fact" that is "verifiable," is that "the Christian religion has never survived the white teachers," something that is not verifiable, because it is false.

7. He cites Darwin and Mendel, as well as Stoddard, but only mentions evolution in a quote from Stoddard.

8. Jackson's *Science for Segregation* describes the continued attempts of various racists to legitimate segregation and white supremacy through

scholarly journals, organizations, and publications, and describes in detail quite a few that do a better job.

9. He also discusses William Ziff's *The Gentlemen Talk of Peace,* "although he has no rating as a scholar," an odd criticism from someone who cites Cox as much as does Bilbo.

10. In general, it is almost a perfect sign of demagoguery that the texts don't represent the opposition fairly, and usually don't include the opposition arguments at all. Granted, Bilbo misrepresents these authors' arguments, but he includes enough of them that the reader can see that it is a misrepresentation; this book is the only case of that I have found among otherwise demagogic texts.

11. The most spirited recent defense of Bilbo's actions is the chapter "Bilbo and the Greater University" in David Sansing's *University of Mississippi: A Sesquicentennial History.*

12. Bilbo may have been motivated by a desire to improve the medical schools, which were inadequate in many ways, but even his defenders admit it was significant "political interference" (see, for instance, the relatively defensive narrative in Quinn 10–14). And my point here is that Bilbo played to the perception that it was him against the professors.

13. Chamberlain's situation was a kind of mirror image. The Germans were the newly politically empowered, and it is a commonplace to see Chamberlain's Germanomania as typical of authors who responded to the need to justify and rationalize the arbitrary boundaries of the new Germany. That is, it was rationalizing the new social order. But, the book was taken up by people like Lord Redesdale and Grant, who wanted to position the new social order as less just than the previous. Again, it was the just-world hypothesis in both cases, but opposing worlds. In each case, the text was read as a jeremiad against the *parvenu* at the same time that others read it as a rationalization of the arrival of the very same *parvenus* and preemptive nostalgia at the possibility they might lose their newly acquired status.

14. For a summary of some of the positions on the issue, see especially Sunstein, Griffin and Newman, and Shane.

15. The website was http://www.1man1woman.net/main-e.html, and it was still fully functional when I first began this research in 2009. It has since disappeared, and I have relied on the Wayback Machine to check quotes, and so on.

16. It appears to me that among the eras and places are ones in which homosexuality was criminalized regardless of the age of the participants (so sex between a twenty-two-year-old man and a seventeen-year-old boy would be criminalized) and eras and places in which heterosexual sex between an

adult and a minor was not criminalized (as in places in which sex between a twenty-two-year-old man and a fifteen-year-old girl would not be considered child molesting). This is, quite simply, invalid data.

17. This way of describing his reasoning is generous. Implicitly, Cameron's definition of "homosexual" is "a male who has sex with other males or females who has sex with other females," thereby assuming what is at stake—that child molesting is within the normal range of sexual practices of homosexuals (thanks to Paul Wallich for pointing out to me the significance of this definition).

18. That first-year composition has not advanced very much in its approach to logic also doesn't help. Many argumentation texts evade the topic altogether, and of the few that do, far too many begin with the premise that a logical and an emotional argument are different categories. The substantial work in informal logic has had depressingly little impact on the teaching of argumentation.

19. Demagoguery can be used for backpedaling on policies, as with Stalin on collectivization, *Prairie Fire*, post-Civil War demagoguery about the "true" causes of the Civil War (which amounted to backpedaling in regard to slavery), and pundits who claimed to have always been against the Iraq invasion. Such demagoguery, it seems to me, rarely involves an admission of error (although it sometimes does) and instead presents returning to an older policy as a way of moving forward, or simply denies that there ever was an older policy.

20. That seems to me an apt description of what actually happens in political debates, but hoping to persuade people to make a distinction between logical argument and rational argumentation may be too ambitious. Hence, throughout this book, I've opted for using "logical" and "irrational" more or less interchangeably, and tried to be precise whether I was discussing a particular set of claims or an argument overall. And, in general, what I've meant is simply how their claims fit together—do they appeal to premises consistently.

Conclusion: Snakes, Vehemence, Snark, and Argumentation

1. And there was opposition. According to Spiro, several speakers explicitly criticized the committee for its reliance on Madison Grant, and his invention of the "Nordic race" (see especially 220–26). Three dissenting congressional representatives wrote their own report, and it put forward strong evidence that the act was "a deliberate discrimination against the so-called newer immigrants" (42), would prevent the immigration of the amount of unskilled labor necessary for various industries (44–45), was not necessitated by an imagined postwar increase in immigration (45), and would prevent the

uniting of families (46). One of their strongest arguments was that the United States benefited from this immigration (45).

2. Much scholarship on the issue suggests that the rise in race-baiting rhetoric after the war was a case of fairly complicated one-upmanship; once one politician engaged in it, then other rhetors felt the need to do so. Several political figures blamed losing elections to their hesitation in race baiting, and then went at it even more in the next election.

Works Cited

"About FRC." *Family Research Council: Advancing Faith, Family and Freedom.* Family Research Council, 2012. Accessed 17 April 2012.

Adorno, Theodore, et al. *The Authoritarian Personality.* John Wiley and Sons, 1964.

Agamben, Giorgio. *State of Exception.* U of Chicago P, 2005.

Allen, Bryce, et al. "Persuasive Communities: A Longitudinal Analysis of References in the Philosophical Transactions of the Royal Society, 1665–1990." *Social Studies of Science*, vol. 24, no. 2, May 2014, pp. 279–310. *JSTOR.* Accessed 5 May 2014.

Allport, Gordon W. *The Nature of Prejudice.* Perseus Books, 1954.

Altemeyer, Bob. *The Authoritarian Specter.* Harvard UP, 1996. Arendt, Hannah. *Life of the Mind.* Harcourt Brace Jovanovich, 1971.

Arendt, Hannah. *Life of the Mind.* Harcourt Brace Jovanovich, 1971.

———. "What Is Authority?" *Between Past and Future.* Rev. ed. Viking Press, 1968.

Aristotle. *Art of Rhetoric.* Translated by J. H. Freese. Harvard UP, 1926.

Aristotle. *Politics.* Translated by H. Rackham. Harvard UP, 1932.

Aune, James Arnt. *Rhetoric and Marxism.* Westview Press, 1994.

Avolio, Bruce, and Francis Yammarino. Introduction. *Transformational and Charismatic Leadership: The Road Ahead.* Emerald Publishing, 2002.

B., G. H. Rev. of *The Passing of the Great Race* by Madison Grant. *Journal of Race Development*, vol. 8, no. 4, 1918, p. 153. *ProQuest.* Accessed 12 May 2014.

Bacevich, Andrew J. *The Limits of Power: The End of American Exceptionalism.* Holt Paperbacks, 2008.

———. *The New American Militarism: Why Americans Are Seduced by War.* Oxford UP, 2005.

Barkan, Elazar. *The Retreat of Scientific Racism: Changing Concepts of Race in Britain and the United States between the World Wars.* Cambridge UP, 1993.

Barkun, Michael. *A Culture of Conspiracy: Apocalyptic Visions in Contemporary America.* U of California P, 2013.

Beevor, Antony. *Stalingrad: The Fateful Siege, 1942–1943.* Viking Press, 1998.

Below the Fold. Fox News. 25 Aug. 2002. Television.

Bendersky, Joseph W. *A Concise History of Nazi Germany.* 3rd ed., Rowman and Littlefield, 2007.

Benedict, Ruth, and Gene Weltfish. *The Races of Mankind.* Public Affairs Pamphlet No. 85. Public Affairs Committee, 1946.

Berkson, Isaac B. *Theories of Americanization: A Critical Study with Special Reference to the Jewish Group.* Teachers College, Columbia University, 1920. *Columbia University Libraries.* Accessed 5 May 2014.

Berlet, Chip, and Mathew N. Lyons. *Right-Wing Populism in America: Too Close for Comfort.* Guilford, 2000.

Bhabha, Homi. *Location of Culture.* Routledge, 2004.

Bilbo, Theodore. *Take Your Choice: Separation or Mongrelization.* Dream House, 1947.

Boas, Franz. "Inventing a Great Race." Rev. of *The Passing of the Great Race* by Madison Grant. *New Republic,* 13 Jan. 1917, pp. 305–07.

———. "Peoples at War." Rev. of *The Passing of the Great Race* by Madison Grant. *American Journal of Physical Anthropology,* vol. 1, 1918, p. 363.

Booth, Wayne. *Modern Dogma and the Rhetoric of Assent.* U of Notre Dame P, 1974.

Bostdorff, Denise M. "George W. Bush's Post–September 11 Rhetoric of Covenant Renewal: Upholding the Faith of the Greatest Generation." *Quarterly Journal of Speech,* vol. 8, 2003, pp. 293–319.

Bowler, Kate. *Blessed: A History of the American Prosperity Gospel.* Oxford UP, 2013.

Bowler, Peter J., and Iwan Rhys Morus. *Making Modern Science: A Historical Survey.* U of Chicago P, 2005.

Brace, C. Loring. "'Physical' Anthropology at the Turn of the Last Century." *Histories of American Physical Anthropology in the Twentieth Century,* edited by Michael Little and Kenneth A. R. Kennedy, Lexington Books, 2010, pp. 25–54.

Brinkley, David. *Washington Goes to War.* Ballantine, 1988.

Bullock, Angela Camille. "Charismatic Leadership Theory." *Encyclopedia of Industrial and Organizational Psychology,* edited by Steven G. Rogelberg, Sage Publications, 2007. Accessed 12 May 2017.

Burham, Gilbert, et al. "Morality after the 2003 Invasion of Iraq: A Cross-Sectional Cluster Sample Survey." *Lancet,* vol. 368, no. 9545, 21 Oct. 2006, pp. 1421–8.

Burke, Kenneth. "Rhetoric of Hitler's 'Battle.'" *Philosophy of Literary Form: Studies in Symbolic Action.* 3rd ed., U of California P, 1978.

Burrough, Bryan. *Days of Rage: America's Radical Underground, the FBI, and the Forgotten Age of Revolutionary Violence*. Penguin Press, 2015.

Burton, Robert. *On Being Certain: Believing You Are Right Even When You're Not*. St. Martin's Press, 2009.

Bush, George W. "Text of President Bush's 2002 State of the Union Address." *Washington Post*, 29 Jan. 2002. Accessed 6 May 2014.

Cameron, Paul. "Homosexual Molestation of Children/Sexual Interaction of Teacher and Pupil." *Psychological Reports*, vol. 57, 1985, pp. 1227–36. *Ammons Scientific*. Accessed 6 May 2014.

Carroll, Wallace. "Scope of Hawaii's Spy Army Told." *Los Angeles Times*, 31 Dec. 1941, p. 2. *ProQuest Historical Newspapers: Los Angeles Times*. Accessed 6 May 2014.

"The Case Made Clearer." *Economist*, 6 Feb. 2003. Accessed 12 May 2014.

Cash, W. J. *Mind of the South*. Alfred A. Knopf, 1941.

Castells, Manuel. *Networks of Outrage and Hope: Social Movements in the Internet Age*. Polity Press, 2012.

Chamberlain, Houston Stewart. *Foundations of the Nineteenth Century*. Translated by John Lees. Adamant Media, 2005. 2 vols.

Chappell, David L. "Seven Disunity and Religious Institutions in the White South." *Massive Resistance: Southern Opposition to the Second Reconstruction*, edited by Clive Webb, Oxford UP, 2005, pp. 136–50.

Chenoweth, Erica, and Maria Stephan, *Why Civil Resistance Works: The Strategic Logic of Nonviolent Conflict*. Columbia UP, 2012.

Chesterton, G. K. "The Shadow of the Shark." *Thirteen Detectives: Classic Mystery Stories by the Creator of Father Brown*. Penguin Press, 1987, pp. 179–97.

Communiqué #1 From the Weatherman Underground. N.p., Students for a Democratic Society, 1970. TXT file.

Coulson, Doug. "British Imperialism, the Indian Independence Movement, and the Racial Eligibility Provisions of the Naturalization Act: *United States v. Thind Revisited*." *Georgetown Journal of Law and Modern Critical Race Perspectives*, vol. 7, 2015, pp. 1–42.

Coulter, Ann. "Make Liberals Safe, Legal, and Rare." *Townhall*. 15 Aug. 2002, townhall.com. Accessed 5 May 2014.

———. "New Idea for Abortion Party: Aid the Enemy." *Ann Coulter*. 23 Nov. 2005, anncoulter.com. Accessed 5 May 2014.

"Council Acts on Cameron Case." *Footnotes*, vol. 15, no. 1, 1987, pp. 4, 6. American Sociological Association. Accessed 25 June 2015.

Cox, Earnest Sevier. *Unending Hate*. N.p., n.p., 1955.

———. *White America*. White America Society, 1923.

Cramer, Jane K. "Militarized Patriotism and the Success of Threat Inflation." *American Foreign Policy and the Politics of Fear: Threat Inflation since*

9/11, edited by A. Trevor Thrall and Jane K. Cramer, Routledge, 2009, pp. 135–52.

Cramer, Jane K., and Edward C. Duggan. "In Pursuit of Primacy: Why the United States Invaded Iraq." *Why Did the United States Invade Iraq?*, edited by Jane K. Cramer and A. Trevor Thrall, Routledge, 2012, pp. 201–43.

Crosswhite, James. *Deep Rhetoric: Philosophy, Reason, Violence, Justice, Wisdom.* U of Chicago P, 2013.

Daniels, Roger. *Prisoners without Trial: Japanese Americans in World War II.* Macmillan, 2004.

——. *Politics of Prejudice: The Anti-Japanese Movement in California and the Struggle for Japanese Exclusion.* U of California P, 1962.

Darsey, James. "Patricia Roberts-Miller, Demagoguery, and the Troublesome Case of Eugene Debs." *Rhetoric and Public Affairs*, vol. 9, no. 3, Fall 2006, pp. 463–70.

——. *The Prophetic Tradition and Radical Rhetoric in America.* New York UP, 1997.

Deporte, Christian. "The Image and Myth of the 'Fifth Column' during the Two World Wars." *France at War in the Twentieth Century: Propaganda, Myth, and Metaphor*, edited by Valerie Holman and Deborah Kelly, Berghahn, 2000, pp. 49–64.

Diamond, Larry. *Squandered Victory: The American Occupation and the Bungled Effort to Bring Democracy to Iraq.* Times-Henry Holt and Company, 2005.

——. "What Went Wrong in Iraq." *Foreign Affairs.* The Council on Foreign Relations, Sept.-Oct. 2004. Accessed 5 May 2014.

DiAngelo, Robin. "White Fragility." *International Journal of Critical Pedagogy*, vol. 3, no. 1, 2011, pp. 54–70.

Douglas, Mary. *Purity and Danger: An Analysis of Concepts of Pollution and Taboo.* Routledge, 1966.

Dowd, Maureen. "Bush Jr. Gets a Spanking." *New York Times*, 19 Aug. 2002. *LexisNexis.* Accessed 5 May 2014.

Duke, David. *My Awakening: A Path to Racial Understanding.* Free Speech, 1998.

Dweck, Carol S. *Mindset: The New Psychology of Success.* Ballantine Books, 2007.

E., J. M. Rev. of *The Passing of the Great Race* by Madison Grant. *International Journal of Ethics*, vol. 28, 1918, p. 295.

Eriksen, Thomas Hylland, and Finn Sivert Nielsen. *A History of Anthropology.* Pluto Press, 2001.

Evans, Richard. *Coming of the Third Reich.* Penguin, 2003.

"Executive Order 9066: Resulting in the Relocation of Japanese (1942)." *Our-Documents.* Accessed 12 May 2014.

Fallows, James. *Blind into Baghdad: America's War in Iraq.* Vintage-Random House, 2006.

———. "The Fifty-First State?" *Atlantic,* 1 Nov. 2002. Accessed 14 May 2014.

Federico, Christopher M., and Grace M. Deason. "Uncertainty, Insecurity, and Ideological Defense of the *Status Quo:* The Extremitizing Role of Political Expertise." *Extremism and the Psychology of Uncertainty,* edited by Michael A. Hogg and Danielle L. Blaylock, Wiley-Blackwell, 2012, pp. 197–211.

Finkelman, Paul, and Melvin I. Urofsky. *Landmark Decisions of the United States Supreme Court,* 2nd ed. Sage Publications, 2007.

Flibbert, Andrew. "Ideas and Entrepreneurs: A Constructivist Explanation of the Iraq War." *Why Did the United States Invade Iraq?,* edited by Jane K. Cramer and A. Trevor Thrall. Routledge, 2012, pp. 73–100.

Franks, Tommy, and Malcolm McConnell. *American Soldier.* HarperCollins, 2004.

Fromm, Erich. *Escape from Freedom.* Hearst-Avon, 1941.

G., C. A. Rev. of *The Passing of the Great Race* by Madison Grant. *Theosophical Quarterly,* vol. 14, 1916, pp. 385–7.

Garver, K. L., and B. Garver. "Eugenics: Past, Present, and the Future." *American Journal of Human Genetics,* vol. 49, no. 5, 1991, pp. 1109–18. PMC. Accessed 5 May 2014.

Gehrke, Pat J. *The Ethics and Politics of Speech: Communication and Rhetoric in the Twentieth Century.* Southern Illinois UP, 2009.

Gerecht, Reuel Marc. "Crushing al Qaeda is Only a Start." *AEI.* American Enterprise Institute for Public Policy Research. 19 Dec. 2001. Accessed 5 May 2014.

Gershkoff, Amy, and Shana Kushner. "Shaping Public Opinion: The 9/11 Iraq Connection in the Bush Administration's Rhetoric." *Perspectives on Politics,* vol. 3, no. 3, 2005, pp. 525–37. *JSTOR.* Accessed 21 Aug. 2013.

"Gobineau, Comte de." *International Encyclopedia of the Social Sciences,* edited by William A. Darity Jr., vol. 3, 2nd ed., Macmillan Reference USA, 2008.

Goldzwig, Steven. "A Social Movement Perspective on Demagoguery: Achieving Symbolic Realignment." *Communication Studies,* vol. 40, 1989, pp. 202–28.

Gore, Al. "A Commentary on the War against Terror: Our Larger Tasks." *Council on Foreign Relations.* Council on Foreign Relations, 12 Feb. 2002. Accessed 18 Dec. 2013.

Grant, Madison. *The Passing of the Great Race.* Charles Scribner's Sons, 1916.

"The Great Race Passes." *Journal of Heredity,* Jan. 1917, pp. 34–40.

Greenberg, Kenneth S. *Honor and Slavery: Lies, Duels, Noses, Masks, Dressing as a Woman, Gifts, Strangers, Humanitarianism, Death, Slave Rebellions, the Proslavery Argument, Baseball, Hunting, and Gambling in the Old South.* Princeton UP, 1996.

Gregor, Neil. *How to Read Hitler.* Granta, 2005.

Gregory, William K. Rev. of *The Passing of the Great Race* by Madison Grant. *Natural History,* vol. 22, 1922, pp. 135–40.

Griffin, John D., and Brian Newman. "Are Voters Better Represented?" *Journal of Politics,* vol. 27, no. 4, 2005, pp. 1206–27.

Gross, Alan G., et al. *Communicating Science: The Scientific Article from the 17th Century to the Present.* Oxford UP, 2002.

Grote, George. *A History of Greece; From the Earliest Period to the Close of the Generation Contemporary with Alexander the Great,* new ed. London: J. Murray, 1888. 10 vols.

Gustainis, J. Justin. "Demagoguery and Political Rhetoric: A Review of the Literature." *Rhetoric Society Quarterly,* vol. 20, no. 2, 1990, pp. 155–61. *Taylor and Francis Online.* Accessed 6 May 2014.

Haard, Jennifer, et al. "Scientese and Ambiguous Citations in the Selling of Unproven Medical Treatments." *Health Communication,* vol. 16, no. 4, 2004, pp. 411–26. *Taylor and Francis Online.* Accessed 5 May 2014.

Haass, Richard N. *War of Necessity, War of Choice: A Memoir of Two Iraq Wars.* Simon and Schuster, 2009.

Haidt, Jonathan. *The Righteous Mind: Why Good People Are Divided by Politics and Religion.* Pantheon, 2012.

Hall, Bolton. Rev. of *The Passing of the Great Race* by Madison Grant. *Public,* 6 July 1918, p. 1340.

"Hans Blix's Briefing to the Security Council." *Guardian,* 14 Feb. 2003. Accessed 12 May 2014.

Hariman, Robert. *Political Style: The Artistry of Power.* U of Chicago P, 1995.

———, editor. *Prudence: Classical Virtue, Postmodern Practice.* Pennsylvania State UP, 2003.

Haynes, Stephen R. *Noah's Curse: The Biblical Justification of American Slavery.* Oxford UP, 2002.

Henderson, Jeffrey. "Demos, Demagogue, Tyrant in Attic Old Comedy." *Popular Tyranny: Sovereignty and Its Discontents in Ancient Greece,* edited by Kathryn A. Morgan, U of Texas P, 2013, pp. 155–180.

Hendrix, Jerry A. "Theodore G. Bilbo: Evangelist of Racial Purity." *The Oratory of Southern Demagogues,* edited by Cal M. Logue and Howard Dorgan, Louisiana State UP, 1981, pp. 151–72.

Herek, Gregory M., editor. *Stigma and Sexual Orientation: Understanding Prejudice against Lesbians, Gay Men and Bisexuals.* Sage Publications, 1998.

Herring, Rodney. "Representational Crisis: Contradiction and Determination in Verbal Criticism." *Rhetoric Society Quarterly* vol. 40, no. 1, 2010, pp. 23–45.

Hetherington, Mark J., and Jonathan D. Weiler. *Authoritarianism and Polarization in American Politics.* Cambridge UP, 2009.

Hibbing, John R., and Elizabeth Theiss-Morse. *Stealth Democracy: Americans' Beliefs about How Government Should Work.* Cambridge UP, 2002.

Hilligoss, Brian, and Soo Young Rieh. "Developing a Unifying Framework of Credibility Assessment: Construct, Heuristics, and Interaction in Context." *Information Processing and Management,* vol. 44, no. 4, 2008, pp. 1467–84. *ScienceDirect.* Accessed 5 May 2014.

Hirabayashi v. United States. 320 U.S. 81. Supreme Court of the United States. 1943. *Justia.* Accessed 12 May 2014.

Hitchcock, Mark. *The End of Money: Bible Prophecy and the Coming Economic Collapse.* Harvest House, 2009.

Hofstadter, Richard. *Anti-intellectualism in American Life.* Vintage, 1966.

Hogg, Michael A. "Self-Uncertainty, Social Identity, and the Solace of Extremism." *Extremism and the Psychology of Uncertainty,* edited by Michael A. Hogg and Danielle L. Blaylock, Wiley-Blackwell, 2011, pp. 19–35.

Hogg, Michael A., and Danielle L. Blaylock, editors. *Extremism and the Psychology of Uncertainty.* Wiley-Blackwell, 2011.

Huntington, Samuel P. "The Hispanic Challenge." *Foreign Policy,* 1 March 2004. Accessed 5 May 2014.

Hyde, Walter Woodburn. Rev. of *The Passing of the Great Race* by Madison Grant. *Bulletin of the Geographical Society of America,* vol. 14, no. 2, 1916, pp. 138–48.

Hyland, Ken. "Academic Attribution: Citation and the Construction of Disciplinary Knowledge." *Applied Linguistics,* vol. 20, no. 3, 1999, pp. 341–67. *Oxford Journals.* Accessed 5 May 2014.

———. *Metadiscourse: Exploring Interaction in Writing.* Continuum, 2005.

Ignatiev, Noel. *How the Irish Became White.* Routledge, 1995.

Ivie, Robert L. *Democracy and America's War on Terror.* U of Alabama P, 2005.

———. *Dissent from War.* Kumarian, 2007.

———. "Fighting Terror by Rite of Redemption and Reconciliation." *Rhetoric and Public Affairs,* vol. 10, no. 2, 2007, pp. 221–48.

Jacobs, Ron. *The Way the Wind Blew: A History of the Weather Underground.* Verso Books, 1997.

Jacobson, Matthew Frye. *Whiteness of a Different Color: European Immigrants and the Alchemy of Race.* Harvard UP, 1999.

Jackson Jr., John P. *Science for Segregation: Race, Law, and the Case against Brown v. Board of Education.* New York UP, 2005.

———. "Whatever Happened to the Cephalic Index? The Reality of Race and the Burden of Proof." *Rhetoric Society Quarterly*, vol. 40, no. 5, 2010, pp. 438–58.

Jervis, Robert. "Explaining the War in Iraq." *Why Did the United States Invade Iraq?*, edited by Jane K. Cramer and A. Trevor Thrall, Routledge, 2012, pp. 25–48.

———. "Understanding Beliefs and Threat Inflation." *American Foreign Policy and the Politics of Fear: Threat Inflation since 9/11*, edited by A. Trevor Thrall and Jane K. Cramer, Routledge, 2009, pp. 16–39.

Jordan, Mark D. *Recruiting Young Love: How Christians Talk about Homosexuality*. U of Chicago P, 2011.

Kahneman, Daniel. *Thinking, Fast and Slow*. Farrar, Straus and Giroux, 2011.

Kahneman, Daniel, and Jonathan Renshon. "Why Hawks Win." *Foreign Policy*, 13 Oct. 2009. Accessed 16 June 2017.

Kaiser, Robert G. "The Long and Short of It: The War on Terrorism Began So Well. Then the Focus Changed. What is the Bush Administration Aiming to Do Now?" *Washington Post*, 8 Sept. 2002, p. B01. *LexisNexis*. Accessed 6 May 2014.

Kashima, Tetsuden. *Judgment without Trial: Japanese American Imprisonment during World War II*. U of Washington P, 2003.

Kaufmann, Chaim. "Threat Inflation and the Failure of the Marketplace of Ideas: The Selling of the Iraq War." *International Security*, vol. 291, 2004, pp. 5–48. *JSTOR*. Accessed 5 May 2014.

Kershaw, Ian. *Hitler: 1889–1936: Hubris*. W. W. Norton and Company, 1998.

———. *Hitler, the Germans, and the Final Solution*. Yale UP, 2008.

Kevles, Daniel. *In the Name of Eugenics: Genetics and the Uses of Human Heredity*. U of California P, 1985.

Kissinger, Henry A. "Phase II and Iraq." *Washington Post*, 13 Jan. 2002. *Henry A. Kissinger*, henryakissinger.com. Accessed 5 May 2014.

Klare, Michael. "Blood for Oil, in Iraq and Elsewhere." *Why Did the United States Invade Iraq?*, edited by Jane K. Cramer and A. Trevor Thrall, Routledge, 2012, pp. 129–44.

"Knox Discloses Losses in Hawaii as 2897 Killed, Six Warships Sunk." *Los Angeles Times*, 16 Dec. 1941, p. 1. *ProQuest Historical Newspapers: Los Angeles Times (1881–1988)*. Accessed 12 May 2014.

Koutsantoni, Dimitra. "Attitude, Certainty and Allusions to Common Knowledge in Scientific Research Articles," *Journal of English for Academic Purposes*, vol. 3, no. 2, Dec. 2004, pp. 163–82.

Kramer, Michael. "The Case for Bagging Saddam." *New York Daily News*, nydailynews.com. 18 Aug. 2002. Accessed 6 May 2014.

Krebs, Ronald R., and Jennifer Lobasz. "The Sound of Silence: Rhetorical Coercion, Democratic Acquiescence, and the Iraq War." *American Foreign Policy and the Politics of Fear: Threat Inflation since 9/11,* edited by A. Trevor Thrall and Jane K. Cramer. Routledge, 2009, pp. 117–34.

Kruglanski, Arie W. "Knowledge as a Social Psychological Construct." *The Social Psychology of Knowledge,* edited by Daniel Bar-Tal and Arie W. Kruglanski, Cambridge UP, 1988, pp. 109–41.

———. *Lay Epistemics and Human Knowledge: Cognitive and Motivational Bases.* Plenum Press, 1989.

———."Lay Epistemic Theory." *Handbook of Theories of Social Psychology,* vol. 1, edited by Paul A. M. Van Lange et al., Sage Publications, 2011. Accessed 15 Apr. 2015.

Kruglanski, Arie W., and Edward Orehek. "The Need for Certainty as a Psychological Nexus for Individuals and Society." *Extremism and the Psychology of Uncertainty,* edited by Michael A. Hogg and Danielle L. Blaylock, Wiley-Blackwell, 2012, pp. 3–18.

Kruglanski, Arie W. and Anna Sheveland. "Thinkers' Personalities: On Individual Differences in the Processes of Sense Making." *The Sage Handbook of Social Cognition,* edited by Susan T. Fiske and C. Neil Macrae. Sage, 2012, pp. 474–94.

Laclau, Ernesto. *On Populist Reason.* Verso Books, 2005.

Lakoff, George. *Moral Politics: How Conservatives and Liberals Think.* 2nd ed., U of Chicago P, 1996.

Lawrence, W. H. "President Warns Foe Could Shell or Bomb New York." *New York Times,* 18 Feb. 1942, p. 1. *ProQuest Historical Newspapers.* Accessed 6 May 2014.

Lears, Jackson. *Something for Nothing: Luck in America.* Penguin Press, 2003.

Lecklider, Aaron. *Inventing the Egghead: The Battle over Brainpower in American Culture.* U of Philadelphia P, 2013.

Lester, Will. "Democratic Hopefuls Careful on Iraq." *AP News Archive,* 12 Aug. 2002. Accessed 6 May 2014.

Lim, Joon Soo. "Authoritarianism." *Encyclopedia of Political Communication,* edited by Lynda Lee Kaid and Christina Holtz-Bacha, Sage Publications, 2008. Accessed 16 June 2017.

Little, Michael. "Franz Boas's Place in American Physical Anthropology and Its Institutions." *Histories of American Physical Anthropology in the Twentieth Century,* edited by Michael Little and Kenneth A. R. Kennedy, Lexington Books, 2010, pp. 55–86.

Locke, Alain Leroy, editor. *The New Negro.* Simon and Schuster, 1997.

Logan, Rayford W., editor. *What the Negro Wants.* U of NC P, 1944.

Logue, Cal M., and Howard Dorgan, editors. *Oratory of Southern Demagogues.* Louisiana State UP, 1981.

Lomas, Charles W. "The Rhetoric of Demagoguery." *Western Speech*, vol. 25, no. 3, 1961, pp. 160–68.

Lombardo, Paul A. *Three Generations, No Imbeciles: Eugenics, the Supreme Court, and* Buck v. Bell. Johns Hopkins UP, 2008.

Lord, Walter. *Day of Infamy.* Owl Books, 1957.

Luthin, Reinhard H. *American Demagogues.* Beacon Press, 1954.

Madsen, Douglas, and Peter Snow. *The Charismatic Bond: Political Behavior in Time of Crisis.* Harvard UP, 1991.

Malik, Kenan. *The Meaning of Race: Race, History, and Culture in Western Society.* New York UP, 1996.

Mann, Michael. *The Dark Side of Democracy: Explaining Ethnic Cleansing.* Cambridge UP, 2005.

———. *Fascists.* Cambridge UP, 2004.

Marquart-Pyatt, Sandra T., et al. "Politics Eclipses Extremes for Climate Change Perceptions." *Global Environmental Change*, vol. 29, 2014, pp. 26–257. Accessed May 2017.

McClintock, Anne. *Imperial Leather: Race, Gender, and Sexuality in the Colonial Contest.* Routledge, 1995.

McCloskey, D. "Keeping the Company of Sophisters, Economists, and Calculators." *Rhetoric and Pluralism: Legacies of Wayne Booth*, edited by Frederick J. Antczack, Ohio State UP, 1995, pp. 187–210.

Mezzano, Michael. "The Progressive Origins of Eugenics Critics: Raymond Pearl, Herbert S. Jennings, and the Defense of Scientific Inquiry." *Journal of the Gilded Age and Progressive Era*, vol. 4, no. 1, 2006, pp. 83–97. *Cambridge Journals.* Accessed 6 May 2014.

Morgan, Chester M. *Redneck Liberal: Theodore G. Bilbo and the New Deal.* Louisiana State UP, 1985.

Morgan, Kathryn A., editor. *Popular Tyranny.* U of Texas P, 2003.

Morse, Samuel. *Foreign Conspiracy against the Liberties of the United States.* New York: B. A. Chapin and Company, 1841. *Internet Archive.* Accessed 6 May 2014.

Murphy, John "'Our Mission and Our Moment': George W. Bush and September 11th." *Rhetoric and Public Affairs*, vol. 6, no. 4, 2003, pp. 607–32.

Neiwert, David. *The Eliminationists: How Hate Talk Radicalized the American Right.* PoliPointPress, 2009.

Noll, Mark A. *The Scandal of the Evangelical Mind.* William B. Eerdmans, 1994.

Noon, David Hoogland. "Operation Enduring Analogy: World War II, the War on Terror, and the Uses of Historical Memory." *Rhetoric and Public Affairs*, vol. 7, no. 3, 2004, pp. 339–64.

Nussbaum, Martha. *Political Emotions: Why Love Matters for Justice.* Belknap-Harvard, 2013.

Nye, Roland F. "The Doom of the Nordics." *Reedy's Mirror,* 21 June 1918, pp. 377–78.

Ober, Josiah. *Mass and Elite in Democratic Athens: Rhetoric, Ideology, and the Power of the People.* Princeton UP, 1989.

———. *Political Dissent in Democratic Athens: Intellectual Critics of Popular Rule.* Princeton UP, 1998.

O'Connor, Jennifer. "Federal Snake Ban Lacks Bite." *PETAPrime.* People for the Ethical Treatment of Animals. 17 Feb. 2014. Accessed 6 May 2014.

O'Hanlon, Michael E. "Iraq without a Plan." *Policy Review,* vol. 128, 2004. *Hoover Institution.* Stanford University. Accessed 6 May 2014.

Okihiro, Gary Y., and Julie Sly. "The Press, Japanese Americans, and the Concentration Camps." *Phylon,* vol. 44, no. 1, 1983, pp. 66–83. *JSTOR.* Accessed 12 May 2014.

1man1woman. 1man1woman.net. Accessed 20 Dec. 2014.

O'Rourke, Sean Patrick. "Circulation and Noncirculation of Photographic Texts in the Civil Rights Movement: A Case Study of the Rhetoric of Control." *Rhetoric and Public Affairs,* vol. 15, no. 4, 2012, pp. 685–94.

O'Shaughnessy, Nicholas. *Selling Hitler: Propaganda and the Nazi Brand.* Oxford UP, 2017.

Osborne, Henry Fairfield. Preface. *The Passing of the Great Race* by Madison Grant. Charles Scribner's Sons, 1916, pp. vii-ix.

Pasher, Yaron. *Holocaust versus Wehrmacht: How Hitler's "Final Solution" Undermined the German War Effort.* UP of Kansas, 2015.

"The Passing of the Great Race." *Wikipedia,* 23 April 2014. Accessed 12 May 2014.

"Paul Cameron." *Southern Poverty Law Center,* n.d. Accessed 25 June 2015.

Pascoe, Peggy. *What Comes Naturally: Miscegenation Law and the Making of Race in America.* Oxford UP, 2010.

Percy, William Alexander. *Lanterns on the Levee: Recollections of a Planter's Son.* Alfred A. Knopf, 1941.

Perelman, Chaim, and L. Olbrechts-Tyteca. *The New Rhetoric: A Treatise on Argumentation.* Translated by John Wilkinson and Purcell Weaver. U of Notre Dame P, 1969.

Personal Justice Denied: Report of the Commission on Wartime Relocation and Internment of Civilians. US Government Printing Office, 1982/3. 2 vols.

Petit, Jeanne D. *The Men and Women We Want: Gender, Race, and the Progressive Literacy Test Debate.* U of Rochester P, 2010.

Plato. *Gorgias.* Translated by W. R. M. Lamb. *Perseus.* Tufts University. Accessed 12 May 2014.

———. *Republic*. Translated by Paul Shorey. *Perseus*. Tufts University. Accessed 12 May 2014.

Polkinghorne, John. *Science and Theology: An Introduction*. SPCK/Fortress Press, 1998.

Prados, John, and Christopher Ames, editors. "The Iraq War—Part II: Was There Even a Decision?" *National Security Archive Electronic Briefing Book No. 328*. National Security Archive. 1 Oct. 2010. Accessed 6 May 2014.

Prange, Gordon W., et al. *At Dawn We Slept: The Untold Story of Pearl Harbor*. Penguin Press, 1981.

Pratto, Felicia, et al. "Social Dominance Orientation: A Personality Variable Predicting Social and Political Attitudes." *Journal of Personality and Social Psychology*, vol. 67, no. 4, 1994, pp. 741–63. *PsycARTICLES*. Accessed 6 May 2014.

Pronin, Emily, et al. "Alone in a Crowd of Sheep: Asymmetric Perceptions of Conformity and Their Roots in an Introspection Illusion." *Journal of Personality and Social Psychology*, vol. 92, no. 4, Apr. 2007, pp. 585–95. *PsycARTICLES*. Accessed 6 May 2014.

Proulx, Travis, and Steven J. Heine. "The Frog in Kierkegaard's Beer: Finding Meaning in the Threat-Compensation Literature." *Social and Personality Psychology Compass*, vol. 4, no. 10, 2010, pp. 899–905.

Quinn, Janis. *Promises Kept: The University of Mississippi Medical Center*. UP of Mississippi, 2005.

Ranciere, Jacques. *Disagreement*, translated by Julie Rose, U of Minnesota P, 1999.

Rendel, Val Perry. "Fuck Bernie Fucking Sanders." *Medium.com*, 19 Apr. 2017. Accessed 26 April 2017.

"Report of the Committee on Homosexuals in Sociology." *Footnotes*, vol. 15, no. 2, 1987, pp. 4, 6. American Sociological Association. Accessed 1 July 2018.

Report of Roberts Commission, 23 Jan. 1942. *New York Times*, 25 Jan. 1942, pp. 1, 5.

Report to the President, March 31, 2005. Commission on the Intelligence Capabilities of the United States regarding Weapons of Mass Destruction. Commission on the Intelligence Capabilities of the United States Regarding Weapons of Mass Destruction. Accessed 12 May 2014.

Rev. of *Germany's Ethnic Pathology*. *American Journal of Physical Anthropology*, vol. 2, 1919, p. 92.

Rev. of *The Passing of the Great Race*, by Madison Grant. *Bookseller*, vol. 10, 1916, p. 724.

———. *Journal of Geography*, vol. 15, 1917, pp. 206–7.

———. *Spectator* 13 Oct. 1917, pp. 385–86. *ProQuest.* Accessed 5 May 2014.

"The Revolt against Civilization." *Spectator,* 28 Apr. 1923, p. 704. *ProQuest.* Accessed 12 May 2014.

Rice, Condoleezza. "Campaign 2000: Promoting the National Interest." *Foreign Affairs.* Council on Foreign Relations. Jan.-Feb. 2000. Accessed 6 May 2014.

Ripley, William. *The Races of Europe: A Sociological Study.* New York: D. Appleton and Company, 1899. *Internet Archive.* Accessed 6 May 2014.

Roberts-Miller, Patricia. *Deliberate Conflict: Argument, Political Theory, and Composition Classes.* Southern Illinois UP, 2004.

———. "Democracy, Demagoguery, and Critical Rhetoric." *Rhetoric and Public Affairs,* vol. 8, 2005, pp. 459–76.

———."Dissent as 'Aid and Comfort to the Enemy': The Rhetorical Power of Naive Realism and Ingroup Identity." *Rhetoric Society Quarterly,* vol. 39, no. 2, Spring 2009, pp. 170–88.

———. *Fanatical Schemes: Proslavery Rhetoric and the Tragedy of Consensus.* U of Alabama P, 2009.

Robinson, Greg. *By Order of the President: FDR and the Internment of Japanese Americans.* Harvard UP, 2001.

———. *A Tragedy of Democracy: Japanese Confinement in North America.* Columbia UP, 2009.

Roediger, David. *Working toward Whiteness: How America's Immigrants Became White. The Strange Journey from Ellis Island to the Suburbs.* Basic/Perseus, 2005.

Ryback, Timothy W. *Hitler's Private Library: The Books That Shaped His Life.* Vintage Books, 2009.

Sansing, David. "Bilbo and the Greater University." *University of Mississippi: A Sesquicentennial History.* U of Mississippi P, 1999, pp. 215–46.

Saurette, Paul, and Shane Gunster. "Ears Wide Shut: Epistemological Populism, Argutainment and Canadian Conservative Talk Radio." *Canadian Journal of Political Science,* vol. 44, no. 1, 2011, pp. 195–218. *Cambridge Journals.* Accessed 6 May 2014.

Saxonhouse, Arlene W. *Free Speech and Democracy in Ancient Athens.* Cambridge UP, 2006.

Schlatter, Evelyn. "18 Anti-Gay Groups and their Propaganda." *Intelligence Report,* vol. 140, 2010. *Southern Poverty Law Center.* Accessed 6 May 2014.

Schmitt, Carl. *The Concept of the Political.* Expanded ed., U of Chicago P, 2007.

Schulz, Kathryn. *Being Wrong: Adventures in the Margin of Error.* Ecco, 2010.

Scowcroft, Brent. "Don't Attack Saddam." *Wall Street Journal,* 15 Aug. 2002. Accessed 5 May 2014.

Semelin, Jacques. *Purify and Destroy: The Political Uses of Massacre and Genocide*, translated by Cynthia Schoch, Columbia UP, 2007.

Shaffer, Robert. "Cracks in the Consensus: Defending the Rights of Japanese Americans during World War II." *Radical History Review*, vol. 72, Fall 1998, pp. 84–120.

"Shamanthropology." *Nation*, 12 May 1917, pp. 139–40. *ProQuest*. Accessed 12 May 2014.

Shane, Peter M., editor. *Democracy Online: The Prospects for Political Renewal through the Internet*. Routledge, 2004.

Shirer, William L. *The Nightmare Years: 1930–1940*. Little, Brown, 1984.

Signer, Michael. *Demagogue: The Fight to Save Democracy from its Worst Enemies*. Palgrave MacMillan, 2009.

Simons, Herbert W. "From Post-9/11 Melodrama to Quagmire in Iraq: A Rhetorical History." *Rhetoric and Public Affairs*, vol. 10, no. 2, 2007, pp. 183–94.

Snyder, Timothy. *Black Earth: The Holocaust as History and Warning*. Tim Duggan Books, 2016.

Solomon, Richard H., and Nigel Quinney. *American Negotiating Behavior: Wheeler-Dealers, Legal Eagles, Bullies, and Preachers*. United States Institute of Peace Press, 2010.

Spicer, Kevin P., editor. *Antisemitism, Christian Ambivalence, and the Holocaust*. Indiana UP in association with the United States Holocaust Museum, 2008.

Spiro, Jonathan Peter. *Defending the Master Race: Conservation, Eugenics, and the Legacy of Madison Grant*. U of Vermont P, 2009.

Staub, Ervin. *The Roots of Evil: The Origins of Genocide and Other Group Violence*. Cambridge UP, 1989.

Stern, Roger. "United States Cost of Military Force Projection in the Persian Gulf, 1976–2007." *Energy Policy*, vol. 38, 2010, pp. 2816–25. *Science Direct*. Accessed 6 May 2014.

Steyrer, Johannes. "Charisma and the Archetypes of Leadership." *Organization Studies*, vol. 19, no 5, 1998, pp. 807–28. Accessed 16 June 2017.

Stiglitz, Joseph E., and Linda J. Blimes. *The Three Trillion Dollar War: The True Cost of the Iraq Conflict*. W. W. Norton and Company, 2008.

Stoddard, Lothrop. *The Rising Tide of Color against White World-Supremacy*. Charles Scribner's Sons, 1921. *Internet Archive*. Accessed 6 May 2014.

Stratigakos, Despina. *Hitler at Home*. Yale University Press, 2015.

Sullivan, Daniel, et al. "An Existential Function of Enemyship: Evidence That People Attribute Influence to Personal and Political Enemies to Compensate for Threats to Control." *Journal of Personality and Social Psychology*, vol. 98, no. 3, 2010, pp. 434–49. *PyscARTICLES*. Accessed 5 May 2014.

Sunstein, Cass. "Forum: Is the Internet Bad for Democracy?" *Boston Review: A Political and Literary Forum*, 1 June 2001. Accessed 4 June 2015.

Swain, Carol M., and Russ Nieli, editors. *Contemporary Voices of White Nationalism in America*. Cambridge UP, 2002.

Tanner, Lindsey. "A Fanatical Fifth Column: The Media's Argument for Japanese Internment." *Young Scholars in Writing*, [S.l.], vol. 11, 2015, pp. 39–46.

Taylor, Charles. *Sources of the Self: The Making of the Modern Identity*. Harvard UP, 1989.

Tetlock, Philip E. *Expert Political Judgment: How Good Is It? How Can We Know?* Princeton UP, 2006.

Tetlock, Philip E., and Dan Gardner. *Superforecasting: The Art and Science of Prediction*. Broadway Books, 2016.

Thucydides. *The Peloponnesian War*. Translated by Steven Lattimore. Hackett Publishing Company, 1998.

Tolan Committee. *Preliminary Report on Evacuation of Military Areas,* House Report no. 1911, March 19, 1942.

Torgovnik, Marianna. *Gone Primitive: Savage Intellects, Modern Lives*. U of Chicago P, 1990.

"Unfinished Business: Dealing with Iraq." *Economist*, 8 Dec. 2001. *Academic OneFile*. Accessed 19 Dec. 2013.

United States, Congress, House. "Appendix VI: Report on Japanese Activities." *Investigation of Un-American Propaganda Activities in the United States: Hearings before a Special Committee on Un-American Activities*. Government Printing Office, 1942. 77th Congress, 1st Session, House Res. 282.

United States, Congress, House. Committee on Immigration and Naturalization. *Restriction of Immigration: Report No. 176, part 2.* (Minority Report to Accompany H.R. 6540). 68th Cong., 1st sess. Government Printing Office, 1924.

———. Select Committee Investigating National Defense Migration. *Fourth Interim Report*. 77th Cong., 2nd sess. Government Printing Office, 1942.

———. Select Committee Investigating National Defense Migration. *National Defense Migration Hearings*. 77th Cong., 2nd sess. Government Printing Office, 1942.

———. Select Committee Investigating National Defense Migration. *National Defense Migration: Report of the Select Committee Investigating National Defense Migration, House of Representatives: Preliminary Report and Recommendations on Problems of Evacuations of Citizens and Aliens from Military Areas, March 19, 1942*. 77th Cong., 2nd sess. Government Printing Office, 1942.

Van Boven, Leaf. "Naïve Realism." *Encyclopedia of Social Psychology*, edited by Roy F. Baumeister and Kathleen D. Vohs, vol. 2, Sage Publications, 2007, pp. 602–3.

van den Bos, Kees, and Annemarie Loserman. "Radical Worldview Defense in Reaction to Personal Uncertainty." *Extremism and the Psychology of Uncertainty*, edited by Michael A. Hogg and Danielle L. Blaylock, Wiley-Blackwell, 2012, pp. 90–112.

Walker, Anders. *The Ghost of Jim Crow: How Southern Moderates Used* Brown v. Board of Education *to Stall Civil Rights*. Oxford UP, 2009.

Waller, James. *Becoming Evil: How Ordinary People Commit Genocide and Mass Killing*. Oxford UP, 2002.

Walton, Douglas. *Appeal to Expert Opinion: Arguments from Authority*. Pennsylvania State UP, 1997.

———. *Witness Testimony Evidence: Argumentation, Artificial Intelligence, and Law*. Cambridge UP, 2008.

Ward, Jason Morgan. *Defending White Democracy: The Making of a Segregationist Movement and the Remaking of Racial Politics, 1936–1965*. U of NC P, 2014.

Warren, Earl. *The Memoirs of Chief Justice Earl Warren*. Doubleday, 1977.

Weintraub, Stanley. *Long Day's Journey into War*. First Lyons Press, 1991.

Westen, Drew. *The Political Brain: The Role of Emotion in Deciding the Fate of the Nation*. Public Affairs, 2007.

Western, Jon. "The War over Iraq: Selling War to the American Public." *Security Studies*, vol. 14, no. 1, 2005, pp. 106–39. *Taylor and Francis Online*. Accessed 11 May 2014.

Whedbee, Karen E. "Reclaiming Rhetorical Democracy: George Grote's Defense of Cleon and the Athenian Demagogues." *Rhetoric Society Quarterly*, vol. 34, no. 4, 2004, pp. 71–95. *JSTOR*. Accessed 6 May 2014.

Whitson, Jennifer, and Adam Gallinsky. "Lacking Control Increases Illusory Pattern Perception." *Science*, vol. 322, 2008, pp. 115–7. *ScienceMag.org*. American Association for the Advancement of Science. Accessed 3 Oct. 2008.

Wohl, Victoria. *Love among the Ruins: The Erotics of Democracy in Classical Athens*. Princeton UP, 2002.

Woods, Frederick Adams. "A Review of Reviews of Madison Grant's *Passing of the Great Race*." *Journal of Heredity*, vol. 14, no. 2, 1923, pp. 93–95.

———. "Scientific Books." *Science*, vol. 48, 1918, pp. 419–20.

Workman Jr., William J. *The Case for the South*. Devin-Adair, 1960.

Wray, Matt. *Not Quite White: White Trash and the Boundaries of Whiteness*. Duke UP, 2006.

Zolberg, Aristide R. *A Nation by Design: Immigration Policy in the Fashioning of America*. Harvard UP, 2006.

Index

action movie comparison, Iraq invasion rhetoric, 43–44
affective markers, 61, 82
Agamben, Giorgio, 10
aggression vs. hostility, assumption errors, 14–15
Alcibiades, 197n1
Allport, Gordon, 20, 189
al Qaeda, portrayals, 37
ambiguity and closure needs, 132–135, 189. See also certainty
American Dilemma, An (Myrdal), 149
American Legion, 73, 201n8, 203n18
American Psychological Association, 160, 164
American Sociological Association, 164
America Return to God Prayer Movement, 156
America's Greatest Problem: The Negro (Shufeldt), 211n5
Ames, Christopher, 46
anti-Catholicism, Morse's, 2
anti-immigration speech, Lodge's, 107, 207n4
anti-intellectualism: complexity of, 151–53; defined, 132; as demagoguery component, 132–33, 171

apocalyptic metanarratives, as demagoguery characteristic, 21–22, 24, 65, 157
Archidamus, 197n1
Arendt, Hannah, 100, 179
argutainment, as validity standard, 142–43
Aristotle, 11, 129, 145, 165
Armitage, Richard, 46
arrows rumor, in sabotage arguments, 77–78, 93, 95
Astoria Chamber of Commerce, 201n8
Athens. See Cleon's Mytilinean speech, elements
attitude markers, as affect signaling, 60, 61–62, 91
Aune, James, 57
authenticity perception, 185–86
authoritarianism, 23–24, 42–43, 58, 196n3
authority appeals, argumentation opportunities, 117–18, 209n13. See also science-oriented demagoguery, as rhetorical puzzle
authority arguments, rhetorical tradition, 164–65
Avolio, Bruce, 180

Cox, E. S. (*continued*)
 hybridity, 211n25; whiteness as
 authority, 143–44
Cramer, J. K., 39
Cramer, Jane, 46
Crosswhite, James, 100–101
cunning projection, 20, 159

Dark Side of Democracy (Mann), 10
Darsey, James, 112
data use. *See* citations/data presentation
dehumanization process, emotionalism
 assumption, 76
deliberation, metacognition requirement, 133. *See also* policy deliberation
demagoguery, overview: anti-intellectualism component, 132–33,
 171; apocalyptic metanarrative
 implications, 21–22; authenticity
 perception, 185–86; authoritarianism element, 23–24; bad behavior
 metaphors, 22–23, 195nn15–16;
 belief as evidence validity, 24–25;
 binaries characteristic, 17–18,
 22–23, 199n13; certainty element,
 24, 133; classical understanding, 11;
 and closure needs, 134–35; consensus requirement, 155; conventional
 scholarship implications, 9–11, 172,
 176; data's functions, 24; defined,
 1–2, 16, 172–74; denial of persuasion process, 28, 195n18; good
 behavior metaphors, 22–23; harm
 assessment criteria, 2–4, 176–77,
 194n4; hostility assumption errors,
 14–15; identities emphasis, 16–18;
 incommensurability responses, 20;
 increase factors, 186–88; individual
 focus error, 1–2, 7–8, 10–11, 26–29,

193n1; logic of, 167–69; masses/
 demagogue power relationship,
 27–29; motivism element, 25; new as
 traditional emphasis, 23; ontological
 category framing, 18–19, 24; for
 policy reversals, 213n19; potential
 responses to, 188–90; projection
 element, 20–21; punitive policy
 element, 22–23, 195n14; rational argumentation compared, 25–26; with
 rationality markers, 91; reductionist
 element, 2, 6–7, 76, 177; role of naïve
 realism, 19–20, 24; scapegoating
 element, 16–17, 20, 177; scholarship
 possibilities, 177–81, 193n2; victimization assertion, 21. *See also specific
 topics, e.g.,* certainty; Iraq invasion,
 rhetorical context; Warren, Earl
 (hearings testimony)
"Democratic Hopefuls on Iraq" (Lester), 35
demophobia, in demagoguery definitions, 9, 172 , 193n1
depersonalized demagoguery, scholarship possibilities, 181
Deporte, Christian, 203n19
DeWitt, John, 70, 93, 199nn17–18,
 204n24
Diamond, Larry, 47, 48–49
Dies Committee report, 200n4
Diodotus, 58, 59
disease metaphors, limitations, 4
dog-biting example, data errors,
 163–64
Dohrn, Bernardine, 177–78, 181
domination/submission binary, 17,
 27–28, 194n9
"do this" or "do nothing" assertions,
 6–7

Patricia Roberts-Miller is a professor in the Department of Rhetoric and Writing and the director of the University Writing Center at the University of Texas–Austin. She is the author of *Demagoguery and Democracy*; *Fanatical Schemes: Proslavery Rhetoric and the Tragedy of Consensus*; *Voices in the Wilderness: Public Discourse and the Paradox of Puritan Rhetoric*; and *Deliberate Conflict: Argument, Political Theory, and Composition Classes*.